Healing the Hurting

Christians for Biblical Equality
122 West Franklin Avenue Suite 218
Minneapolis, MN 55404-2451
Ph: 612-872-6898 Fax: 612-872-6891
Email: cbe@cbeinternational.org
Website: http://www.cbeinternational.org

Healing the Hurting

*Giving Hope and Help
to Abused Women*

*Catherine Clark Kroeger
and James R. Beck, editors*

Baker Books
A Division of Baker Book House Co
Grand Rapids, Michigan 49516

Published by Baker Books
a division of Baker Book House Company
P.O. Box 6287, Grand Rapids, MI 49516-6287

Printed in the United States of America

Library of Congress Cataloging-in-Publication Data

Healing the hurting : giving hope and help to abused women / Catherine Clark
    Kroeger and James R. Beck, editors.
    p.   cm.
    Includes bibliographical references.
    ISBN 0-8010-5831-7 (pbk.)
    1. Church work with abused women. 2. Wife abuse—Religious aspects—
Christianity. I. Kroeger, Catherine Clark. II. Beck, James R.
BV4445.5.H43 1998
261.8'327—dc21   98-26721

For current information about all releases from Baker Book House, visit our web site:
http://www.bakerbooks.com

Contents

Part 2   And the Healing

Introduction

Working Together to Listen and Learn

Catherine Clark Kroeger

The inner prison door slid shut behind me as I started down the tunnel-like corridor. In one of the cubicles that lined the wall sat a member of Christians for Biblical Equality—a man who had killed his wife and two children. As president emerita of the organization, I had come to tell him that he was not beyond God's love and care. The terrible tragedy could not be undone, but he could still experience God's forgiveness, and he could still know the healing grace of repentance.

He told me that when the realization of what he did sweeps over him, he stuffs a pillow in his mouth so that others cannot hear him screaming. As I was leaving, the horror of the ghastly murders flooded over me, and I too wanted to scream. Clearly, membership in Christians for Biblical Equality had not been enough to prevent this terrible crime, nor had his long-standing profession of faith in Jesus Christ as Lord and Savior. Both he and his wife had been raised in evangelical Christian families and had committed themselves to Christ. Had the wider Christian community—the churches, pastors, Christian therapists, and friends—failed them both?

This case is far from unique. In America, three thousand women are slain by their domestic partners each year, and thousands of others are permanently injured. Children are abused and murdered at a lower rate than women, but the blood of these innocents cries out to those who will listen.

Even though abuse happens in Christian homes at nearly the same rate as in society as a whole, Christians do not recognize it or do not properly address it. Few pastors have received training in the treatment of domestic abuse, and in one survey, less than ten percent of Christian therapists, when provided with case studies, were able to identify abusive family situations. Often, abused wives are mistakenly told they are partly to blame for the abuse and that greater submission or more prayer will solve the problem. Nowhere in the Bible are wives told to submit to abuse. The Bible does tell us, however, that the wrongdoing of a Christian is to be corrected by other believers.

For many evangelicals, the uneasiness associated with confronting abuse in Christian homes springs in part from their perplexity in interpreting certain biblical passages. If the Bible is our only infallible rule of faith and practice, then our standards must be consistent with its directives. Distortion of Scripture can prove dangerous as we go farther than is warranted by honest exegesis. Evangelicals also long to see families harmoniously united. In our zeal to hasten the process, we sidestep the slow and painful steps that can lead to true transformation and healing.

Churches can make major blunders. I remember another visit that Christians for Biblical Equality asked me to make. Angela, an emaciated young missionary, stood in the middle of her mother's living room looking at me with frightened eyes. Her first words were, "Don't tell me I have to go back to him." Already crippled with a permanent spine injury caused by her abusive husband, she cringed at the thought.

The story was a sad one. Angela had endured years of abuse, hiding it from her family and fabricating excuses for her injuries. At last, she had become too ill and traumatized to continue in the parachurch ministry she shared with her husband, Peter. Only after her parents brought her and the children back to their home did she discover that her daughters had been violated by their father.

At first Peter had stayed half a continent away at the headquarters of the mission organization they served. Angela's requests that he attend a Christian batterers' group went unheeded even though an excellent facility was available near the mission's main office. After six months without a reconciliation, the church that had commissioned and supported Peter and Angela became aggressively involved, insisting that they both return to the pastor and the congregation.

Two lines of argument persuaded Angela that she had little choice in the matter. First, she was told that only in this way would she be doing the will of God, and Angela wanted desperately to be obedient to her Lord and Savior. It was made clear to her that any other course of action would be dishonoring and displeasing to God. Her wounded spirit could not bear the thought of abandonment by the heavenly friend who had been her only consolation through so much abuse and degradation.

Second, the church offered to provide her with a place to live and help with expenses. She would even be given counseling with a Christian therapist, albeit one who had no previous experience with battered women. With no other way to provide for her children, Angela was compelled to yield despite her fears. She was caught in the twofold trap that forces so many women back into life-threatening situations: religious pressure and financial duress. The pastor's wife told her, "Angela, even if this does not lead to reconciliation, you will be able to stand before the Lord and say, 'I gave it my best shot.'"

Initially, Peter won the support of the church members with his charm, persuasive tactics, and feigned repentance. He was considered the high priest of the home, and it was Angela's duty to submit. Despite being forewarned that couple counseling was not a proper technique in cases of abuse, the pastor insisted that both Angela and Peter take part in joint counseling sessions every Sunday afternoon at his house. During these sessions, Peter found ways to avoid admitting his responsibility. He used phrases such as, "I had anger, rage." Never did he say, "I did terrible things to her. I am so sorry."

As the congregation became increasingly aware that Angela truly had been abused, Peter was obliged to make a public confession, one that was forced by the circumstances. There were no other signs of repentance, and Peter resented having to go through such an exercise. Yet, Angela was still the one who was held responsible for the marital crisis. For the most part, Peter was artful enough to dodge the demands for accountability that were being made on Angela.

The pastor's wife later reported to the mission organization under which the couple had labored:

> I confronted Peter. Whenever anything went wrong this past year, he blamed Angela. Except for the one time he made the public confession in church, he blamed everyone else for his problems. He lost his jobs because his bosses were unfair; he couldn't go to our church because of Angela; the girls didn't want to visit him because Angela turned them against him; he didn't have any money because he and Angela were separated. . . . He has called Angela on the phone and verbally abused her for all that has happened. He came uninvited into her house one night when bringing the children home. He would not leave until he said what he wanted to say. We have told him over and over again not to go in the house unless invited. The girls will not go with him now as a result of all this.

Angela could not understand how the church could be so hard on her and so lenient with Peter. Finally, she wrote a letter to the church leaders. In part she said,

> I feel I have done my best, but I have not had the support I needed from you, the leaders. I feel church discipline was not there when my husband needed to be confronted on many issues.
>
> I was asked one and one half years ago to come here at your request in hope of reconciliation. But Peter continued his abusive ways to me, the children, and himself. Because of the situation, I suggested separate counseling, but you did not listen. Marriage counseling was not the answer, so I asked Mark [the therapist] to become my mediator and to hold back everyone to give me time to pray and to think.
>
> It became apparent that Peter has a drinking problem, and it was decided that he needed to get help for his substance abuse through a drug and alcohol program. He never completely followed through with the counseling for substance abuse. He quit going, and nobody ever got in contact to see how he was progressing at the rehab. Again, Peter was running the show. Perhaps if the church would have followed up on Peter's progress, they would have found out that he had quit the program and still continued to drink. Maybe you could have helped him or disciplined him then if you would have gotten involved. I had asked the leaders, "Do you know Peter is still drinking?" "Yes," was the reply. "Are you going to confront him?" Your response was

that he has a spiritual problem. I know that, but what are you going to do?

Angela was left with the knowledge that the church had excommunicated Peter not because he had abused his wife and children but because of his drinking. Several church members admitted that in their well-meaning efforts they had abused Angela more than had her husband.

In retrospect, the pastor's wife reported:

> If I had to do it over again, I would do what one of her counselors recommended. We should have sent Peter to a physical abusers' group. The problem was that the closest one was an hour's drive away. There is now one in this city. I am convinced that going through a program with a group of men with the same problems would have done far more than we were able.

Angela continues to live in the community and to participate in the life of the church. She leads a Bible study for abused wives and seeks to bring healing to troubled situations. The haunted expression is gone from her face. She has gained weight and is a beautiful woman. Peter has asked what he must do to win her back, and she was able to spell out, clearly and firmly, what would be necessary.

She knows that the church cares deeply for her and her children. Members of the church have apologized to her for their ignorance and mishandling of a very delicate matter. Others, including the pastor and therapist, have expressed deep regret for their bungled efforts and have vowed that if they are confronted with a similar situation in the future, they will handle it differently.

Through a sad experience, these church members learned that it is necessary to address the abuser directly, to hold him accountable, to mentor and monitor him, and to show zero tolerance for his behavior. They now realize that a forced confession brings only resentment from the husband and more hardship for the family. They know they did not utilize the help that was available from resources outside the church. They have learned that the Bible's directive of stern discipline for an offender is the most effective remedy (Matt. 18:15–17; 1 Thess. 5:14; 2 Thess. 3:14–15; 1 Tim. 5:20; Titus 3:2–11; James 5:19–20).

These Christians have learned that blaming the victim only intensifies her suffering. Support, on the other hand, can help to rebuild lives and to sustain the family's faith in the God of love and justice. This is a church that is ready to serve another family caught in the terrible web of domestic violence.

Angela believes that both abuser and victim can be transformed and that a community of faith can do much to help. God is in the business of healing. That is the message of this book.

In 1994, Christians for Biblical Equality held a conference on women, abuse, and the Bible. We sent out a call for papers, and proposals flooded in from theologians, biblical scholars, pastors, therapists, social workers, sociologists, psychologists, survivors, and even an offender. Although we ran three concurrent series of presentations, we still could not make room for all the papers and all the concerns that were raised. We knew that the material must be made available to Christian communities around the world.

The first set of papers, dealing largely with theological and theoretical issues, was published as *Women, Abuse, and the Bible* and is available in both American and British editions. But theory alone cannot solve the problem of abuse.

This second collection of essays is intended as a sequel that moves our concerns forward to basic application and moral imperative. We present here the more practical papers—papers that provide insights into the souls of frightened, hurting people and point to realistic paths of prevention and healing. This book is intended to help Christians confront both the reality and the potential for remedy.

The time has come when we must both listen and learn. Only as we perceive the evil in our midst, prayerfully bring the Word of God to bear on it, and take appropriate action can we become agents of reconciliation and healing.

God calls us to deliver the helpless from the hand of the violent and to correct the way of the sinner. We must heed that call.

Part 1

All the Hurting

Power, Patriarchy, and Abusive Marriages

1

Cynthia Ezell

A young pastor receives into his office for a counseling session an attractive young woman from his congregation. She is married to a man who also attends this pastor's church. The young woman has bruises on her face and on her arm, but the young pastor decides not to mention them for fear of embarrassing her. He waits for her to tell him that her husband caused the bruises. He asks her, "Why did he hit you? Is he jealous?" He then counsels the young woman to curtail her social and career activities so as not to give her husband an opportunity to become jealous. He suggests that she try to praise her husband more frequently so that he will feel more confident that she loves and admires him (Wicks, Parsons, & Capps, 1985).

This story reflects both the theology and the sex-role beliefs of the pastor. This is not an extreme example. Another account of a similar counseling session is presented by Carole R. Bohn: "While our children were still small and I was being battered, I went to our pastor for counseling. I realized that he meant well, but he laid a heavier burden of guilt on me. His advice was to 'pray harder, have more faith, and be grateful for your six fine children'" (1989, p. 107).

Both of these stories highlight some of the elements that make patriarchal thinking so dangerous for women, especially married women. In the first story, the pastor hesitates to name the abuse, and then, in his ignorance, he looks to the woman to provide an answer as to why the abuse occurred. In neither story did the pastor address the woman's safety. Both women were expected to control the abuse by being more attentive and subservient and by taking responsibility for the abuse. Patriarchal beliefs about marital relationships make women vulnerable to abuse and powerless to protect themselves once abuse occurs.

This chapter will explore the ways, both subtle and overt, that patriarchal attitudes founded in religious beliefs contribute to the abuse and subjugation of women within marital relationships. A brief look at the history of religious ideology concerning the place of women in families will shed light on the foundations of patriarchal sex-role beliefs. Factors that contribute to the victimization of women that are maintained by patriarchal beliefs will be discussed, and alternate ways of relating and an egalitarian model for marriage will be suggested. Implications for therapists, ministers, and lay counselors will also be discussed.

The Burden of Inequality

In 1980, a United Nations report cited the burden of inequality for women. While women make up half the world's population, they do two-thirds of the world's work, earn one-tenth of the world's income, and own one-hundredth of the world's property. Despite the fall of repressive governments and the growing representation by women in corporations, the 1993 United Nations Human Development Report found that in no country are women treated as well as men. In spite of the progress of democracy worldwide, the UN still reports a "global epidemic of violence against women" (Mac-Farquhar, Seter, Lawrence, Knight, & Schrof, 1994, p. 44).

Over the last twenty years, the feminist movement has dramatically influenced sex roles for men and women in America. While feminist ideology has certainly made an impact on women in the context of family and church, its effects have been muted by traditional religious teaching. Religious teachings that support the primacy of males, still a dominant thread in the fabric of our society, are woven into the beliefs we have about marital relationships. At their worst, such teachings have served not only to keep women silent but also to keep them vulnerable. A survey of third world women's groups conducted in the 1980s found violence to be the chief concern for women. Feminists are beginning to realize that addressing abortion rights is less important to the average woman than the issue of violence against women. Because of the pressure from feminists, the United States Congress will soon consider a bill that will make violence against women a civil rights offense (MacFarquhar et al., 1994).

For Christian women, the influence of religion in defining their role in the family has not been a positive one. Several authors discuss the fact that adherence to traditional religious beliefs about sex roles contributes to the depression, suppression, and victimization of women in families (Neuger, 1993; Shupe, Stacey, & Hazlewood, 1987; Stoudenmire, 1976).

The term *patriarchy* has been defined as a type of social organization in which the father is the head of the family. The husband is the final authority, and wives and children are legally dependent upon him (Russell, 1990; Saussy, 1991). Patriarchy has also been described as a social system of male domination structured by racism, sexism, classism, and colonialism (Freedman, 1993). One of the tasks of feminism has been to point out the ways that patriarchy permeates our culture and limits the options of women in defining themselves and their roles. When religious teachings support and even prescribe those patriarchal beliefs, then those beliefs can be even more limiting for women and their partners.

History of Patriarchy

The interplay of religion, myth, and tradition in shaping our cultural beliefs about men and women is complicated (Lerner, 1986). Separating religion from culture is impossible. Admittedly, the biblical texts that are used either to support or to refute asymmetrical sex roles are bound up in the culture of that time. The exclusion of women from certain roles in ancient Israel cannot be equated with the exclusion of women from those roles in our society. Taking those ancient injunctions, lifting them out of their time-bound culture, and applying them to present-day marriage roles is risky and ridiculous. The church, however, has traditionally used the biblical text to serve and support its purposes, whether political or religious. The church fathers have used the biblical text to maintain a hierarchical model of marriage wherein woman is subservient to man.

The writings of Irenaeus, Tertullian, Augustine, Jerome, Thomas Aquinas, and Martin Luther provide us with information regarding the sources of Christian misogynism (Farley, 1976). "Hopelessly entangled in the sources for Christian misogynism are not only myths of the Fall and Hellenistic dualisms, but also ancient blood taboos and Hebrew connections between nakedness and shame. The notion of woman became theoretically entrenched in theologies of original sin" (1976, p. 165). M. Farley cites these two briefly mentioned sources of sexual inequality in Christian thought: the concept of woman as responsible for sin entering the world and the concept that the fullness of the image of God is found only in males. She states that "neither line of thought is finally compatible with assertions of sexual equality." Both lines of thought "lead irresistibly to conclusions regarding role definitions that exclude both women and men from important opportunities for reciprocity in a shared Christian life" (p. 165).

One important interface between religion and culture is found in the observance of religious rituals. Rituals are one of humanity's ways of making and expressing meaning and transmitting those meanings and values through generations (Neville, 1974). Women experience and learn the roles they are to take through community interactions and socially prescribed rituals. Every worship service, Sabbath, or Mass is a miniritual reenacted weekly; this ritual confirms to all that women are to be passive, separated, and silent because they are not allowed to pass out the sacraments, lead in prayers, or have contact with the holy vessels.

In contrast to the male-only rituals that permeate much of religious practice, Christianity brought with it the inclusive ritual of baptism. With this ritual, which was available both to men and women, a door was opened for new patterns of relationship. In spite of texts such as 2 Corinthians 5:17 and Galatians 3:28, the patriarchal forces of society and the need of males to dominate led to entrenchment in the familiar pattern of seeing man as made in God's image and seeing woman as made of something other.

Many of the social and religious teachings of Jesus reflect a mind-set that was remarkably egalitarian. Jesus stood against the patriarchal leadership of his day and modeled a new way of relating (Bohn, 1989). The New Testament church in some places afforded women more opportunities for leadership than many present-day churches do. There were prophetesses and women church leaders such as Lydia. The church, however, became more patriarchal as it aged.

Some feminist exegetes want to liberate the Scripture from its patriarchal bias. Some believe the text is irreparable and have serious questions about canon and the extent of biblical authority. Others suggest an acceptance of the text as patriarchal but are willing to overlook that bias in an effort to extract the larger truths. "Christian feminist apologetics asserts that the Bible, correctly understood, does not prohibit but authorizes equal rights" (Fiorenza, 1993, p. 789). Feminist theology is concerned with naming the patriarchal structures of the past and finding new ways of applying and interpreting Scripture that affirm the equality of all persons.

Religious tradition and teachings are relied upon to provide the basis for social structures and laws. In the same way, religious traditions are called upon to provide justification for existing social norms. Bohn refers to this phenomenon as the "chicken-and-egg nature of a theology of ownership" (1989, p. 105). The first laws enacted to regulate family and property issues were based on the accepted social norms of the time. Often religious teachings and traditions were cited as the basis for those laws.

In Roman law, a woman was considered to be the property of the man on whom she was financially dependent—whether father, husband, or brother-in-law. In the Islamic faith, a husband had, and to some degree still has, almost total control of his wife's activities. In the Middle Ages, a wife who refused to obey her husband or who was considered unruly in a social sense could be flogged, chained, or publicly punished for her disobedience (Hauser, 1982). Marriage laws in western precapitalist Europe maintained a husband's right to batter his wife. The legal and moral codes of the day recognized the family as the domain of the husband. Christian religious tradition provided ideological reinforcement for the continuation of such practices. In England, a husband's absolute power over his wife was abolished in 1829 (Schechter, 1982), but she still could not have real legal and social autonomy. As late as 1874, police in North Carolina who investigated domestic disputes were told not to interfere in a husband's battering of his wife unless the wife was critically injured as a result (Hauser, 1982). Richard J. Gelles and C. P. Cornell (1985) report that in fairly recent history many local criminal justice systems followed an informal "stitch rule," by which a woman could not have her husband arrested for assault unless she was injured severely enough to require a certain number of stitches.

American social norms are the product of the melting pot of immigration. Each ethnic group that immigrated to America brought with it a blend of culturally and religiously based sex-role expectations and practices. The patriarchal social and relationship norms that we struggle with result from this great stew of cultural and religious beliefs. Historically, marriage has not been a place of equality for women. Often it has not been a place of safety. The patriarchal forms of relationship between men and women have contributed to making marriage a place of violence for many women.

Marital Violence

Marital violence is so serious a problem that it is being addressed in a significant way by the crime bill proposed by the White House (1994). This bill includes $610 million in expenditures to prevent spousal violence, $900 million to address crimes against women, $30 million to combat rural domestic violence, and $600,000 to help educate judges in how to handle gender crimes (Klein, 1994).

Violence in families is underreported. Some couples experience violence on such a regular basis that it becomes a normative experience, hardly worthy of complaint. Generally, the more intimate the victim, the less seriously people consider the assault. This is especially true in the case of marital sexual assault (Finkelhor, 1983). More severe forms of family violence carry social shame and a greater threat that outside forces will move in to disrupt the family, so authorities do not always see the real extent of violence (Straus, 1977–78).

Murray A. Straus's landmark study on marital violence was conducted with two thousand couples who were chosen in such a way that they were representative of American couples. He used a Conflict Resolution Techniques (CRT) scale to see how couples settle conflicts between themselves. Found within the CRT scale is a Physical Violence Index that contains items defining the behaviors considered abusive:

throwing things at someone

pushing, shoving, and grabbing

slapping

kicking, biting, hitting with an object

hitting spouse with an object

threatening spouse with a knife or gun

assaulting spouse with a knife or gun (Straus, 1977–78)

Studies show that couples reporting physical violence report a median of 2.4 serious assaults per year (Hampton & Coner-Edwards, 1993; Straus, 1977–78). A survey made of admissions at a Yale emergency room during one month showed that 3.4 percent of the women entering for treatment had been injured by their partners. Because incidents of battering are underreported, the actual number was estimated to be as much as ten times higher (Hillard, 1988).

Some of the most significant factors in creating a marital climate in which spousal abuse is likely are provided by Straus (1977–78):

social isolation

lower opportunities for employment for women

socialization of women for subordinate roles in marriage

use of violence as a legitimate resource to maintain power

poverty

assumption that the husband is the head of the house

assumption that the wife is responsible for the success of the marriage and the care of the children

abuse of alcohol

Violence occurs in families at all socioeconomic levels. Researchers have repeatedly found violent families to be characterized by high levels of social isolation, rigid sex-role stereotyping, poor communication, and extreme inequalities in the distribution of power (Belenky, Clinchy, Goldberger, & Tarule, 1986). Unequal social power and sex-role socialization cause many of the problems women face, especially emotional, sexual, and physical abuse (Enns, 1988).

Marital violence often results from the husband's attempt to use physical force to gain control of his wife and her behavior. Husbands are also the victims of physical violence, but because women are usually not as strong as men, the potential for physical harm to men is greatly reduced. Studies suggest that when women batter, it is in self-defense not in an attempt to use physical force to gain power (Rosenbaum & O'Leary, 1981). Evidence shows that the risk of violence in marriage is greater when all the decision making is in the hands of one partner. Violent husbands report that they "need" to hit their wives to show them who is in charge (Gelles & Straus, 1988). "It only takes one such beating to fix the balance of power in a family for many years—or perhaps for a lifetime" (Straus, 1977–78, p. 446).

Most battering incidents between married couples follow a predictable pattern with three phases. In the first phase there is a buildup of tension: the beginning of an argument or the accumulation of alcohol and its effects in the batterer. The second phase is the acute phase, in which the actual emotional and physical assault takes place. The last stage is the stage of loving contrition, wherein the batterer becomes profusely apologetic and begs forgiveness. Often the woman nurtures the illusion that this will be the last time her husband hits her. She may begin making downward comparisons in this stage to convince herself that the relationship is really not that bad (Walker, 1987).

The Battered Wife

Students and researchers of marital abuse have tried to delineate the personality characteristics of women who remain in battering relationships. This concern with finding the differences between battered and nonbattered women obscures the issues of power and control that are at the heart of marital abuse. Studies suggesting that battered women are different from women who are not battered are "methodologically indefensible" since much of the literature on spouse abuse is sexist and rife with misogyny (Wardell, Gillespie, & Leffler, 1982, p. 71). Research repudiates the myth that women who are battered are masochistic and feel they deserve it, or that they set themselves up. Women stay in abusive relationships because they have few viable options. They often feel that it is safer to stay than it is to leave (Walker, 1987). The special pressures in religious women to stay in abusive relationships will be discussed further in this chapter.

Several authors conducted extensive research to find out how and why women stay with abusive men (Herbert, Silver, & Ellard, 1991). They found that women who stay in these marriages are able to make downward comparisons that reframe the relationships in a more positive light. They are able to form and maintain the illusion that the marriage is better than it really is by saying to themselves, "Well, at least he doesn't drink," or "At least he doesn't hit the kids or run around on me." The greater the verbal abuse, the less able these women were to frame the relationship in a positive light. The psychological damage done by verbal abuse may be ultimately more damaging than the physical abuse (Strube & Barbour, 1984). The ability of these women who were being beaten to deny their own suffering and frame the relationship as better than it is, points to what Valerie Saiving (1979) calls the sins of women. She says the sins of women are rarely about excessive pride or overt abuses of power but are more likely to be sins against the self and others born out of a self-destructive tolerance and self-sacrifice.

The Battering Husband

In a study of men involved in a treatment program for male batterers, researchers developed a profile of men who are violent toward women (Adams, 1989). The violent and controlling behaviors included in the profile range from physical force and violence to frequent, demeaning criticism, possessiveness, restrictiveness, and emotional withholding. Men who physically or sexually abuse their wives typically

  believe in male superiority over females
  believe in traditional sex roles for men and women

either see women as weak, or idealize women

expect women to be caretakers

are intolerant of women's anger

project responsibility for their own feelings

see their wives as extensions of themselves

have relationships with other men that are superficial and limited

are interested in looking strong to other men

Men may resort to violence in response to perceived powerlessness (Hampton & Coner-Edwards, 1993). If a man believes he is supposed to be superior to his wife but he makes less money or is not as intelligent as his wife, he may believe that his physical advantages of size, weight, and strength are the most effective ways of letting her know that he is still in control. Unemployed men are twice as likely to batter their wives as men who are employed. Men who have less status in their jobs than their wives have are more likely to batter their wives (Gelles & Cornell, 1985). Men who abuse alcohol are more likely to commit spousal abuse than men who do not drink. In fact, the abuse of alcohol is the most significant factor in marital abuse (Straus & Sweet, 1990). Abuse of alcohol provides a man with an excuse for his behavior, allowing him to displace responsibility for battering his wife.

Men who batter use various defenses to justify their behavior (Adams, 1989):

They minimize the seriousness of their violence.

They claim their intentions were good. ("I just wanted her to listen.")

They blame the abuse on the fact that they were drinking and therefore not responsible.

They claim loss of control.

They blame their wives for provoking them.

C. Greenblat (1983) examines the argument about loss of control that batterers so often use to explain their behavior. She asserts that most people who act violently have on some level at first reflected on the likelihood that they will suffer negative consequences as a result of their behavior. If a man believes that the chances of his being arrested or of his wife leaving him as a result of the abuse are low, then he is less likely to make the judgments necessary to prevent him from acting out his feelings of rage. The rewards of battering her into submission may outweigh the possible costs. "An individual will attempt to obtain a desired outcome or reward at a minimum cost. If a man lacks legitimate power, he can use violence as a low cost alternative" (Hauser, 1982, p. 23). The husband who has other resources for validating his superior position over his wife is not likely to use violence (Hauser, 1982). Inherent in these research findings is the cultural and religious concept of a relationship model in which the man is entitled to be in charge.

The Role of Culture

Our culture says that men are to assume powerful roles in sexual relationships and that women are to assume submissive roles. Clyde W. Franklin (1984) says that part of male sexual socialization includes learning to objectify the female, fixating on parts of her body considered sexually stimulating, and conquering the woman through intercourse. Sigmund Freud believed that violence is a component of the sexual instinct in men. Franklin (1984) contends that sex-role socialization is responsible for linkages between sex and violence in our culture. Men learn certain traits associated with masculinity that include both sexual aggression and sexual dominance. Sex-role rigidity and violence are positively correlated. Rigid sex-role beliefs are the breeding ground for both the devaluation and the idealization of women. Some men believe the myth that women enjoy being subdued or conquered. Warren Farrell (1993) postulates that men are violent because women and children need them to be. He argues that women have covertly requested that men be violent to protect them and fight wars for them. He seems oblivious to the fact that political power has been and still is primarily in the hands of males. Although Farrell makes an interesting argument about the historical disposability of young males, many of his arguments appear to be another attempt to blame women for their own victimization.

Kathleen H. Hofeller (1982) relates the story of Joe and Ruth, a typical violent man and his wife. In the past few years, Joe's alcohol use has increased and his behavior has become irrational and erratic. If Joe goes out drinking and Ruth keeps his dinner warm for him, he accuses her of having fixed it for her lover, and he beats her. If she does not keep his dinner warm, he calls her a lazy, good-for-nothing bitch who does not take care of her husband, and he beats her. Afterward he is apologetic, but he always adds, "Why did you make me do it? If only you wouldn't act that way, I wouldn't get so angry. You are the only person in the world who could make me do this" (p. 64).

In this vignette, Joe shifts the responsibility for the abuse onto Ruth. He expects that Ruth should take care of him emotionally and take responsibility for controlling his anger. Ruth has left Joe several times, but she always goes back. She has told several people about the violence, and they all suggest she get a divorce. However, she has never worked, has no job skills, and would not be able to support herself and her children. Ruth's reasons for staying in this abusive marriage highlight her lack of options, her dependency on Joe's income for financial support, and the prospect of being solely responsible for the children. Whether to take care of herself by leaving or to take care of her children by staying is her dilemma.

For many religious women who are in abusive marriages, the greatest dilemma comes from having to repress their anger at their husbands because they believe they must not challenge the husband's authority. This repression of anger and resentment often leads to depression for women who believe they must be submissive on the outside. Many people believe that religion plays a part in creating and maintaining life situations that contribute to depression in women (Stoudenmire, 1976). They feel that suppressed anger is a significant factor in the evolution of their depression.

The Role of Religion

The relationship of religion to family violence has largely been ignored. Those within the religious community have been unwilling to examine the connections, have ignored the prevalence of family violence in religious homes, and have generated little research on the topic. Secular researchers who look at religious aspects of family violence often do not adequately address the dynamics of the religious family system.

A study was conducted with more than five hundred residents of Texas (Shupe et al., 1987). Religious participation was one of the correlates being studied in relation to family violence. Those persons who participated in traditional religious groups had more traditional sex-role attitudes and were less likely to state that spousal rape was unacceptable. For comparison purposes, the study grouped religious denominations into two categories: conservative and moderate. The results, while not statistically significant, suggest that conservative religious denominations had more incidences of life-threatening abuse than moderate denominations.

The Austin Family Violence Diversion Network and the Tyler Family Preservation Project, both based in Texas, help abusive couples and families discover ways to handle conflict without physical violence. Batterers in these programs are challenged concerning their patriarchal sex-role beliefs. Religious belief of the batterer is one of the areas in which the programs strive to create an attitudinal change. "The hardest men to counsel are the older, religious men. They are stubborn and they never stop referring to the Bible," says John Patrick, a counselor with the Family Preservation Project (quoted in Shupe et al., 1987). The men in these programs who mention their religious beliefs typically appeal to the Bible to justify their use of violence. They often use the word *submit* concerning their wives' failure to bow to their demands. Some of the men said that their wives must submit to them in order to be submitting to God. These men used religion as a rationale to dominate women and to excuse occasional violence as necessary discipline (Shupe et al., 1987).

William J. Hauser (1982) reports on a study done by Allen and Straus in 1977 that looks at several correlates of abusive marriages. Religious participation by both spouses was one of the correlates being studied. Religious participation was found to increase the positive correlation with physical abuse. Hauser reports that "when the husband is perceived as having the greater power in the family, religious participation by either spouse may serve to reinforce the traditional notions of the husband as the head of the household, and therefore, enhance the possibilities for the use of physical abuse to maintain that status" (1982, p. 56).

When the husband is seen as having more power than the wife, religious participation by either spouse can reinforce his perceived right to use force to maintain that status. The results of this study support the assertion that traditional conservative religious belief is positively correlated with spousal abuse.

Marital Rape

Sexual violence against women is a horrifying almost normative occurrence in America. Any woman who travels alone, dates, goes to work, or takes a walk in a park must be vigilant in protecting herself from unwanted sexual contact. Statistics consistently point to the fact that one out of four women in our country will experience unwanted sexual contact by the time she is eighteen years old.

A form of sexual violence that receives little attention is marital rape, the least reported form of sexual assault. Sexual assault by husbands occurs twice as often as rape by a stranger (Schwendinger & Schwendinger, 1983). One-third of women who report being battered by their husbands also report being raped by them. More than two-thirds of those who report being battered also report that their husbands frequently pressure them into having sex (Frieze, 1979). Diana Russell (1990), in her classic work on marital rape, questioned hundreds of women about their experiences with marital abuse. Of 644 married women interviewed, 14 percent reported being sexually assaulted by their husbands, with 12 percent of those reporting forced intercourse. David Finkelhor and Kersti Yllo (1983), in their study of more than three hundred women, found that 10 percent had been forced to have sexual intercourse with their husbands. Richard J. Gelles and Murray A. Straus (1988) found that of the one thousand women they questioned, 8 percent reported having been forced by their husbands to have sexual intercourse. Finkelhor and Yllo (1983) cite several studies on marital rape, all of which show that about 35 to 37 percent of women who have been battered by their husbands have also been raped by their husbands. If one were to add the objectionable sexual acts that husbands force their wives to perform, the percentage of women reporting sexual abuse within marriage would be even higher.

Finkelhor and Yllo (1983) conducted in-depth interviews with women who had been raped by their husbands. They delineated three types of rapes that husbands perpetrate on their wives. The battering rape occurs in a marital relationship in which the rape is part of a larger picture of abuse and is usually the culmination of a battering episode. The nonbattering rape grows out of general conflicts about sex. The husband in this case uses rape as a means of getting what he wants sexually. The husband will often initiate the rape while the woman is sleeping. The third type of rape that Finkelhor and Yllo describe involves bizarre sexual obsessions. These men are usually addicted to pornography and demand that their wives help them play out their sexual fantasies. Often these men need to experience ritualized or debasing sexual activity in order to become aroused. They shame or ridicule the wife into participating in their ritualized activity by accusing her of being selfish, frigid, or uptight about sex.

Many women who experience marital rape do not name it as rape (Gelles, 1979). One woman describes her experience: "He thought I was a cold fish. He told everyone I was frigid. Well, I suppose I was cold. I mean, he would come home after being out the whole night and he was drunk and reeking of beer. I didn't feel like it [sexual intercourse]. But he wanted it. We didn't argue. He just got his way" (Gelles & Straus, 1988, p. 94).

Marital rape was not a crime until the 1970s (Hampton & Coner-Edwards, 1993; Russell, 1990). Although all fifty states now have marital rape laws, many include exemptions that protect husbands from being fully prosecuted. As of 1990, only sixteen states and the District of Columbia had no marital exemptions in their marital rape laws. Twenty-six states have some form of marital exemption, and in eight states, husbands cannot be prosecuted for marital rape unless the couple is living apart or is legally separated, or if one spouse has filed for divorce or an order of protection. Studies reveal that while many people see rape as a heinous crime, they do not see spousal rape as a serious problem (Finkelhor & Yllo, 1985).

The church has been particularly silent concerning marital rape and its consequences for the women who are so assaulted. The first accounts in the writings of the Catholic church concerning marital

rape are from the 1600s. The issue in question was not how to protect wives from rape by their husbands but whether the woman had
a right to expel the semen from her body after the rape (Bayer, 1985).

The concept that females are the property of males is the key to
understanding the history of marital rape and the origin of marital
rape exemption laws. From the seventeenth century onward, rape
laws protected individual women only if the rapist was not the husband. English common law of coverture (laws that insured the husband's place as supreme authority in the home) gave the husband
the right to use physical violence if needed to maintain control of
his wife. The woman's money, property, and body belonged to the
man after marriage (Schwendinger & Schwendinger, 1983). The marital rape exemption says to a woman that she is indeed the property
of her husband.

Gender Inequality and Marital Rape

Gender inequality is one of the four variables that Larry Baron and
Murray A. Straus (1989) assert are the main causes of rape in our society. They believe that the domination of women is built into society
in the opportunity and reward structures of our culture. Women are
systematically disadvantaged in obtaining socioeconomic resources
that provide power and are socialized to accept being victimized.
Peggy Reeves Sanday (1981) looked at marital rape through a sociological lens. She hypothesized that the occurrence of rape would vary
according to the degree of power and status afforded women in any
given society. She found higher incidences of rape in societies in which
women are excluded from positions of status and power. In contrast,
in societies that afford women relatively equal access to positions of
power, rape is much more infrequent. Other factors Baron and Straus
found to be significant in contributing to rape occurrence included:

  economic inequity between classes and sexes
  social disorganization
  the age structure of the population (most rapes are committed by
    those under the age of forty)
  degree to which violence is normative and accepted

availability of pornography

patriarchal domination of women

A perception exists that once a sexual relationship has been established, subsequent sexual refusal is less legitimate. R. Lance Shotland and Leonard Goodstein (1992) found that after a woman consented to have sex with a man on as few as ten occasions, her refusals against further sexual involvement were perceived as losing their legitimacy. Both men and women believed that prior sexual activity establishes a precedence that makes future sexual refusal less legitimate. This attitude is perhaps one of the roadblocks to getting rid of all exemptions to marital rape laws. Another roadblock to ending exemptions is the fear that marital rape laws give women a weapon to use against men. According to Warren Farrell, spousal rape legislation "gives the woman a nuclear bomb" (1993, p. 338).

The media obsession with the case of Lorena and John Bobbitt has brought out fears of both sexes concerning marital rape. After Lorena Bobbitt was allegedly raped, she took a kitchen knife and sliced off her husband's penis, which was later recovered and surgically re-attached. She was acquitted of malicious wounding. John Bobbitt was acquitted of raping his wife. During the trials, a picture of a typical abusive relationship emerged. Lorena described frequently being raped by John, especially when he was drunk. Many men were horrified and frightened at the viciousness of Lorena Bobbitt's attack on her husband, but many women felt that it somehow evened the score for all the thousands of women who are raped by men.

Role of Religion in Marital Rape

In an extensive study of the impact of religious attitudes on marital rape, C. Jeffords (1984) looked at demographic variables in attitudes toward marital rape immunity laws. Approximately two-thirds of the respondents did not believe wives should be able to accuse their husbands of rape. This was particularly true of older respondents. Women were more likely to favor legislation limiting exemptions than were men. These results are from 1982, and it is likely that if a study were done now, general attitudes toward spousal immunity might be less lenient. This study found that persons with traditional religious beliefs concerning sex roles were less likely to see marital rape as a serious offense. Both religiosity and religion were positively correlated with traditional sex-role attitudes. These results lend credence to the claims of feminists that patriarchal ideology has slowed down the abolition of spousal immunity for marital rape (Jeffords & Dull, 1982).

Diana Russell (1990) examined the religious upbringing and current religious preference of victims of marital rape in her landmark study. Almost half of the victims of wife rape were brought up in Protestant religions. Thirty-five percent were reared as Catholic, 6 percent as Jewish, and 7 percent as some other religion. More than one-third of the victims of wife rape had no religious preference. Twenty-four percent described their preference as Catholic, 23 percent as Protestant, 5 percent as Jewish, and 13 percent as some other religion. These percentages reflect the distribution of the sample as a whole and are therefore seen as representative of society. Russell looked only at religious affiliation in this study. Had Russell studied the content of the women's religious beliefs and the degree of personal religious integration, the results would have had more usefulness in learning about the effects of religion on marital abuse. It is the content of individuals' religious beliefs and the way those individuals apply those beliefs in their lives that affect their relationships. One can be a staunchly patriarchal Jew just as easily as one can be a staunchly patriarchal Methodist.

A 1983 study provides a multivariate analysis of the effects of religion on the crime of rape (Stack & Kanavy, 1983). The theoretical foundation for the study is an acceptance of the Durkheimian model of deviant behavior. A theory relating low religious involvement to relatively high crime rates is constructed from Durkheim's social integration theories of deviance. S. Stack and M. J. Kanavy believe that the crime of rape is particularly sensitive to variation in the religious component. Their hypothesis is that the greater an individual's religious integration, the less likely he is to commit rape. They look at the degree of religious integration or regulation as being the antidote to the deviant behavior of rape. The results of their study showed a positive relationship between degree of religious integration and propensity to commit rape. It makes sense that the more deeply integrated a man's sense of religious ethics, the less likely he is to assault and rape a stranger. The applicability of their findings to marital rape is vague. If a man's religious conviction is that his wife is to be under his authority and that her body belongs to him, his religious integration may contribute to, rather than mitigate, the likelihood that he would rape his wife. The pivotal issue is not how deeply held religious convictions are but the content of those beliefs concerning marital relationships and equality, as the story of Mary and Gray illustrates.

Mary entered therapy asking for help with her feelings of depression and hopelessness. She was a full-time homemaker with three school-age children. She had been married for twelve years to Gray, who was a part-time preacher and a schoolteacher. Mary had never worked outside the home and had given up her plans for college in order to care for her young children. Both she and Gray were deeply committed to their religious beliefs, and much of their time was spent on church activities. Mary's complaints centered on her feeling that her life had little meaning and that she did not feel appreciated or loved by her husband.

In subsequent interviews with Gray and the children present, a picture emerged of a highly patriarchal family structure. Gray ruled the family, using frequent spankings to control the behavior of the children. Gray's chief complaint about the marriage was Mary's lack of interest in being sexual with him. He used passages in 1 Corinthians and Ephesians to shame Mary into submitting to his sexual desires. At one point Gray confided to Mary's father, who was also a preacher, that Mary was not fulfilling her "wifely duties." Mary related that her father advised Gray, "Women hate sex, but you just have to make them do it." Gray proceeded to pressure, coerce, and threaten Mary into submitting to his sexual demands. Gray stopped short of raping Mary, but the emotional bond of the marriage was irreparably damaged by his beliefs that he had a God-given right to demand sexual contact.

There are passages in the Bible that speak beautifully about the sexual relationship between a man and a woman. The Song of Solomon is one of those texts. First Corinthians 7 contains the apostle Paul's advice on marriage and sexuality. He says, "The wife hath not power of her own body, but the husband: and likewise also the husband hath not power of his own body, but the wife" (v. 4 KJV). Paul describes a fairly radical approach to marriage relationships in which the husband is as responsible for and committed to meeting his wife's sexual needs as she is for meeting his. In the account of creation, the man and woman are entreated to become "one flesh" in their spiritual and sexual union. As male leaders have interpreted these texts, they have become a weapon that a Christian husband uses to demand sexual intercourse whenever he wants it. This unity doctrine, or one-body concept, still affects marital laws, especially as they relate to the physical and sexual abuse of women (Schwendinger & Schwendinger, 1983).

Treatment Issues for Therapists and Pastoral Counselors

The minister, pastoral counselor, or therapist is often the only person outside the family in whom the abused woman will confide. Providing for the woman's physical safety should be the first priority. Concern for the woman's physical safety must override any need on the professional's part to keep the couple together. If the battering continues, then the professional needs to encourage the woman to get into a women's shelter, file a restraining order, or, if necessary, file charges against the husband. Getting both partners into a treatment program is essential.

For the woman, outpatient therapy needs to include assertiveness training, exploration of identity, and defining what her needs and expectations are for a marital relationship. She should also be involved in some type of group therapy with other women who have been battered or raped. She needs to have a supportive community, which may include her church community, but only if the church can support her right to be physically and emotionally safe. If the church community tries to push her into living with her husband even though she is being abused, or if they tell her that she must not divorce, they may sabotage her treatment.

In treatment, both partners may believe initially that the woman is partly responsible for the abuse. The counselor must herself believe and help the couple to see that the husband is solely responsible for the battering. Both spouses need to be educated that every person is responsible for his or her own actions and that the woman cannot make her husband hit her. The couple will need direction in developing a safety plan if future battering is threatened. These plans may include fully complying with any court orders, helping the woman find a safe place to go if she anticipates a battering episode, or addressing issues of alcohol abuse.

Helping the couple learn to communicate assertively and respectfully is important. The abusive husband will need to learn to communicate frustration without being aggressive. The wife may need to be more assertive in setting limits on how much verbal abuse she will allow before she needs to get away from her husband. Conventional feminine goodness means being voiceless, so one task of the therapist or counselor is to help the woman find and use her voice for her own good (Belenky et al., 1986).

Treatment for the husband should include therapy and involvement in a batterer's program for men. Violent men believe that violence is a legitimate way of solving problems and that it is acceptable for men to control women (Adams, 1989). Outpatient individual therapy alone is not usually sufficient to help the husband change his behavior and thinking. He needs to explore the battering behavior in the company of other men who can challenge and support each other toward change. The group can become an alternative peer culture apart from the culture that has contributed to his sexist beliefs. Treatment goals for the husband include learning to accept ambiguity and loss of control, developing acceptance of women's anger, and recognizing the sexism in himself and in society (Adams, 1989). He needs to be encouraged to recognize and own his feelings of powerlessness. Helping the man to recognize the thought patterns that trigger his urge to use violence is important. The therapist can encourage the husband to construct for himself a new definition of manhood that includes valuing and respect for the feminine. Gershen Kaufman states that the most fundamental problem in the patriarchal construction of manhood is the assumption of male centrality (Gray, 1992). Men must accept that they are not the center of the human world but partners with women in defining humanity.

The therapist who is not a member of the clients' religious group may need to let the clients educate him or her about their religious beliefs about marital relationships. In order for the therapist to be effective in helping the religious couple, he or she must understand the belief system under which they are operating. Questions such as, "Where did you learn that women must be submissive to their husbands?" or "What do you believe are the responsibilities of wives in a marriage relationship?" or "What does the Bible teach about sex in marriage?" will give the therapist valuable information into what beliefs define their roles. The therapist can then begin to question the efficacy of those beliefs in establishing an honest, intimate relationship. With Christian men, a pastoral counselor may want to examine Jesus' standard of behavior toward women.

A primary responsibility of the counselor will be to provide education and modeling for relationships based on equality and respect. "There can be no intimacy without equal, overt power" (Beavers, 1994). If the balance of power is equal in a marital relationship there is little danger of violence. Democratic households have the lowest levels of violence (Gelles & Cornell, 1985). The therapist can work toward helping the couple see the significant psychic and relationship costs for assuming polarized roles in which the man is solely responsible for financial leadership of the family and the woman is solely responsible for the emotional health of the family and the needs of the children (Enns, 1988). Both partners and the children are cheated by these polarized sex roles. When responsibilities are assigned based on the interests and skills of the partners instead of on their gender, the couple will be more productive.

Implications for Religious Leaders

What are the implications of the research on marital abuse? It suggests that the role of religion in providing answers to the problem of spousal abuse has been negligible, as the experience of one woman demonstrates: "I had a pretty strong faith. I tried everything I learned in the church. The scriptures say the woman who is submissive is the one who excels in God's sight and who is treasured. I knew my husband wasn't acting in faith. I couldn't reconcile his behavior with what I heard in church. I wanted God's love, but I began to have my doubts. As far as the pastor was concerned, the husband had a right to beat his wife. He said he would pray for me and I should submit to it" (Jacobs, 1984, p. 164). However, religion could and should be used to provide solutions to the problem of spousal abuse (Shupe et al., 1987). Although religious groups have created and funded most women's shelters, the religious dialogue about spousal abuse has been sparse.

Pastors can break the silence about spousal abuse in religious families. They can encourage models for marriage based on equality and respect instead of submission and headship. They must first recognize the patriarchal ideology and teaching in Scripture and in the history of the church. They must be willing to challenge old forms of relating.

Ministers can publicly value and encourage assertive self-care in women. They must not only prize the long-suffering, sacrificial woman in Scripture but also teach about strong female leaders in church history. The Christian woman will need encouragement to find a balance between caring for others and caring for herself, balancing her own needs for self-development with responsiveness to the needs of others (Gilligan, 1982). "When the values of religion are perceived as sacred, commitment to those values functions as a more powerful motivation than does freedom to pursue personal goals. It means seeing autonomy as less important than mutual interdependence and mutual responsibility, both of which are divinely sanctioned" (McClain, 1979, p. 41).

Ministers can challenge the men in their churches to change their ways of relating and can model relationships of mutual submission and respect by extending women equal partnership in the life of the church. Church leaders should pay attention to what the church's rituals and processions communicate about relationships (Harrison, 1976; Neville, 1974). Are women represented in visible leadership roles? Are they included in the rituals of the church? Are they cocreators with males of church policy? Are their talents fully utilized in the service of the church or are they restricted in the roles they are allowed to fill? The church must embody the unity and diversity of God's image. It can become more fully representative of the nature of God by allowing men and women in all of their sexual distinctiveness to be equal partners in the ministry and work of the church. Service based on gifts not on gender affirms the contribution of each sex.

Ministers must publicly challenge traditional theological assumptions about the nature of God. They must affirm in their ministry and in their conversation that the image of God is fully represented in woman as well as in man (Farley, 1976). Ministers need to examine their feelings about feminism, which is a commitment to social, political, economic, and religious equality for all men and women.

Pastors and ministers can train themselves to use nonsexist language when speaking about God. They can highlight at times the many Scriptures that depict God as a nurturer and caretaker, affirming that both traditional masculine and feminine qualities are a part of the Divine. This beautiful passage from the Book of Job illustrates the richness of Scriptures that speak of God the Mother:

> Who shut up the sea behind doors
>   when it burst forth from the womb,
> when I made the clouds its garment
>   and wrapped it in thick darkness,
> when I fixed limits for it
>   and set its doors and bars in place,
> when I said, "This far you may come and no farther;
>   here is where your proud waves halt"?
>
> Job 38:8–11

Mary Stewart Van Leeuwen (1990) writes about the five "acts" of the biblical drama that unfold in Scripture. The five acts in sequence are creation, the fall, redemption, Pentecost, and renewal. She calls Pentecost "Women's Emancipation Day" because at Pentecost, with the outpouring of the gift of the Holy Spirit, women shared equally with men in the receipt of spiritual gifts. Women proceeded to break bread and participate with men in the worship services, even assuming positions of leadership in church gatherings. This kind of equality was considered scandalous before Pentecost. Jesus' teachings and actions were intended to reverse the consequences of the curse after the fall for both man and woman. Pentecost was to have been the beginning of new forms of relationship in the church.

Justice, Equality, Intimacy

The role that religion plays in Christian marriages is significant. Religious beliefs help shape concepts about marital roles and about personal identity. The research on patriarchy and marital abuse supports the clinical experience of this author: Traditional, patriarchal beliefs about marriage make establishing an intimate marital relationship harder than it has to be.

Patriarchy is not responsible for an individual husband's violent action toward his wife. It does, however, create an environment ripe for abuse. A weakened immune system does not create the virus that leads to deadly infection, but it provides the environment in which the virus can thrive and do its killing. Patriarchal beliefs weaken the marital system so that the deadly virus of violence can gain a stronghold.

W. Yates (1990) provides four dominant principles for a modern model of marriage: love, justice, freedom, and order. He relates that the concept of justice in marriage is a twentieth-century concept that comes out of our concerns with justice in society. The church can be in the forefront of the struggle for justice by affirming the equality of all people. The biblical text can and should be used as a resource for bringing justice to marital relationships. For the text to be used in a reparative way, it must first be wrested from the grasp of the patriarchal interpretations that overshadow its messages of mutual submission and interdependence. Marital relationships based on old models of submission and headship limit both partners in their ability to experience true intimacy. "The rhythm of a real, healing and empowering love is take and give, give and take, free of the cloying inequality of one partner active and one partner passive" (Harrison, 1976, p. 51). The love we need and want is a deeply mutual experience.

It is time for the church to sanction and encourage models of equality and mutuality in marriage. It is time for ministers, priests, pastoral counselors, and theologians to recognize the destructive power of patriarchy and its contribution to violence in marriage. It is time for the church to actively refute the claims of patriarchy. With the church taking a leadership role, Christian couples can begin to construct marital relationships that affirm the embodiment of the Spirit of God that resides in both partners. The fullness of the image of God can be represented in a union that values both the feminine and masculine aspects of humanity.

When Right Becomes Scriptural Abuse

2

Melissa Kubitschek Luzzi

Come to me, all you who are weary and are carrying heavy burdens, and I will give you rest. Take my yoke upon you and learn from me, for I am gentle and humble in heart, and you will find rest for your souls. For my yoke is easy and my burden is light" (Matt. 11:28–30 NRSV). These words of Jesus have brought comfort and encouragement to countless weary souls throughout the centuries. Christ offered his yoke as a replacement for the heavy and burdensome yoke of the law. Unfortunately, the evangelical church, the very community that is to be salt and light to a decaying and hurting world, appears to hinder many abused women and their children from experiencing this rest and learning that Jesus offered.

During the previous two decades, a growing public awareness of domestic violence has developed. One of the first books written about woman battering, *Scream Quietly or the Neighbors Will Hear,* was published in 1977. It puzzled the British author, Erin Pizzey, that Americans had been silent on the topic of wife beating. Perhaps Mildred Daley Pagelow's response of twenty years ago should be heeded by the evangelical church today: "In the still somewhat puritanical United States, citizens do not like to question their most sacred institutions. We prefer to believe that we are too civilized [and as Christians, maybe too spiritual] for brutal behavior, and that these problems can't happen here" (Pizzey, 1977, p. 147).

The experience of Jim and Phyllis Alsdurf, authors of *Battered into Submission,* an important book about wife abuse in Christian homes, appears to support this observation. "Eight years ago we were not aware that wife abuse even occurred in Christian homes" (1989, p. 9). The belief that all family life is safe and secure is continually shattered by the alarming frequency of violent incidents spanning all age groups, races, ethnic and religious groups, educational levels, and socioeconomic groups. The Christian community is beginning to admit and address the pervasiveness of abuse within its church families and not just the violence in unchurched homes.

In *Gender and Grace,* Mary Stewart Van Leeuwen wrote that "conservative religiosity is currently the second-best indicator of wife abuse" (1990, p. 245). In addition, the Alsdurfs (1989) suggested that the majority of abuse against Christian women is not physical but rather emotional abuse and manipulation. "In fact, men who perceive their position before God as superior to that of women generally will not need to resort to physical abuse. When a man can psychologically overpower his wife and justify his actions through a misapplication of Scripture, physical violence is less necessary" (1989, p. 150). Thus, a Christian woman who is taught from childhood to submit to men because that is God's ordained order can earn the labels "unsubmissive," "rebellious," or "feminist" if she questions the behaviors of her husband and the advice of mainly male clergy. This teaching may also predispose her to question her own inner voice even more than she may already be doing.

For Christians to ignore, deny, or minimize the reality of abuse is often to limit or deny Christian women who have been battered physically, emotionally, and/or spiritually a support system that shares and encourages her values and commitment to biblical principles. Christian women with strong religious beliefs and values have unique needs as well as resources. Using biblical language to guide in understanding and confronting the abuse augments her integration process. Utilizing a woman's Christian faith also assists her in more fully tapping God's power that is available to her. God is her ally and partner instead of her accuser.

This can prove to be a difficult task, though, because many of the commonly taught biblical instructions, when they are placed within an abusive relationship, can become harmful, destructive, and abusive themselves. The right becomes wrong. Consequently, the woman may feel guilt, anger, or shame, and may question her relationship with God when she decides not to obey such teachings. The power of the Holy Spirit is then perceived as being less available. Furthermore, access to the church, the body of Christ, as a support system, which is so vital to recovery, can be easily lost.

A woman's faith and her connectedness with the church exemplify Mary Ann Dutton's view of mediating factors that affect the level of psychological trauma and the strategies used to protect the woman from abuse: tangible resources and social support; personal strengths/inner resources; and current stressors (1992, p. 10). If the church does not counteract the psychological effects of abuse among battered women and reinforce strategies for the protection of these women, their children may also be denied the emotional and spiritual support and education that are so vital for their healing. The church can help to provide support systems outside the immediate family and develop a good relationship with at least one parent—two factors that have been demonstrated to increase a child's resilience to domestic violence (Jaffe, Wolfe, & Wilson, 1990, p. 73). This good relationship is made possible because the mother has found nurturing, care, and support within the church and with her God. Thus she may be able to better nurture, relate to, and be with her children.

To assist in this complicated sorting process, I will focus on some commonly accepted traditional evangelical teachings: the husband as the spiritual leader of the family, sacrificial love, and "total acceptance of your man" (Rainey & Rainey, 1986). How such teachings can become destructive when they are coupled with abuse will be exemplified in various case studies. This discussion is intended not as an end but rather will focus on an area that will benefit from further clarification.

Christians should not be surprised that distorted application of the truth has occurred. It is consistent with Satan's character and with fallen human nature. Consider Satan's temptation of Christ. By taking God's words out of the contextual whole, their misuse became a vehicle for the attempted purpose of perpetuating evil. Relationship became a secondary concern when exaggerated dominion supposedly became available. Satan did not say, "If you fall down and worship me, your relationship with the Father will become more intimate!" Christ resisted the temptation to usurp dominion and thereby maintained his commitment to intimate relationship with the Father.

It is of interest to note that what Satan lost by his rebellion was his intimate relationship with God. Satan still has power, at least for the present time. However, the close relationship that he once shared with God is no longer possible. Perhaps one of Satan's greatest desires is not only total disruption but also the destruction of every possible harmonious and intimate relationship of the Creator with his creation. Deplorably, this disintegration of relationship, protected by the guise of male headship and authority, is often reflecting Satan's heightened focus on dominion. This sin is repeatedly ignored in abusive marriage relationships within the evangelical church today.

The Husband as Spiritual Leader of the Family

Hierarchical theology teaches the submission of wives to husbands. The husband is viewed as the leader of the family and has the final authority for making all the decisions. The wife is to be in subjection to him.

> The Christian woman must be in subjection to her husband! Whether she likes it or not, subjection is a command of God and her refusal to comply with this command is an act of disobedience. All disobedience is sin; therefore, she cannot expect the blessing of God on her life unless she is willing to obey God. (Based on Genesis 3:16) (LaHaye, 1968, p. 106)
>
> A Christian man is obligated to be the ultimate decision-maker in the home. (*Focus on the Family*, 1992, p. 4)

This obligation includes that of being the spiritual leader. One aspect of being the spiritual leader is claiming the responsibility and authority to ultimately decide the amount to be tithed. The wife is to submit to the decision even though she may disagree, since it is God's plan that the husband be in charge. This is true even if it means she does not tithe at her husband's request. (Or is command more accurate?) Her submission to her husband's authority is paramount (Burkett, 1987).

What a dilemma for the mother of four children whose father gave so much to missions that the children had to wear shoes with holes in them during the snowy winter. Despite the woman's guilt regarding her disobedience to her husband and thus ultimately to God, the mother chose not to honor her husband's final tithing decision. She clearly stated her objections and spent a portion of the family's money from the next paycheck to buy adequate shoes for the children.

Her husband's reaction filled her with anger, frustration, and questioning, not only of God's provision but also of the reality of her relationship with God. The woman's husband continually reminded her that she clearly had been taught and knew that God had appointed him to provide leadership. In addition, he was an elder at the evangelical church that they regularly attended. Therefore, as spiritual leader of the family and the church, he knew she obviously could not be a Christian because of her obsession with materialism.

As a result, this woman found herself extremely depressed and spiritually barren. When searching for counsel, she was told to share with her husband how she was feeling. In this relationship, where control was disguised as God-ordained, the feelings and opinions of the wife were not regarded. To meet the needs of the children, the wife had to act contrary to what she had been instructed was God's will. She believed her choices were to care for her children as she deemed appropriate or to disobey her husband, the spiritual leader of the family. Thus, her salvation was put into question as she was continually told that she loved mammon more than God.

This case study exemplifies how a hierarchical interpretation of the Bible can contribute to the spiritual abuse of the wife as well as the neglect of the children. To allow the husband such ultimate, unquestionable authority and power in decision making is to protect the continuation of inappropriately applied scriptural instruction or "sexism intrinsic to certain doctrinal positions" (Hubbard & Hubbard, 1990, p. 46).

Lest some of you wonder why a woman would find herself in such a quandary, consider the assumption of most Christians that God, although he is often mysterious, is logical. If a woman of faith believes, as she has been religiously taught, that women were not created for leadership, she will not consider questioning her husband's, her pastor's, or her Bible teacher's interpretation of Scripture or deciding for herself whether Scripture is being used appropriately. Instead, she will continually feel condemned by her spouse, her pastor, the Scripture, and God. A Christian wife who considers the Bible her standard of behavior would reasonably succumb to the manipulation of a husband who uses God's words for his unchallengeable means of control (Hubbard, 1992a, p. 28; Rinck, 1990, p. 72).

Numerous authors and experts recommend that parents present a united front in matters of discipline and interactions with their children. Each parent is instructed to support the other, and if there is disagreement, it should be settled in private. In a home where there is mutual respect and love between parents, such a model has merit and contributes to the security and the stability of the home. A husband's unchallengeable means of control, however, is transferred into his role as father. What if one parent is abusive toward a child? What then is the basis for action? Most people agree intellectually that abusive treatment of children needs to be addressed. Ethical and legal standards are continually being revised to help protect those children who are in destructive situations. Social service agencies have become the keepers of many families.

Francis Schaeffer and C. Everett Koop recognized child abuse as a violation of human rights and challenged Christians to act and to take a sacrificial stand on such overwhelmingly important issues (1979, p. 29–31). "If, in the last part of the twentieth century, the Christian community does not take a prolonged and vocal stand for the dignity of the individual and each person's right to life—for the right of each individual to be treated as created in the image of God . . . we feel that as Christians we have failed the greatest moral test to be put before us in this century" (p. 195).

If the abusive parent is the mother, the father obviously has the responsibility as well as the God-mandated authority to protect the children by whatever means is appropriate. What if the abusive parent is the father? Some would say that since he is obviously disobedient to God's way, the mother has the obligation to protect her children. It seems unfair, though, to expect a woman who has been taught that her husband is the leader and her spiritual function is to rely on him to have the skills, confidence, and strength to make a far-reaching decision contrary to his. In those situations where there is clear physical and sexual abuse, the correctness of the decision may be easier to determine. It is still difficult to act on, since it is not uncommon for the mother and the children to be in greater jeopardy during the separation process.

Cases in which the abuse is not as obvious and is not "illegal" present an even greater moral dilemma in regard to the mother's responsibility to protect the children from a psychologically and spiritually abusive father. It seems realistic to assume that if verbal abuse of wives is common as a means of control for Christian husbands, such interaction would include verbal and spiritual abuse of the children. If this is the situation, should a Christian mother attempt to counteract the harm inflicted by a father who will not or cannot realize the impact of his behavior? What effect does it have on the child if the mother supports the father in his behavior and verbalizations because he is the spiritual leader and, after all, he is not physically bruising the child? What is the spiritual effect on a child whose Christian father, by God's supposed decree to lead, inflicts repeated shaming?

By contrast, what effect does it have on the child if the mother chooses to name the sin inflicted by the father? She may be viewed as nonsupportive of her husband and divisive, especially by the church community. At a time when open dialogue is so needed, there are too few resources available to sort through these complicated issues and to assist the mother in determining the wisest course to pursue.

The following case study illustrates the challenges facing many Christian women.

It was Christmas night. The children, Jackie and Paul, were playing a game while adult relatives and their parents observed. Paul was five years younger than Jackie and relished continually changing the rules of the game for his benefit. Thirteen-year-old Jackie finally had enough and began a loud lecture on Paul's unfairness. Father became furious at their interaction, rose from his chair, struck Jackie on the arm, and told her to grow up. She was extremely embarrassed as she ran to her bedroom.

After the company left, Jackie apologized to her brother for calling him a cheater. She told her father that she was humiliated by the way he treated her in front of company and requested that his disapproval of her be displayed in ways other than hitting. Father angrily told Jackie that he had every right to do what he did and that God has commanded him to discipline his children as he sees fit. In fact, he does not have a choice in the matter.

Not wanting to be divisive, but realizing that the incident needed to be discussed and corrected rather than ignored, Mother spoke with Father in private. His reaction was one of disbelief. He had not done anything inappropriate, he said, and it would have been wrong for him not to intervene. Father then demanded that Mother agree with him and support him in his earlier discipline. She felt that to do so would defraud the children and would do greater damage than had already been done. This was becoming a usual occurrence, and Mother chose to verify the children's reality that humiliation of another person and angry hitting are not righteous behavior.

For Mother, the result of not supporting Father in his decision was a threat of divorce. He then recklessly drove away, only to return a short time later and demand that Mother move out, since he makes most of the money and she obviously cannot care for the house and the children's needs.

This woman had chosen to stay home with the children instead of pursuing a career, and what was the result? Perhaps God was not pleased with her lack of submission, and the threat of having to leave her home and find another place to live was the consequence. How can she seek God with this consciousness of nonsubmission in her life? It is not uncommon for Christian women to face these psychological and financial dilemmas with a simultaneous spiritual battle.

A theology that reinforces a woman's limited ability to make choices can translate to depression and a lower valuing of self (Hubbard, 1992b). The shame imparted to this wife became a formidable barrier hindering the woman's experiencing her incredible value as endowed by her Creator: "I praise you, for I am fearfully and wonderfully made. Wonderful are your works; that I know very well" (Ps. 139:14 NRSV). That which could have been a source of strength in a difficult situation was illusive.

For three reasons it is important for the evangelical Christian community to recognize and confront such spiritual abuse. First, the secular world cannot adequately understand how a person's primary motivation is to live a righteous and holy life: "For the message about the cross is foolishness to those who are perishing, but to us who are being saved it is the power of God" (1 Cor. 1:18 NRSV). Religious issues are primary issues for the Christian. For the church to remain silent is to abandon those women who struggle with the complex task of defining and following the truth regarding spiritual leadership. The hierarchical teaching on male leadership contributes to the destruction of herself and her family. A united voice is needed in supporting the abused woman as she confronts such manipulation of Scripture.

Second, it can be beneficial to understand and address scriptural abuse as a category of verbal abuse. The Scripture is used as a tool to champion a misuse of power and authority. The woman is discredited and her position as wife and mother is disabled. According to G. H. Ketterman (1993), verbal abuse does not have to be tolerated. Victims speak of the damage that words have had on their emotional and physical state. What are a Christian woman's options, especially if the abusive words come from the mouth of her husband, the man who is her spiritual leader, the authority in her life? On what basis can she make an informed and righteous decision, since her husband is the disseminator of spiritual truth? If a woman is taught that she needs to be protected and that she cannot have a close relationship with God if she does not acknowledge her husband's position of authority over her, how can she feel competent to discern scriptural abuse, let alone say no to the abuser?

Unless a woman accepts her ultimate calling as that of a disciple and follower of Jesus Christ, a woman who can hear the word of God and obey it (Luke 11:28), it is unlikely that she can choose to withstand abuse. She need not "demonstrate her obedience to Christ by obeying her husband" (Page, 1975, p. 33). The armor of God (Eph. 6:10–18) is equally available and equally protective of both male and female, wife and husband. A wife's submissiveness to her husband's authority is not her shield of protection against Satan's devices (Christenson as quoted by Page, 1975, p. 36).

Therefore, when Julia's husband, Bill, would forcibly sit on her, pray in tongues, and then spit in her face because God told Bill that he was displeased with her behavior, as she was able, Julia could recognize and acknowledge the abuse, hold her husband accountable, and feel affirmed and strengthened in her relationship with God.

She did not feel abandoned, because she knew that God, not her husband, was her protector, spiritual leader, and final authority, and God would lead her.

Third, acknowledging spiritual abuse assists in untangling a woman's spiritual identity from traditional roles. Adherence to hierarchical theology in regard to gender has made it acceptable for a woman to avoid personal responsibility in the name of obedience to men and seeming fidelity to the Word of God; indeed, such submission is often perceived to be a more spiritual way (Hubbard & Hubbard, 1990). Recognizing the woman's tendency to defer her appropriate dominion in order to maintain her relationship (Van Leeuwen, 1990) can assist in empowering a woman to bring change to what appears to be a hopeless situation. A woman can further develop self-sufficiency, accountability, and responsibility for her God-mandated dominion. Especially during this transition, it is essential to sincerely interact with an abused woman "as a person with gifts and personal worth of equal and complementary value to those of a man" (Glazer & Moessner, 1991, p. 136). Romans 14:12 assumes a new dimension when a wife sees herself as spiritually separate from her husband. She will be the person giving an account of herself to God.

Sacrificial Love

Sacrificial love is an important element of Christian theology. As John 3:16 teaches, God loved the world to the extent that he sacrificed his Son, Jesus Christ, to redeem his creation and restore the intimate relationship experienced before the fall. Likewise, Christians are to love their neighbors, doing them no harm (Rom. 13:10), and their enemies (Matt. 5:44).

The biblical command to love is given to both men and women. Within passages regarding husbands and wives, the instruction to love is directed more to the husband, and the direction to submit is directed more to the wife. E. White (1965) wrote that the primary and supreme command in the husband's role is "love your wife" and the primary task of the wife is accepting her role in subordination. The husband "is to be the sacrificial agent with whom no cost is too great to pay to express his love for his wife" (p. 79). For the wife, "subordination is clearly seen to be voluntary. . . . The wife voluntarily accepts her role for the well-being of the relationship, not because she fears a tyrant husband" (p. 80). Consequently, the love of the husband is to be demonstrated by his sacrificial headship or leadership for the wife and family, with the emphasis being on leadership. For the wife, an indicator of her spirituality is her submission to her husband's leadership. (It is interesting that male leadership is central to both the husband's and the wife's roles.)

Is it not reasonable that such an instruction means that self-denial becomes a common focus for the wife? This self-denial may be further reinforced by the common concept that Eve was Adam's "helpmate" rather than "a help meet" (Gen. 2:18, 20 KJV).

A practical example of what appears to be an overemphasis on a wife's duty of self-denial is explicated in *Building Your Mate's Self-Esteem,* which suggests that a married woman's responsibility as wife should be "her number one focus" (Rainey & Rainey, 1986, p. 222). To make a husband's or a wife's role one's primary focus could border on idolatry (Van Leeuwen, 1990, p. 174). Total dedication to mate and/or family can undermine loyalty to Christ, his message, his kingdom, and his body. Such a narrow focus can also dull individuals' faith as well as their witness. How can Christians be light and salt if they cloister themselves in their homes and Christian communities where they feel comfortable and where everyone supposedly subscribes to the same roles, or could it be said, rules?

For a dedicated Christian who is in an abusive relationship, such family and congregational isolation can generate a tension that is hideous to acknowledge because it should not exist. How can a wife voluntarily submit to a tyrant whom she fears? How can following God's guidelines for a happy and successful marriage, guidelines that were designed to eliminate marital problems, cause anxiety? Instead of reexamining the guidelines and the prejudiced patriarchal viewpoint from which they proceed, the woman blames herself for difficulties or denies that they exist.

Such guidelines often include a narrow understanding of sacrificial love. The component of truth is excluded. Teaching on love rarely distinguishes "between attention to needs and submission to exploitation" (Outka, 1972, p. 277). To sacrifice oneself as an indication of love is to fall into the trap of unprofitable martyrdom. "If I give all I possess to the poor and surrender my body to the flames, but have not love, I gain nothing" (1 Cor. 13:3). Does God ask us to sacrifice ourselves to perpetuate evil? Christ voluntarily sacrificed his life to save humanity and to bring life. In contrast, sacrificing oneself for abuse sanctions destruction. The female predisposition to relationship (Van Leeuwen, 1990) frames peace at any price as a godly quality. Stability is supposedly being maintained. Codependent behavior is valued instead of truth and honesty.

Besides the drain on self-esteem that an abusive relationship causes, guilt and continuous, futile striving to improve the relationship can become a depressing oppression for a Christian woman whose relationship with God is of utmost importance. Stress can result from denying the hidden conflict that often culminates in a destructive and violent outburst (Alsdurf & Alsdurf, 1989, p. 151). Encouraging abused partners to turn the other cheek, meaning to ignore the occurrence of violence, is tolerating sin and violence. Enduring an abusive marriage does not respect human dignity or protect the dignity of marriage and the rights of children. Rather, it disdains Christian marriage by covering abuse with scriptural justification. How contrary to the loving, mutual submission taught in Ephesians 5:21: dominion tempered by love and relationship tempered by responsibility to Christ.

Total Acceptance

Total acceptance of a mate has become a popular instruction: "Give him your complete acceptance, even if you don't understand totally. It may be necessary to ask God to help you accept your husband, for your situation may not be easy to live with" (Rainey & Rainey, 1986, p. 224). Such a suggestion may be incredibly close to the moral indifference found in both the church and the culture. Total acceptance frequently becomes synonymous with exempting a man from the consequences of his behavior within marriage.

If a person's behaviors tend to be abusive, that person probably lacks the empathy required to understand the effect of one's behavior on another and to accept the consequences. If the victim adheres to the principle of total acceptance, she does not consider the probable consequences of her spouse's behavior. Responsibility and accountability, two important characteristics of Christian discipleship, become secondary to maintaining the marriage. The abuser is excused for the abusive behavior and the abused is excused from addressing the evil of sin. Since marriage is "for better or for worse," mere physical survival may depend on denying the devastating effects of a psychologically and spiritually abusive relationship. Steeled by the commonly accepted belief that divorce (unless, perhaps, for infidelity) is not an option for an evangelical Christian, the wife enables her mate, in the name of obedience to God's teaching on marriage, to abuse her.

In my understanding, the problem is not total acceptance of another person but its narrow explanation. For an abused spouse, total acceptance of one's mate is required to recognize the abuse cycle (Walker, 1979). It takes courage and self-awareness to tear down the defenses of denial and minimization that assist in perpetuating the destructive relationship. If a woman accepts and is aware of her husband's abuse, she may dissolve the relationship rather than maintain it.

Perhaps Ephesians 5:6–7 contains appropriate considerations for the wife of an abusive husband. An abusive relationship lacks the righteous living and mutual submission that are required to fulfill the Christian model of marriage (see vv. 21–33). "Let no one deceive you with empty words, for because of these things the wrath of God comes on those who are disobedient. Therefore do not be associated with them" (Eph. 5:6–7 NRSV). Interestingly, an abusive marriage is filled with empty words and broken promises, a phase that Lenore Walker (1979) called kindness and contrite loving behavior. Through defenses such as denial and minimization, the battered spouse is deceived into thinking that the abuse will never happen again. This deception serves to perpetuate the cycle unless the behavior is recognized and confronted. To halt the cycle is not to take part in it. The specifics depend on the person and the complexity of the situation.

To condemn women who have accepted their role in God's created order for responsible dominion (Gen. 1:28) and who have chosen not to participate in perpetuating abusive evil is a travesty. Much respect is given to those who raise their voices against the practice of abortion. A day is even dedicated to enhance the voice. Yet men and women who address the sin of abuse are often considered to be the weaker brothers and sisters, the unaccepting and the unforgiving. For example, Amy, a mother of two children, was praying and seeking God's wisdom in regard to divorcing her abusive husband. An older Christian woman responded, "I admire Joanna [a woman married to an incredibly abusive man]. She has chosen to focus on the positive and not the negative in her husband." The message was clear: Joanna is the spiritual woman because she does not allow the abuse to bother her.

A narrow explanation of total acceptance assumes unconditional love and forgiveness, apart from mutuality, as the desired basis for a marital relationship. Merely being an extension, as Howard Hendricks (1973) describes a wife, clearly does not an intimate relationship make (p. 35).

Total acceptance, unconditional love, and forgiveness are imperative in a healthy relationship. In an intimate, loving relationship, there must also be mutual accountability and responsibility. Mutual submission, as Ephesians 5:21 teaches, provides the necessary solidity for marriage, and the verses following in chapter 5 expound on that concept. Without mutuality, total acceptance can become license to exert unwarranted control over another. This is not unlike the misunderstanding that Paul addresses in Romans 6:1–2: "What shall we say, then? Shall we go on sinning so that grace may increase? By no means! We died to sin; how can we live in it any longer?" Total acceptance does not allow moral irresponsibility, just as grace does not warrant increased sinning.

Acknowledging mutuality as a required basis for unconditional acceptance, forgiveness, and love within an intimate relationship strengthens rather than weakens the marriage commitment. Why are basic principles for relationships with another person set aside when people are married? Who would consider it necessary to go to lunch with someone who batters and shames? Yet many women are daily living, frequently by necessity, with such persons. By emphasizing total acceptance apart from responsibility for personal behavior, the church and the culture encourage or even require abused women to attempt to develop intimate relationships with men who destroy their personhood and perhaps their physical and sexual safety.

It is significant to remember that even though Jesus loved the rich young man (Mark 10:17–22), the man's heart and the choices that he made precluded his becoming a disciple. An appropriate response from the young man was a prerequisite for this special relationship with the Master. Why would it be different for a dedicated Christian attempting to be a soul mate to someone whose basic lifestyle continually exhibits desires of the sinful nature and shows no repentance or fruit of the Spirit? Mutual love and accountability are required for an intimate relationship.

Conclusion

I wrote this chapter with much prayer, thought, consultation, and fear. It is an awesome responsibility to teach about God, the Creator of the universe, and his ways. In God's providence, however, he chose humanity to assist in the giving of his message. Just as Christ was the first incarnation, so Christians are the second, and by God's grace, power, and plan a laywoman can be instructed by the Holy Spirit (John 14:26; Acts 17:11). This is my mind-set: I embrace myself and others by loving my God. It is a lifelong partnership rooted in God's words. For truth to be complete, the objective facts need to be morally lived within relationship. This is my goal, and I believe it to be consistent with Scripture.

From studying the dynamics of abuse and from working in the field, I have known too many women precluded from such a relationship, a relationship with God that is intended to sustain in and be strengthened by life's trials. For women who have been controlled, manipulated, and battered by husbands who were supposedly God's provision for earthly guidance, protection, and sustenance, it can be emotionally wrenching and cognitively dissonant to then trust not only a male-dominated church and religion but also a "male" God. Biblical translations that use exclusive language potentially forestall instruction and solace. Women who have been abused by their partners tend to make generalizations about all males, especially those in authority, including God. To care for and to save themselves and their children may mean a choice between distancing from the Christian faith and its teachings or being destroyed emotionally, physically, sexually, and/or spiritually.

Kate sat quietly, her eyes downcast and her usually fluid speech faltering. As a child, an adolescent, and an adult, Kate had experienced emotional, physical, and sexual abuse at the hands of men she had trusted. Now, while she was courageously facing her abuse issues and becoming attuned to her feelings and the personal effects of the abuse, Kate realized a deep desire for physical comfort.

While Kate was in bed that night, thoughts of how alone she felt and how nurturing and sustaining it would be to feel the embrace of God's arms filled her being. But, as she contemplated the arms of God as being ideally strong, muscular, and manly, she felt repulsed and betrayed. Kate did not want a man to touch her and hurt her again!

Kate then thought of the soft, warm arms of a mother. How she longed for that intimate nurturing and the sense of God's presence. Such peaceful thoughts were quickly forced from her mind. Guilt suffused the images of being held by a woman. Maybe she was a lesbian, Kate thought, and God would be even more displeased with and unaccepting of her.

What a travesty that what could have been a healing balm for Kate was banned from her experience. Within a male-centered religion, the words of Isaiah are too often foreign: "As a mother comforts her child, so will I comfort you" (Isa. 66:13); "Can a mother forget the baby at her breast and have no compassion on the child she has borne? Though she may forget, I will not forget you!" (Isa. 49:15).

Rossi writes that "clients with deeply religious convictions often experience what they call 'progress towards God.' . . . One of the ways clients understand this is through their image of God" (Stern, 1985, p. 55). It frequently becomes imperative for healing that an abused woman must identify with God as other than a representation of maleness. As Genesis 1:27 states, both male and female are made in the image of God. Thus, especially during the healing process, is it necessarily abhorrent to focus on those characteristics of God that are culturally viewed as female? Without such refocusing, the victim may be unknowingly revictimized by the very words that God intended to bring consolation, understanding, and peace, and also be restrained from the only true source of love—an intimate relationship with God.

Part of the healing process for an abused person is to be able to recognize personal needs and to assume responsibility in seeking to have those needs appropriately met. As a person reconnects with and reclaims his or her emotions, including pain, the person seeks and establishes safe, healthy relationships within which such processing can be accomplished. If males have been the primary abusers in a woman's life, it is realistic to suppose that men initially will not be trusted and that relationships with other women, including therapists and advocates, will provide the beginning bonds for healing and reconstructing life.

An article in *Focus on the Family* (March 1994) appears to substantiate such an idea. An interview with a woman who had been in lesbian relationships for five years revealed that her father frequently abused her mother and terrorized the family with violence. As a young adult, the woman hungered for love, but she found sexual relationships with men to be unsatisfying. She sought out a female soul mate and became involved in the homosexual lifestyle. Her aching for genuine love and acceptance was eventually met through a relationship with God, who, she testified, is changing her desires and her heart (pp. 3–4).

Evangelicals consider practicing homosexuality to be a sin. To be consistent, evangelicals must also be willing to examine their part in perhaps contributing to a climate in which the temptation for such female bonding is increased and even encouraged. How deplorable if Christ's disciples' insistent use of predominantly masculine language and leadership contributes to making a chasm between a woman and the most important thing in life—a right relationship with her God!

Relationships are complex, and it would be arrogant for me to indicate that I thoroughly understand the correspondences between Christ and the church and the relationship between husband and wife. Thus, upon rereading Ephesians 5, a key passage for this discussion, my eyes rested on verse 32: "This is a profound mystery—but I am talking about Christ and the church."

It is a mystery. Unraveling the many relational intricacies, in God's timetable, is a process. There are many more questions to be asked, answers to be sought, and issues to be confronted. It is a privilege and a challenge to live in a day when egalitarian insights and teachings are being studied and discussed in the quest to bring Christ's message, in word and deed, to people in the church as well as to those who hesitate to enter.

Battered Christian Women

3

Elizabeth Pearson

As a specialist working with abused children, I received a call in 1984 from a thirteen-year-old girl whose father had been convicted of sexually abusing her and one of her younger sisters. He was appealing the conviction and was free on bond under a restraining order prohibiting him from unsupervised contact with his family. The restraining order had been given in part because of the abuse conviction but also because he had been battering his wife, who was unable to insure her own protection or that of her children. The thirteen-year-old called because her father had moved back home and had started sexually abusing her seven-year-old sister. His appeal bond was revoked that day, and he was returned to the county jail.

The next morning, a minister came to my office to explain that I had obviously misjudged a troubled yet devout Christian who was a member of his church. He wanted to help me understand the underlying reasons for the problems in this family. The minister had been counseling the couple to resolve some marital problems, and he believed this father would "no longer be provoked to violence or need to go to his daughters for sexual fulfillment if the wife would recognize her duty to submit in love to her husband."

Many studies of domestic violence have noted a correlation between rigid male and female role expectations and an increased incidence of spousal violence (Dobash & Dobash, 1979; Straus, Gelles, & Steinmetz, 1980). A relationship between religious belief and rigid role expectations is sometimes assumed, although the majority of studies that have included religion as a variable have not examined this relationship in enough detail to make that assumption. This study focuses on the way in which personal religious beliefs enter into the decision-making process of a battered woman. The religious beliefs of the respondents and the need for response from the church community, health-care providers, and therapists are examined.

Religion and Battering

If religion is considered at all in many family violence studies, it is often categorized simply by religious affiliation. No specific questions are asked about the respondents' own beliefs or what influence those beliefs have or had on their reaction and response to being abused. Rather, religion is considered an epiphenomenon, that is, a secondary phenomenon rather than a primary motivator. This is usually reflected in one of three ways: Religious belief is either minimized, marginalized, or pathologized.

Religious belief is minimized in family violence studies because patriarchy is viewed as the underlying motivator (Dobash & Dobash, 1979), and a person's religious preference may be used merely as a "behavioral indicator" of patriarchy. Patriarchy is seen as the base structure that makes it necessary for society to make up a religion to support it. A fit metaphor would be viewing patriarchy as the body and religious belief as clothing. Clothing styles vary widely among cultures and individual members of cultures. However, most cultures use clothing either to adorn or to cover up the body, and although there are variations among individuals, human bodies are all basically the same. In the same way, the meaning of religious affiliation or preference varies among groups and individual members of those groups. To identify a person as Protestant, Catholic, or Jew provides only a vague outline of some basic beliefs he or she may hold and tells nothing of the complexity or depth of those beliefs. Studies that allow minimum input by asking only about religious preference or affiliation deny the primary motivating power of the beliefs and practices of the individual respondent. Those beliefs and practices, which may be rooted in patriarchy, are more than cloth-ing styles designed to adorn or to cover up a patriarchal power struc-ture. Viewing all historically patriarchal religious groups as the same results in a loss of valuable information, particularly when one attempts to analyze a complex social issue.

Religion may also be marginalized by clinicians and researchers. They may value it in the same way a hobby is valued. If it increases self-esteem or if an individual finds it "helpful," then it will be added to the list of positive ego strengths for that individual. If it is an area that appears to be hindering personal growth or, in the case of domestic violence, placing the battered person in continued dan-ger, there are numerous other religious options to replace it. Mar-ginalizing religion dismisses the reality that religious faith is intri-cately woven into the tapestry of many people's lives. The threads are not interchangeable nor can they be easily replaced without risk of destroying the entire pattern.

Religion is also sometimes considered pathological. Clinicians who know of my interest in this topic often ask, "What kind of ego deficits do you think these people have that draw them to conser-vative religion?" If I as a clinician view a person's religion as a rela-tive indicator of pathology, at best I lose complex information needed for thorough assessment, and at worst I have put up a tremendous roadblock to a therapeutic relationship. The result is that we often do not ask in any meaningful way how a person's reli-gious belief influences his or her reaction to trauma. But when a per-son experiences trauma of any kind, that trauma often disrupts his or her assumptions about the world, assumptions that are neces-sary to maintain healthy denial of the tenuousness of our existence. These assumptions are that the world is benign and meaningful, that the self is worthy, and that people are trustworthy (McCann & Pearlman, 1990). When a person experiences disruptions in these assumptions, it is essential that he or she have a way of making sense of the experiences. It is not surprising, therefore, that religious faith often becomes a primary issue in response to any trauma, includ-ing domestic violence.

As Christians, we say our faith is a primary issue in all areas, but we too treat it as secondary when the area in question is abuse within a Christian family. We make it secondary when we hear about a husband battering his wife and then concentrate our examination, evaluation, and response almost completely on the woman, rather than looking with a critical eye at our theology of the family.

I am dismayed by the language used in a great number of books written about Christian families. Military language is often used to describe the marital relationship when the comments are addressed to husbands. For example, terminology such as chain of command, obedience, and authority is used rather than terminology such as friendship, respect, and love (MacArthur, 1982; Narramore, 1978; Gothard, 1978). This is also true when the discipline of children is discussed. Parent-child relationships are often described in terms of winning, overpowering, or breaking the will (Dobson, 1970, 1978; Fugate, 1980; Hyles, 1972; Tomczak, 1982).

Wives are often encouraged not to challenge their husbands' authority but to be covertly manipulative in order to influence his decision making. Many Christian writers who address the issue of abuse usually begin by stating that the husband is responsible for his own abusive behavior. However, that statement is frequently negated by a shift of focus to the wife. This shift usually results in a lengthy discussion about a woman's proper attitude and behavior in a Christian marriage and the devastating results of her failure to adequately follow what the writer believes to be the biblical model of marriage established at creation. Special emphasis is placed on biblical passages that emphasize a wife's submission to her husband, the obligation to forgive those who hurt us and to tolerate suffering, and prohibitions against divorce. The influence of church teaching in these four areas (submission, suffering, forgiveness, and divorce) on the reaction and response of Christian battered women served as the framework for this survey.

Surveying Battered Women

A nonprobability sample of sixty-five women from seven states made up the group taking part in the study. These women range in age from nineteen to over sixty. Most are well educated, with 66 percent having college or graduate degrees. Most are married, middle-class, and white. They are actively involved in their church com·

munities, with the majority (78.7 percent) attending services more than one time per week. The majority of the women (59.6 percent) report that they are still in abusive relationships. Given the descriptions of some of their marriages, this percentage may be higher.

The questionnaire was divided into five areas. The first involved general demographics. The second area contained a set of statements about abuse and a four-choice Likert-type scale the respondent used to indicate her level of agreement with each statement (see table 1 on page 68). The third section listed sixty-five specific abusive behaviors. A respondent marked those she had experienced and listed her relationship to the abuser (see table 2 on page 68). The fourth area dealt with the respondents' attempts to receive help. The respondent was asked whom she had told about the abuse, and then she used a scale of 1 to 10 to rate the effectiveness of the help she received from that person (see table 3 on page 69). The last area contained four open-ended questions asking respondents to describe the way in which church teaching influenced their reaction and response to the abuse. Several beliefs or events that were most influential in their response to being abused were identified. It is important to remember that these statements reflect what the women believed to be the Christian ideal at the time of their abuse (see table 4 on page 69).

How does this information translate into tangible suggestions for ministers, therapists, friends, and health-care providers who want to provide effective assistance to battered Christian women? For each of these groups, some possible suggestions emerged.

The Need for Response

Ministers and Church Leaders

A strong relationship existed between a respondent being told by a minister that she was responsible for the abuse and the likelihood that she was staying in that abusive relationship. Eighty-six percent of the women who were still being battered were told by a minister that the abuse was their fault. They were also more likely to believe that

wives are primarily responsible for the emotional well-being of
their families

abusers are violent only when they are out of control

they will not be forgiven if they do not forgive their abuser promptly

forgiveness means forgetting

Encouraging a woman to submit to violence is wrong. Many women
reported that they were told the abuse would stop if they would be
more submissive to their husbands. Submission to abuse will not lead
an abusive husband to repentance; it increases the likelihood of continued or increased violence (Jobling, 1974; Thorman, 1980). Focusing heavily on the submission of women helps perpetuate the violence.

A good place to start advocating nonviolence in the home is from
the pulpits of our churches. The sin of abuse needs to be addressed as
actively as any other sin within the body of Christ. We need to talk about
forgiveness in a helpful way, recognizing the process of forgiveness and
emphasizing the responsibility of the abuser to confront his behavior
honestly. Forgiveness does not mean forgetting, nor does it mean trust
should be restored, unless the abuser's behavior shows evidence of
true change over a long period of time. We need to emphasize that Ephesians 5 is not the only biblical passage that relates to marriage and
that it does not start with verse 22.

The Church Community

Although most people would probably want to help a member of
their church community who is being abused, many women reported
feeling shamed within their church families, and 70.2 percent left their
church because of the abuse. Good intentions are clearly not enough.
The participants in this study offered church members the following
suggestions:

Do not engage in verbal voyeurism by spreading details of the abuse
through a prayer group.

Before you offer assistance to a woman, make sure you realize what
you are offering. Mean what you say and do what you say you are

going to do. Do not make offers of help that you cannot follow through on.

Realize the need for your own boundaries and respect the boundaries of the person you want to help. Opening your home to victims of battering without setting up ground rules for privacy, availability, and safety concerns can be problematic for everyone.

Get training through your local battered women's shelter or host training sessions in your church with qualified therapists or legal experts who can assist you.

Establish a safe house or safe apartment that can be maintained through cooperation with other local churches. The concrete needs of abused women and children can be costly, both financially and emotionally. By working in conjunction with others in your community, you can provide more effective assistance to a greater number of families.

Health-Care Providers

Health-care providers must educate themselves so they can recognize signs of abuse in their patients. Many women tell their doctor or other health-care provider about the abuse. The low level of effective help from physicians (see table 3 on page 69) is due in part to the lack of training in most medical schools about domestic violence. This is changing, and hospitals are now required by their accrediting organization to have domestic violence protocols in place in all emergency rooms.

Many women who are abused come through hospital emergency rooms and physicians' offices. Recognizing the pervasive nature of some of the beliefs articulated by the participants of this survey can be helpful for health-care providers. Asking patients how they make sense of the trauma they have experienced can provide information for successful treatment planning in any health-care discipline.

Therapists

Therapists need to include questions about religious faith in their psychosocial assessments, using language that will be comfortable for the client. For example, a Christian woman may have a difficult time admitting to suicidal thoughts. Asking if she ever prays that something bad would happen to her or that she would die in an accident might elicit a more realistic response.

Therapists should also recognize the pervasiveness of shame that most battered Christian women experience. Many of the women in this study reported that in order to survive they had acted against long-held beliefs, and they felt shame about doing so. This is most likely to happen if they separate from their husbands. Many times these women lose the support of their community when they separate, and they report feeling hopeless and powerless to change their lives. Many of them join twelve-step groups that provide community support, which they do not find in their church.

Reading the writings of biblical scholars who challenge interpretations of Scripture that seem to support the subordination of women is also helpful. These writers provide a clear picture of Christianity that breaks into a patriarchal world and stands against the abuse of power rather than a picture that perpetuates the abuse of women and children. As a clinician, it is important to try to understand the importance of that picture. It is the missing piece that can provide real hope to abused Christian women. Therapists use phrases such as "working through" or "dealing with" problems of shame, grief, and guilt. By working in conjunction with biblical scholars and church communities that are confronting the issue of abusive power, therapists can help battered Christian women also find freedom.

The women who participated in this survey began their relationships with hope, and they believe in the so-called traditional biblical model of marriage. In fact, one of the more traditional groups included the younger married women. When these women are abused, however, they have a difficult time making their experience fit with what they believe to be the Christian ideal. In order to survive, they begin questioning their traditions and changing what they tell themselves about Christianity. At that stage they are more likely to separate from their husbands and feel shame about their decision. Their hope is that God will somehow work out the details, but they can no longer tolerate the abuse even if it means going against long-held beliefs about the sanctity of marriage and the obligation to tolerate suffering.

Religious belief is clearly a primary motivator for battered Christian women. The debate that has been going on within the Christian church throughout its history about the proper role of women in ministry, in the family, and in society is not an academic debate for these women.

The Christian church has been slow to recognize that family violence is a problem in our communities. For the most part, Christians have given over the moral high ground to the secular community when it comes to responding to domestic violence. Unfortunately, the majority of social scientists do not understand the dilemma that a Christian battered woman faces.

May God who created each of us in his own image grant us grace to contend fearlessly against evil and to make no peace with oppression so that we may reverently use our freedom to seek justice in our communities, churches, and homes.

Table 1

Attitudes about Abuse	% agree	disagree
Marriage counseling is a good way to stop violence in a relationship.	74.5	25.5
Drinking or drug use can cause battering or other abuse.	74.5	25.5
People who abuse others do so when they are out of control.	66.0	34.0
As a child I was allowed to express my feelings.	19.1	80.9
I feel hopeless much of the time.	27.7	72.3
As a child I was encouraged to make choices for myself.	44.7	55.3
I am able to express my feelings in front of others.	66.0	34.0
As a child I witnessed abuse between my parents.	53.2	46.8

Table 2

Abusive Behavior	%
Threatened with physical harm to gain submission	91.5
Threatened with harm to possessions or animals to gain compliance or secrecy	91.5
Isolated from friends or family	91.5
Own child witnessed the abuse	78.7
Denied money to keep from leaving	66.0
Choked	63.8
Raped	61.7
Struck with an object	57.5
Hit with an open hand	57.5
Bruised	57.5
Hit with a closed fist	44.7
Threatened with physical harm to children to gain submission	44.7
Internal injuries	44.7
Head injury	38.3
Cut	31.9
Kicked	31.9
Beaten	31.9
Bones broken	31.9
Stalked	25.5
Threatened with a gun	19.1
Tied up and photos taken	12.8
Killed pets	12.8

Table 3

Help-Seeking Behavior

Source of Help	Percentage of Victims Seeking Help from This Source	Effectiveness of Help Received: Mean Scores*
Mother	25.5	5.5
Sibling	34.0	5.3
Other family member	25.5	5.3
Minister	83.0	3.1
Church leader	57.4	3.0
Friend	93.6	7.0
Health-care provider	44.7	5.4
Therapist	57.4	7.5
Police	31.9	5.2

*Rated on scale from 1 (very ineffective) to 10 (very effective)

Table 4

Christian Teachings and Beliefs about Abuse	% agree	disagree
God's forgiveness is conditional and based on my response to the abuser.	36.2	63.8
As a Christian I am obligated to forgive the abuser each time he apologizes and believe with faith that the abuse will not happen again.	87.2	12.8
I believed I was being abused because of my own sin.	36.2	63.8
Suffering should be expected as a Christian. God will not give me more than I can handle.	99	01
I felt hopeless when Bible passages about suffering were read or were the topic of sermons.	57.4	42.6
My minister told me I was responsible for the abuse.	70.2	29.8
My husband told me the abuse would stop if I would submit properly.	78.7	21.3
I believed it was my duty to submit to my husband despite being abused.	61.7	38.3
Other people in my church knew about the abuse but told me they couldn't get involved because they didn't want to appear to be promoting divorce.	66	34
I stayed married as a Christian witness to my children.	61.7	38.3

Testimony of an Abuse Survivor

4

Lydia

At this time in my life I choose not to use my given name. You may call me Lydia. I experienced mental, emotional, physical, and sexual abuse. The sexual and physical abuse occurred regularly from the time I was in preschool until I was twelve or thirteen. The mental and emotional abuse continued into my adult life.

I was reared in a home that probably would not be called churched or Christian. My father, one of my perpetrators, never claimed to be a Christian, nor did he attend church. He insisted, nonetheless, that the children go to Sunday school, and he used the Bible as his source and foundation for the concept that he was head of the home. Thus, what he wanted defined the guidelines for our family. Another perpetrator was a neighbor and a friend of my parents who served as a deacon in one of the local evangelical churches.

My goal in sharing my testimony is to encourage others. Although each situation of abuse is as individual as the person experiencing it, many threads of similarity exist concerning the impact. I am not alone in the abuse I have experienced, nor in its impact. You are not alone either.

We live in a fallen world. I believe abuse has taken place since the fall of humankind, is taking place, and will take place until Christ returns. I believe the abuse I experienced in my childhood and adolescent years was sent from the devil to destroy me. There is one, however, whose power is greater: God, the Father, Son, and Holy Spirit. He has the power to turn it all around; instead of my destruction, glory has been and will be brought to my creator, God. Satan was defeated when Jesus Christ gave himself on the cross and rose from the dead.

I accepted Jesus Christ as my Savior when I was about five. Within my abusive experiences, Jesus became my Savior in a concrete way. He is the reason I am alive today. Over the past three years, as I have actively sought to confront the abuse I experienced and its effect on me, this truth has become real to me.

Although I had Christ in my life, I did not escape the paralyzing effects that abuse has on a person. Because of my frailties, I have an opportunity to experience an intensely personal relationship with God and a great opportunity to experience his power.

As a result of my abuse, I learned many lies and integrated them into my belief system. Confusion set in: Who is who and what is what do not get answered without a great deal of thought and searching. For many years, the thinking and searching were done on my own. After all, who can you trust to have the answers?

What lies did I learn about Jesus Christ? Although he is my salvation and truly loves me and is my only friend and I can trust him, he is powerless to protect me.

What lies did I learn about God the Father? He gave his only Son to die for me, but he does not love me personally. He is the supreme head, neither available to me nor desiring to be a part of my life.

I remember learning the Lord's Prayer and saying it at night before I went to bed. I knew that I had a Father in heaven, but the prayer was like a dream of what I hoped my heavenly Father was to me. His will was not done on earth, I felt no daily provision in love, and being delivered from evil was certainly foreign. My heavenly Father was a hope, a dream that I longed for but did not understand and did not dare to believe was for me. I would only be let down.

What lies did I learn about the Holy Spirit? The Holy Spirit is an it, impersonal, out there somewhere, playing a part, I know not what.

What lies did I learn about the devil? He is all over the place, and I am powerless against him, totally at his mercy or lack thereof.

What did I learn about Christians and the church? I learned skepticism. The name "Christian" means nothing. Anyone can call himself or herself a Christian. If someone claims to be a Christian, it does not mean that person can be trusted. I learned that being deceptive is part of being a Christian. You pretend that what you learn in church is the truth while you are there, but it is not necessary to live out that truth. The organized church is a manmade system, not God's church.

What lies did I learn about men? Men certainly are not to be trusted, and Christian men in particular are not to be trusted. Men are more important and more valuable than women. Men can do what they want; that is their right as men. All men are the same. Men are not people. Men are evil. No man deserves respect.

What lies did I learn about women? Women are helpless or at least are supposed to act that way. Women are not to argue with men. They are subject to men, at the mercy of men. Women are stupid and are not capable. Women are less than human, weak, and not to be considered or respected.

What did I learn about family? Family is not safe. Family is not where I feel accepted and loved for being. Family is not what it is supposed to be. A man owns his wife and children. If my husband has all the say and I need to depend on him to be my spiritual leader, I would choose never to get married. Why would I? It only means further destruction for me.

What did I learn about myself? I had no value. I was less than a dog. Esteem was nonexistent. I was wrong to feel; I was not supposed to feel. I had no right to choose. It was everyone else's right to have me do what they wanted, and I was responsible for their choices.

What did I learn about authority? Authority cannot be trusted and does not deserve my respect. Those in authority are supposed to know all the answers but they do not. Their answers are wrong.

What other issues preoccupied me? I struggled with trust; intimacy; nightmares about being attacked; terrorizing dreams about crying out for help to Jesus without any help coming; shame, guilt, and self-hate; loss of identity and childhood memories. The abuse and its effects seemed to engulf me.

I said I wanted to be an encouragement to others by sharing my story. Are you wondering how this story is encouraging? Have the last few pages lifted your spirits? I suspect not. To me it is encouraging beyond words to be on this end of nearly three years of intense counseling. It is encouraging to know help and healing are available. Unlearning lies and learning the truth has been a long process that I suspect will continue until I die. In looking back, I believe that the truth, the blocked memories, began to work their way out about thirteen years ago.

I believe the true healer is Jesus Christ. He spent ten years preparing me so I would be able to deal with the truth and be rid of the bondage. He offers us tools to use along with the truth of his Word, tools to help us unlearn the twisted truth we have learned as a result of abuse. We can break the cycle; we can feel and be whole. It does take a lot of hard work, but God has provided me with an exceptional therapist. She, God, and I have made a good team as I obtain the healing I desire.

I cannot express how I feel—I, who was so deeply damaged by regular abuse experienced over many years. I, who felt I would never be "normal," can know and experience healing. I am not alone. You are not alone. There is hope. I have experienced healing and will continue to receive healing. Healing is there for you too.

Reflections of an Abuse Survivor

5

Marge Cox

This story is about a beautiful Christian woman I came to know ten years ago when her family started attending my home church. When they first came, the wife was withdrawn and seldom spoke. The man was outgoing and at one time served as the teacher of the adult Sunday school class even though he was not a member of the church. As the months went by we learned, to everyone's dismay, that things were not right in their home. This is Betsy's testimony.

Before we were married, my husband raped me. He threatened suicide if I did not comply—not in the sense of, "Oh, if you don't, I'll just kill myself," but rather, as was pointed out to me by a Ph.D., "I *will* kill to get what I want." That message came through over the next two decades, sometimes subtly, sometimes much more strongly.

But what has had an infinitely more profound effect has been his abuse of Scripture, theology, and doctrine to manipulate me and others for his indulgence and to our destruction. After raping me he pointed out a portion of the Mosaic law, Deuteronomy 22, which says that since we were in the city and I did not cry out for help, I was to be stoned to death. He did not mention that the law gave instruction for both the man and the woman to be stoned to death. He did blend that text into the following verses, which say that if a man rapes a girl who is not engaged, he must marry her. Again, he ignored part of the text, the part about paying her father a fine. He told me that because this incident had "happened," I was obligated to marry him as my punishment. Perhaps this was the foundation for his continuing abuse, since his reasoning for much of it was that he was God's instrument to punish and correct me. [In Deuteronomy 22, it says that the man was to marry the girl and never divorce her. Betsy stayed in this battering relationship for sixteen years, until her husband sexually molested their oldest daughter, age twelve. Betsy finally stood up to him, and he was forced to move out of their home. Now, twenty-two years later, after six years of separation, he has recently filed for divorce.]

> For the husband is the head of the wife as Christ is the head of the church, his body, of which he is the Savior.
>
> Ephesians 5:23

"Since I am your 'head,' like Christ is the head of the church, whatever I do to you is right. In fact, it is loving."

> My son, do not make light of the Lord's discipline, and do not lose heart when he rebukes you, because the Lord disciplines those he loves, and he punishes everyone he accepts as a son. Endure hardship as discipline; God is treating you as sons. . . . If you are not disciplined, . . . then you are illegitimate children and not true sons.
>
> Hebrews 12:5–8; see also Psalms 94:12; 119:75

"I do these things to you because I love you; they are good for you. They will help you. You are too greedy, selfish, sinful, and you need someone to teach you how not to be. You need someone to chasten you and correct you like God does to the sons he loves."

> God is light; in him there is no darkness at all. If we claim to have fellowship with him yet walk in the darkness, we lie and do not live by the truth. . . . If we claim to be without sin, we deceive ourselves and the truth is not in us. . . . If we claim we have not sinned, we make him out to be a liar and his word has no place in our lives.
>
> 1 John 1:5–6, 8, 10

"If you resist me, you are saying that I don't love you, and then you are a liar too."

For Adam was formed first, then Eve. And Adam was not the one deceived; it was the woman who was deceived and became a sinner.

1 Timothy 2:13–14

"Eve was deceived, not Adam. Therefore, all women are deceived and cannot know truth. So whatever you believe, the opposite is true. This is why women are not allowed to teach in the church— and you do not question your own husband who is the 'head.' That is what it means; I am your head, I do your thinking for you. It is your responsibility to carry it out without question—to question it, even in your own heart, is to question God and call him a liar."

Marriage is honorable in all, and the bed undefiled.

Hebrews 13:4 KJV

"God said that marriage is honorable in all and the bed undefiled. This means that whatever happens as long as you are married is honorable. No matter what is considered bad outside of marriage, in the bed of marriage anything goes and should be welcomed on your part because it is purified, even the things that are considered vulgar, wicked, evil, disgusting, and debasing out in the world."

The LORD saves his anointed;
    he answers him from his holy heaven
with the saving power of his right hand.

Psalm 20:6

He who spares the rod hates his son,
    but he who loves him is careful to discipline him.

Proverbs 13:24

"God used a rod to chasten his people. He said that was his way to correct children and save them from destruction. He saves us by his 'strong right arm.' According to Psalm 23:4, you should be comforted by the rod of discipline."

The man said, "The woman you put here with me—she gave me some fruit from the tree . . ."
The woman said, "The serpent deceived me, and I ate."

Genesis 3:12–13

"This is what I am doing—I am saving you from destroying yourself and others. Because you are deceived, you don't know what is best for you; so God provided me to help you with that."

For man did not come from woman, but woman from man; neither was man created for woman, but woman for man.

1 Corinthians 11:8–9

"Actually, you are supposed to be my helpmate. You are supposed to meet my needs. But since you don't, you need to be corrected and disciplined."
[This perpetrator was asked to meet with the elders of the church he was attending after they learned of his incest. He attempted to defend his incestuous act with Scripture, but two elders stopped him. His wife had anticipated that he would justify his actions; he had explained to her, "You didn't meet my needs as my helpmate . . . at least this was kept within the family. It is not like it involved anyone outside." The daughter later told her mother that her father had informed her that she was a better wife to him than her mother was.]

No discipline seems pleasant at the time, but painful.

Hebrews 12:11

"You are supposed to be my helpmate, but here I am meeting *your* needs. But that's okay; it's called 'grace.' When you need discipline and I help you, even when it is hard work, I do it out of grace and mercy, even when I don't want to."

Despise not thou the chastening of the Lord, nor faint when thou art rebuked of him.

Hebrews 12:5 KJV

"If you resist what comes your way, it is further proof of your arrogance and pride that need to be broken. You need someone who will consistently keep you from pride. God says he hates a proud heart. Be glad I am committed to helping you with that."

> Your desire will be for your husband,
> and he will rule over you.
>
> Genesis 3:16

"Since God honors husbands more than wives—by giving husbands a higher place—you should too. It shouldn't be a surprise to you that I am more important in God's eyes."

> Jesus entered the temple area and drove out all who were buying and selling there. He overturned the tables of the money changers and the benches of those selling doves.
>
> Matthew 21:12

"Yes, you are right, Jesus is my model for behavior. Have you noticed what he did to those who didn't agree with him?"

> "How could you agree to test the Spirit of the Lord?" . . . At that moment she fell down at his feet and died.
>
> Acts 5:9–10

"Whenever you take matters into your own hands and do your thinking on your own, it is doomed to failure. That is clear all the way through the Bible."

> For this is the way the holy women of the past who put their hope in God used to make themselves beautiful. They were submissive to their own husbands, like Sarah, who obeyed Abraham and called him her master. You are her daughters if you do what is right.
>
> 1 Peter 3:5–6

"Helpmeet means it is your job to make sure people don't get the wrong idea about me—that I don't look bad. If you get it into your head to start talking and making things up, people get the wrong impression and you are directly sinning against what God intended for you—you are not being a helpmeet."

> The overseer must be above reproach . . . not violent but gentle. . . . He must manage his own family well and see that his children obey him with proper respect.
>
> 1 Timothy 3:2–4

"I wouldn't have done _____, but you drove me to it. I hope you have learned a lesson. I didn't want to, but you left me no choice. You should be glad I don't do it out of anger like some men. This is what proves I love you—I'm not angry."

> Women should remain silent in the churches. They are not allowed to speak, but must be in submission, as the Law says. If they want to inquire about something, they should ask their own husbands at home; for it is disgraceful for a woman to speak in the church.
>
> 1 Corinthians 14:34–35

"You need me to keep you from making a fool of yourself in church. Well, you sure made a fool of yourself this time. You should have listened to me. If you would just keep your mouth shut and let me handle everything, you would not have to embarrass yourself this way."

> An unmarried man is concerned about the Lord's affairs—how he can please the Lord. But a married man is concerned about the affairs of this world—how he can please his wife.
>
> 1 Corinthians 7:32–33

"I would have gone into the ministry a long time ago, but I was patiently waiting for God to get hold of you and straighten you out. There's no way I could have had any kind of a ministry with a wife like you. You have purposely kept me from it. Why wouldn't you want me to have my own ministry? I just know you would make a disaster out of anything I would attempt as far as a ministry. I'll just keep working with you and try to bring you around, but it is going to take a lot of changing on your part. You always seem to be opposed to God's will."

What did he think he was doing to me (us) all those years? Was he really totally deceived? And did he genuinely believe all that stuff, or was he using manipulative bullying tactics?

Too much of the time the church supported his views. I had heard far too much about what constitutes a godly woman. There is a proliferation of counsel that the solution to a difficult marriage is for the wife to submit more. Yet the more I submitted, the worse it became.

I believe that some churches, perhaps unknowingly, have created an environment conducive to abuse, as illustrated by Betsy's testimony. Because men translated the Bible, wrote Bible commentaries, interpreted and preached that only men can hold offices in the church, a male-controlled environment has emerged.

Perhaps church doctrine should be studied and rewritten to eliminate the statements that men are the authority in the home. I say this because some men cannot handle this power that they believe the church has given them.

There is such a need for Christian women to be trained to help other Christian women. They should be recognized as wonderful followers of Jesus who seek to bring God's joy back into the broken lives of hurting women who are being abused in our homes and churches today. I am so thankful that I serve a gentle shepherd, Jesus, who loves us with a "love that passeth all understanding."

minute to the next whether her husband will be loving or livid, kind or cruel, tender or terrible. By switching his behaviors, the misogynist keeps her off balance, unsure, confused. She feels crazy—and when she asks him why he does it, he responds, "Well, if you weren't so_____, then I wouldn't have to act this way." This kind of remark keeps the wife blaming herself and trying harder to please. Yet the misogynist is never pleased—or what pleased him yesterday infuriates him three days later. The woman and often the children feel as if they are walking on eggshells all the time, never knowing when the switch will happen again.

Aren't misogynists just chauvinists with a new name? Aren't all male chauvinists really just misogynists?
  Chauvinism, a form of prejudice, is a fanatical devotion to one's own group or country based on the belief that one's group or country is superior to another group or country. Male chauvinism, then, is fanatical devotion to maleness, based on the belief that males are superior to females. In my experience, while some misogynists are also chauvinists, not all misogynists believe women are inferior to men. They usually know better and assent intellectually that women are equal to men. Despite their belief, they find themselves acting antagonistically toward the women in their lives. I believe that this conflict between what they believe and how they act produces some of the shame that keeps misogynists from seeing their hateful behavior for what it is. The misogynists to whom I have spoken, and who have come out of their denial, feel deeply embarrassed that they acted in a way so contrary to their professed Christian beliefs.
  As to whether all male chauvinists are misogynists, I believe there is a fine line between having prejudice for or toward my own group and having a prejudice against another group. Not having sampled the entire population, I hesitate to say that all chauvinists are misogynists. The problem is we may start out merely being for our group and find that subtly, over time, we have learned to be against the groups that are different from ours. This shift from being for something to being against something is a risk for men and women. Many women started out trying to promote women's rights (being for women) on the basis of justice rather than female chauvinism (belief that women are superior to men). Some women, however, crossed that subtle line and

became anti-men as well as pro-women. Suddenly they found themselves believing women are superior after all. The risk is there: Whenever we become afraid of those who are different from us, we become
defensive, antagonistic, prejudiced, and potentially abusive. If prejudice is based on fear and chauvinism is a prejudice toward one's own
group that leads to fear, hatred of that other group is not far behind.

*What can help a man come out of denial about his misogynistic
behavior?*
Denial is one of the most difficult defense mechanisms to understand and with which to work. It is insidious and powerful and keeps
people enslaved to lies. Although no one can make someone else
come out of denial, the following suggestions may help.

1. *A new perspective due to introduction of new information or data.*
Feedback is a powerful tool when used in a loving manner and by the
right person. In misogynistic relationships, the woman generally has
little power or influence with her husband. Any confrontation by her
is usually discounted or rationalized away. Thus the new data, feedback, or information must come from an outside source. Sometimes
a pastor, a male friend, or a respected family member can broach the
topic of the emotional or physical abuse with the misogynist. Some
men have reported to me that a friend or a family member gave them
my book to read. Sometimes a planned intervention by family and
friends, when directed by a trained therapist, can be helpful. A person can rationalize or discount what one individual says to him, but
it is much more difficult to do so when the comments come from a
group of people he loves and from whom he wants acceptance.

2. *New behaviors and boundary-setting by the wife.* Although a
misogynist may discount his wife's direct verbal confrontations,
ignoring her changed behavior is more difficult. A therapist trained
to work with abused women can teach a woman how to respond
directly to her husband. Women who are married to misogynists
have been quiet and unassertive, so they need help to see alternative behaviors.

For example, Joe refuses to tell Mary when he will be home for dinner each evening. She fixes a meal and waits for him to come home.
He gets home anywhere between 5:00 P.M. and 8:00 P.M., although his
office closes at 4:30 P.M. Mary has repeatedly asked Joe to call her at

3:00 or 3:30 P.M. to let her know how late he will be that day. He does not want to be "controlled" by her, so he refuses to call, although he could easily do so. Mary has tolerated this behavior for ten years and thinks she has no alternative but to have dinner prepared by 5:00 P.M. and hope Joe gets home before it is dried out. A therapist working with Mary could teach her how to set boundaries with Joe in this and other areas. Mary could learn to say, "Joe, I will be cooking dinner so as to be ready to eat by 6:00 P.M. I plan to eat at 6:00 P.M. whether you are here or not. If you call me to say you'll be late, I'll save you a plate. If you do not call, I'll assume that you will fix your own leftovers when you arrive home or stop and get something on the way home." By setting up her boundaries and sticking to them, a woman can begin to change how she and her husband interact.

Learning and using assertive responses to abusive bullying is another behavior change that can make a difference. For example:

> "Talking to me in that manner used to work, but it is not going to work anymore."
>
> "I will not stay here and listen to you when you are so out of control. I'll be back in two hours and we can talk then if you are calm."
>
> "I guess we disagree. It's okay with me if we don't see eye to eye about this."
>
> "It is not okay for you to react to me in this manner."
>
> "I used to be intimidated when you started pouting and withdrawing, but it isn't going to work anymore."
>
> "I will not be manipulated by your screaming and yelling."
>
> "Things have changed. I'm not the person you seem to think I am."
>
> "I will no longer accept comments or so-called jokes that diminish or disparage me or put me down."

Learning to set limits and to be assertive is difficult for the partner of a misogynist because in order to do so she must give up her usual ways of handling situations. No more explaining again and again what she really meant. No more trying to be clearer, more precise in her wording when she speaks to him. No more trying to figure out what went wrong so he will not be angry anymore. She has to begin to understand what Patricia Evans (1992) points out in *The Verbally Abusive Relationship:* The abuser is in a different reality and all the explaining and trying in the world is not going to change him. All she can do is set limits as to what she will and will not tolerate.

Sometimes this type of assertiveness leads to a genuine shift in the relationship. The man may begin to adjust his behavior, although he still will have some significant denial. At other times the misogynist switches tactics and becomes sweet, apologetic, and repentant. (Christian wives are especially susceptible to this tactic.) If being sweet does not work, he may become distant or even violent. Remember, a woman's assertion of any independence is a direct threat: His fear of abandonment goes into high gear. The wife needs to remember that her husband is much more dependent on her than she will ever be on him. Despite that fact, the woman needs to leave quickly and go somewhere safe if her husband becomes violent. There are no guarantees that assertiveness will bring him out of denial. Sometimes the wife's assertiveness within the relationship works. At other times it does not.

3. *A crisis.* When boundary-setting, assertiveness, and confrontation by others fail, creating a crisis may be the only way to get a misogynist's attention. The one crisis that has the most chance of succeeding is to leave the relationship. Remember, the misogynist does what he does because he is terrified his wife will abandon him if he does not keep her subjugated. By separating, the woman gives his fears a chance to surface.

Unfortunately, many times a misogynist, even a Christian misogynist, decides his wife is "crazy" and within weeks finds a new woman who is bowled over by his charm. Thus, the misogynist's anxiety and fear never have a chance to surface. However, because of their Christian values, some Christian misogynists do not seek out other women. In these cases, there is more of a chance for the marriage to be healed since the root problems come to consciousness. Sometimes, if the new woman leaves the man, he starts to face his pain. Even then, it takes a lot of time, therapy, and prayer to renew the marriage relationship. In my experience, separation may be the only thing that finally breaks through a misogynist's massive denial.

What do you do when a man is a misogynist but his wife, besides being codependent, has other compulsive problems (such as addiction to shopping, overeating or undereating, alcoholism, gambling, workaholism)? Isn't some of his anger against her justified? How do you get her to see her problems so as not to blame everything on her husband's misogyny?

It is not unusual for codependent women, whether or not they are married to misogynists, to have other compulsive/addictive problems. When the situation is complicated by the fact that the man is misogynistic, it can be tempting to blame all the problems on him. Focusing only on him is not fair, nor is it helpful. Sometimes the wife has blamed only herself for so long that she swings to the other side and for a while blames only her husband.

I try to shift the focus from blaming and shaming to what works and what is helpful. Building a mutually respectful relationship takes a willingness for each partner to look at himself or herself. Once a good trust level has developed and the woman realizes I believe her story as she sees it, I try to shift her focus in therapy from blaming the husband to family-of-origin work. By looking at three or four consecutive generations of her family, she begins to see patterns that were previously unrecognized. We look at her family members and any codependent, addictive, or compulsive behaviors they exhibit. Sometimes, as she recognizes the behaviors in others, she comes out of denial about her own behaviors. I then do whatever is professionally helpful to continue stimulating the woman to get out of her denial. Keeping a journal, learning more about codependency and other addictions, or being in a women's therapy group can help. I have her read my book *Can Christians Love Too Much? Breaking the Cycle of Codependency.* Chapter 5, on addictive behaviors and codependency, has been helpful to many people by pointing out the links between their codependent acting out and other acting-out behaviors.

Is the misogynist's anger justified by the woman's addictive acting out? His anger toward his wife is surely complicated by her actions. It is as if his anger is a mixed bag: misogynistic anger based on fear, hurt, and shame, and normal anger that anyone would feel if he were living with a person with addictions. The misogynist tends to blame his wife for everything, so when she does mess up, her actions only feed his irrational sense that it is all her fault. Since he can point at some inappropriate behavior on her part, his misogyny makes him excuse the inappropriate behavior on his part. The matter here becomes one of how he handles his anger: Is he straight and clean with it, or does it merely fuel his misogyny? A person may be understandably angry, but that fact does not excuse inappropriate behavior.

Again, each partner in the relationship must be willing to be responsible for his or her own behavior. The husband's behavior does not justify the wife's acting out any more than her behavior justifies his acting out. By helping each person do some work on developmental issues dealing with personal responsibility, this impasse can be crossed.

What do you do when a man is not only misogynistic but also chemically dependent or a workaholic?

As is true when the woman is an addict and codependent, the main goal initially is helping the man out of denial. Just as the woman needs to come out of her denial regarding her codependency and other addictive behaviors, so the man who is misogynistic and addicted needs to overcome his denial system. Addictive behaviors tend to distance relationships, so it is not surprising that they crop up in misogynistic and codependent homes. Sometimes it is necessary to intervene to help the man see his misogyny and/or other problems. If he is chemically addicted, he will need to get off chemicals before marital therapy can be helpful. When the brain is clouded with chemicals, it does not work well on other problems!

A misogynist tends to be somewhat narcissistic, that is, he is self-oriented. He finds it difficult to take another's view into account, so direct feedback in an intervention is not always well received. Many times the individual's addictive thinking only reinforces the craziness of his misogynistic belief system. I have found that consequences can get a misogynist's attention—whether or not he is also chemically addicted or a workaholic. I know of two cases in which a woman finally had to leave her husband and not see him for six months before his denial system cracked. Both men, supermacho types, had such severe depression that they were hospitalized. Both men were workaholic misogynists. Until their wives left them and refused contact with them, they had no understanding of their own pain, shame, and abusive behavior. Since both men were committed Christians, neither found another woman to assuage his pain; hence, their underlying issues became conscious enough to lead to healing. After six to twelve months of individual therapy and marital counseling, both couples reconciled. (The women also received individual therapy.)

Once a man is out of denial about his misogynism, what are the treatment/recovery issues he must face?

One of the most important things that must be done is to help the man switch his worldview. Stephen Covey, in *The Seven Habits of Highly Effective People* (1989), says that to see something differently, I must be different; that is, my character must change. The misogynist must learn to see things differently: his wife, his actions, his view of things around him. It is not enough to learn to be gentle or patient. If he still sees the world from an arrogant viewpoint, all the communication skills in the world will not help. If his focus continues to be on his wife ("If only she'd . . .") and not on himself ("I can be more patient . . ."), any changes will be new attempts to manipulate those around him. One part of the problem is that he fundamentally views himself as the victim. He thinks he has given and given and is to be commended for putting up with such a burdensome wife. His actions tend to be totally reactive rather than responsible. He sees himself as a helpless reactor whose behavior would change immediately if those around him would change. In order for this type of man to grow into a healthy relationship with his wife and family, he must start seeing himself as a responsible chooser—someone who is not merely reacting to things around him but is choosing his behaviors. The flaw is not only in his outward behaviors but also in his inward character.

To have a healthy relationship, a person must have deep integrity and fundamental character strength. What we are communicates much more than anything we say or do. These men try to compensate for their lack of character by "borrowing strength" (Covey's phrase) from their perceived position, authority, physical stature or size, or symbols or achievements. He thus uses force and overpowers his wife to get things done. This only reinforces his inner weakness, since it allows him to rely on external rather than internal strength. It also develops weakness in his wife in that such power tactics stunt the development of independent reasoning, growth, and internal discipline. This borrowing of strength also weakens the marital relationship as fear replaces cooperation. Instead of giving the man more influence over his wife, this process ends with her eventually deciding she is incompetent and weak and thus incapable of doing anything he would want her to do. It reinforces any weakness she already feels. (For more on this concept, see Covey, 1989.)

To help a man change his view of things and hence his character, therapy must involve four areas: knowledge, attitudes, behavior, and skills (KABS). All of these components are important, and if any one component is left out of the therapy or treatment, the person will relapse. By working in these four character-building dimensions, a man begins to internalize biblical principles into his life via habits. As a Christian therapist, I rely heavily on the guidance of the Holy Spirit through prayer and discernment about where to start. Knowledge tends to be necessary for a man to come out of denial; that is, he must know or learn that his behavior or attitudes are inappropriate before he can begin working on them. He must learn and begin to see what he has been blind to previously. Knowledge, however, is not enough. Attitudes and behaviors are often deeply rooted in unconscious fear and shame, and knowing the truth does not magically change things. Besides the unconscious forces, we all have a sinful nature that still tries to control us. Even the apostle Paul wrestled with it (see Romans 7). Also, as Ephesians 6 reminds us, we battle not against flesh and blood but against the principalities and powers of the evil one. Thus we, and our clients, must be aware of the spiritual nature of our work.

What kinds of knowledge help a man continue to stay out of denial and give him new building blocks for the future? In what areas does he need to be reeducated as to his role as a man, husband, and father?

Self-knowledge. Despite their narcissistic focus on themselves, misogynists are usually quite lacking in self-awareness. All of their energy has gone into controlling those closest to them, so they have had little time, energy, or even inclination to get in touch with themselves. They are frightened at the prospect, because they have been running away from themselves for a long time. Although it seems contradictory that people who act so selfishly can have such self-loathing and shame inside, it is true. Misogynists try to avoid noticing the emptiness they have inside by focusing on controlling their wives.

Thus, misogynists need to learn to feel what they feel and know what they know about the present and the past. Often the only emotion they are aware of is anger. They tend to be unaware of guilt, shame, arrogance, depression, or anxiety. Learning to feel and label their feelings is an important first step. Many misogynists confuse their thoughts and beliefs with feelings. I have found that a men's therapy group can be helpful in breaking down denial and in helping them see and label emotions in others first. After watching other men for a while, many misogynists are able, with the help of a therapist, to recognize their own feelings. Being in a group with other men also gives them a chance to tell their stories and be accepted and loved by other men—something most men experience only rarely (Meth & Pasick, 1990).

Respect and boundaries. Another area of knowledge involves boundaries and respect for others. Misogynists tend to heedlessly trample over boundaries in their primary relationships. These men need to learn what is acceptable and what is not. Harry, a man I worked with for a while, was quite a bit taller than his wife. His favorite tactic was to start raising his voice, and if that failed, to stand up and shake his fist or his finger at his cowering wife. One day, when he could not manipulate the therapy session, he pulled out this tactic. He stood above me shaking his fist and shouting. When he stopped to take a breath, I said calmly and without standing up, "Harry, that may work with your wife, but it will not work with me. Sit down." He looked shocked and abruptly plopped back down in his seat.

A misogynist, like most people, tends to confuse respect and admiration. He holds his wife in extreme contempt while also professing to love her. He thinks that if someone is to receive his respect, that person had better earn it. It is here that a misogynist confuses admiration and respect. Respect is something we offer all other human beings because they are created in the image of God. Respectful behavior entails listening attentively, looking the other person in the eye, asking clarifying questions, assuming the best of the other person, and allowing for differences. Admiration, by contrast, can be earned. I may or may not admire a person's behavior, but I owe that person respect because he or she is created in the image of God.

C. S. Lewis, in his magnificent essay "The Weight of Glory," reminds us that the weight or burden of our neighbor's glory is a burden we should daily take seriously: "The dullest and most uninteresting person you talk to may one day be a creature which, if you saw it now, you would be strongly tempted to worship. . . . There are no ordinary people. . . . It is immortals whom we joke with, work with, marry, snub, and exploit" (1966, p. 15). If we could see other people in their potential glorified state, with the image of God unmarred within them, we would be awestruck and reverent. Thus, with regard to that awesome potential, we owe each other respect due such a weight of glory.

Sometimes knowledge alone will help shift a person's attitude; at other times it is not enough. Some misogynists know that what they are doing is wrong and violates their Christian values. Most Christian misogynists, however, tend to use God-talk, the Bible, and theology to bolster their views, beliefs, and attitudes. Attitude transformation is a tricky business. It takes time, and it is often difficult to tell from outward behavior what a person's attitude is.

I asked a misogynist in an individual session if he could possibly say something like the following to his wife: "Honey, I really don't understand why you feel so hurt by my behavior, but I love you, and I feel grieved and sad you feel so badly." His response was, "Sure I could say it! But if you want my real feelings, I think it's a bunch of ____!" Despite many months of marital therapy and some individual therapy, this man's attitude had not budged a bit, even though he had been told by counselors, pastors, and friends that he needed to make changes. So while knowledge is an important factor in changing behaviors and attitudes, for some men it is not enough. These men need what Covey (1989) calls a paradigm shift: a radical altering of the way they see life, the universe, and everything.

In my experience, it usually takes a drastic threat to security—enough to trigger a fear of abandonment and make it conscious—along with the appropriate information, plus the divine intervention of the Holy Spirit for these men to have a change of heart or attitude. If, faced with his own pain and shame but bound by his Christian faith, a man does not rush out to find another woman to take his wife's place, then, through the experience of pain and loss and through openness to the Spirit, change of attitude happens. It is difficult, and giving up his position as master of the universe is painful for such a man. Feeling out of control is terrifying to misogynists, and only by trusting God to be in charge can they survive it.

Attitude change often comes through prolonged exposure to the feared object without the usual defense. For misogynists, it involves developing new cognitive (mental) maps about women; creating new emotional habits involved with letting go of control; learning what attitudes are godly and what attitudes are from the pit; growing spiritually and developing a new reliance on God as the one in control; and developing a deepened self-awareness.

Once the misogynist gets out of denial, has developed some self-awareness, knows what behaviors are off-limits, and has begun working on his basic attitude toward his wife, he will also need training in some new behaviors and skills. He will need help with

> thinking for himself without unconscious impediments of fear and shame and without being reactive
>
> checking out the appropriateness of boundaries for the self and others
>
> problem-solving (He uses control as the way to solve problems.)
>
> learning how to "take orders" rather than give them (He is not used to letting others have authority or responsibility over him. Even if he has no ability in an area, he tends to want to be the one in charge.)
>
> learning how to appropriately express anger without bullying or manipulating
>
> learning to let others (especially his wife) differ, disagree, or be separate from him without feeling terrified of abandonment
>
> learning how to monitor his tendency to act as though he is master of the universe
>
> learning how to speak directly about what he needs and to trust others to care and be there for him
>
> learning to handle the inherent anxiety that any intimate relationship engenders, including learning to ask for help when under stress
>
> learning to use many resources or options and to be patient since all problems are not solved quickly
>
> taking the initiative to meet his own needs rather than demanding that others do so

accepting his underfunctioning, "weak" emotional side, and revealing this side to his family

Skill develops with practice and by focusing on developing godly
habits that lead to radical character change. Under the guidance of
the Holy Spirit, a misogynist begins to take control of the one thing
he can control—himself. By using his God-given imagination, will,
conscience, and new self-awareness, he begins to find that his relationships can improve.

I attend a church where it seems the entire system is misogynistic.
Over the last few years, more and more women have either left or been
kicked out of the church. I know (from personal relationships with
those individuals) that many of the incidents were related to misog-
yny. For example, a man committed adultery and the staff took the
position that his wife was "rebellious" because she was hurt and could
not ignore his behavior. I feel I have three options: to leave the church,
to ignore these incidents and keep a superficial relationship to the
church, or to confront the church. What resources are there for some-
one in my position?

The problem of misogyny and sexism in the church is one that
both men and women have mentioned to me. I have had phone calls
and letters from pastors, elders, and laypeople expressing this concern. In answering such a question, I would be sure to tell the person that his or her dilemma is not unique.

No one can tell another to stay in or leave a church. All available
options should be explored. There may be other women and men
with whom this concern could be quietly and prayerfully shared. It
is always wise to seek out support and counsel in the family of God.
Beyond this first step, I would make the following recommendations.

Covenant together to pray daily for the church and its leaders regarding this issue. We can never overemphasize the need for earnest prayer.

Gather weekly for at least a few months and study together some
of the fine books listed in the Christians for Biblical Equality (CBE)
book list. These and other works will provide the education necessary for any change-oriented movement.

As your fellowship grows, begin to formulate a plan as to how to
help your church grow in a broader understanding of misogyny and

sexism. Some people have offered an alternative Sunday school class for a six- to eight-week period, using such topics as "Abuse in the Christian Home" or "Hidden Problems in Christian Families." Misogyny could be just one of a number of hidden problems addressed. Alcoholism, drug abuse, sexual abuse, sexual addiction, and infidelity are others. If it does not seem the church will accept teaching from your group, I suggest finding a Christian psychologist or social worker who might be willing to do the teaching. CBE and other groups have excellent videos and books available that can be the basis of a class or Bible study.

There may also be resources in your area if you are in a denominational church. Sometimes, resources coming from outside the church are less of a threat. Most denominations have committees that help people resolve conflicts or that are set up to investigate abuses. I would caution that you should speak, as a group if possible, to your pastor or leadership team about your concerns before you choose this route. That type of action is a last step as it is a drastic move. You will need to develop a strategy before speaking to your pastor. By focusing on cases of outright emotional or physical abuse, you can approach the broader issue of misogyny indirectly at first. If you offer your concern and support to the pastor gently, he is less likely to feel threatened. Rather than confronting him with broad statements such as, "You know, pastor, we really think this whole church system is misogynistic and sexist!" approaching him with a specific case is a way to build trust. Perhaps you could say, "Pastor, we are sure you are aware of the [name the type] abuse Mary has been going through. [If Mary cannot meet with the pastor, be sure to have her permission to talk to the pastor.] We are concerned for her and for our church. We've been studying spouse abuse and we'd like to offer a Sunday school class for one month on this important topic." This approach is apt to be better received than a frontal assault. If you do not think your pastor is approachable, seek out another staff member or an elder or a deacon who might advocate for your idea or concerns.

Remember, change takes patience, prayer, and time. It may take years before the church as a whole is where we would like to see it on this issue. Scattered confrontations rarely are helpful, since the person or group confronted will usually label the confronter "crazy," "sinful," "out of fellowship," or "demon-possessed." When we strategize with others in the body of Christ and prayerfully seek God's plan, changes can happen. There will be setbacks and disappointments, but God will honor perseverance. Even if group efforts are rebuffed, participants will have gained some deeper relationships with those with whom they have studied and prayed. If some decide later to leave the church, they can do so in good conscience, knowing they first took the time to pray and work for change. Seeds planted may flourish even after we are gone. May God bless our efforts.

The Silent Killer of Christian Marriages

7

Amy Wildman White

Emotional abuse, as well as all other forms of abuse, is on the rise in our society, and the Christian community is not exempt. Emotional abuse in the marital relationship is often undetected or misdiagnosed. It is hoped that this text will be an informative tool to aid those who are in an abusive relationship or those in ministerial capacities to better counsel victims and their abusers. Effecting change is essential, as emotional abuse over time will destroy a marriage.

This text provides a diagnostic framework to help identify the victim and the abuser, includes a theological statement responding to the question of whether abuse is legitimate grounds for divorce, and offers a case study of emotional abuse. It is hoped that this material will be used to promote the growth of successful, fulfilling marriages and to provide the stimulus for further study and research. It is in no way intended to promote divorce.

Erica desperately wanted out of her marriage with Jack, but she could not connect her feelings of despair and an almost overpowering desire to escape with anything overtly destructive Jack was doing. Jack was a good father, had no problem with alcohol or drugs, did not chase other women, was a good provider, and had never harmed her physically. By contrast, Erica was aware of her own shortcomings as a wife and mother. She experienced guilt, feelings of inadequacy, and embarrassment over her inability to respond sexually to her husband.

Frequently, this is the presenting picture of a woman in an emotionally abusive marriage. In the absence of physical abuse, neither the woman nor the pastor she seeks out for help is likely to recognize that the emotional climate of the marriage is squeezing the life out of her.

There is little room for disagreement over what constitutes physical abuse, and its damaging or even lethal potential is recognized by almost everyone. The nature and impact of emotional abuse, however, is not so easily nor widely recognized. Although the signs of emotional abuse are not always clear, the abuser's behavior is not obvious, and the immediate results are not dramatic as in physical abuse, emotional abuse represents an oppressive and insidious process that strikes deeply at the hearts of its victims.

Even in cases of physical abuse, the most damaging element is not the violence that is done to the body but the violence that is done to the human spirit—a violence that is dehumanizing and leaves its victims feeling confused, vulnerable, trapped, and worthless. How then do we define emotional abuse?

It is fair to assume that in one relationship or another each of us has been emotionally hurtful but not necessarily abusive. That is, by something we have said or done, or by withholding love, we have caused emotional pain to someone. The frequency of these patterns varies among individuals. At what point do we identify a person as an emotionally abusive individual?

The Characteristics of Emotional Abuse

Emotional abuse cannot be reduced to a single list of negative behaviors. One must look deeper to identify and understand the motivational factors beneath the behaviors that create the oppressive, controlling climate a woman feels destined to live in.

The Traits of an Abusive Husband

The key motivational factor that defines an emotionally abusive person is a deep-seated need to be in control. Because of the abuser's insecurities, feelings of inadequacy, and distorted beliefs about women and marriage, he feels he must control his wife or lose her. The abuser will use manipulative and heavy-handed tactics to keep his wife off balance. For example, the abuser may resort to

- intimidation
- eliciting fear, guilt, pity, or anger
- making a person feel vulnerable, in danger, unprotected, or helpless
- put-downs, criticism, or verbal abuse
- causing shame or humiliation
- controlling another's schedule
- keeping another ignorant regarding herself, the world, finances, or others
- keeping a person in crisis, and thus occupied and off balance
- conspiracy and turning others away from aiding the person
- creating situations in which there is no way to win
- lying or gossip
- threatening self-harm or suicide
- possessiveness and jealousy

Although the behaviors in and of themselves are forms of abuse, it is the constant climate of destruction that leaves a woman believing she is trapped, with no confidence or hope that there is a way out. A woman in an emotionally abusive marriage does not believe she has any choices. She believes she carries the responsibility for the bad marriage and that if only she could change, her marriage would improve. No matter what she does differently, however, the marriage never gets better.

The abuser has a typical profile. Like his wife, the abusive husband has low self-esteem, and his worth is often tied to his performance, image, or personal charm. He has a strong sense of insecurity that includes a fear of losing the love and esteem of others. He is generally distrustful of others and believes he does not have a secure place in important relationships.

The abusive person is self-referenced, meaning he sees things from his own frame of reference rather than empathically looking at things from another's perspective. This is not the same as being selfish. It can be said that the self-referenced person would give you the shirt off his back, but he doesn't know you need it. The self-referenced person frequently violates the marriage partnership by acting without thoughtfully considering his partner's point of view and needs.

The abusive individual is also emotionally dependent, feeling that he is less than complete, of diminished worth, inadequate, or unable to live without the other person. The dependent person tends to assume responsibility for another, taking on the role of rescuer, enabler, or controller (e.g., "I know what is best for you."). The intent of the abuser is to prevent the loss of the partner because he is emotionally dependent on her. It is understandable, then, why possessiveness is another characteristic of the abuser. He tries to monopolize the time and attention of his wife, or claims exclusivity in areas when others move close to the object of his love.

For anyone who works with abusive men, the most frustrating characteristic is their lack of insight. When interacting with this type of individual, one is often left feeling as if he or she has just gone in circles. Issues presented are minimized, denied, or turned around to make someone else responsible, or a host of other topics are brought in to sidetrack the conversation. The process of change is most often slow or nonexistent.

The Traits of an Emotionally Abused Wife

Every woman in an emotionally abusive relationship can be characterized as having low self-esteem. Although low self-esteem is always characteristic of an abused woman, it is not always obvious. Many women with low self-esteem appear confident and in control, and many seem to "really have their act together."

Low self-esteem makes a woman vulnerable to the controlling tactics of the abuser. Because she feels she has little value, she looks to her husband's acceptance of her as the measure of her worth. Instead of mirroring to her the truth about her value and dignity, he pulls her down even further by his critical and nonaffirming posture toward her. He exercises a form of mind control that results in the victim's taking on the frame of reference of the abuser, developing feelings of guilt and inadequacy for not meeting his standards and needs. This is complicated even more by her need for the marital relationship.

A woman's identity is often based on her relationships. This is generally not true for a man. Men need relationships, but they tend to draw their identity from vocational expression, academic achievement, athletic success, or material gain. Because a woman's identity is often based on relationships, she is vulnerable to being involved in an abusive relationship. A strong part of her identity is being a wife, and she will do anything she can to maintain that identity. As a result, she forms a false sense of dependency, believing that she cannot stand emotionally without her partner. The husband reinforces this with statements such as "No one will ever love you like I do," "All you are to men is a sex object," or "You can't make it on your own financially." A victim of emotional abuse believes her husband is right, or at the least she has strong doubts about herself.

One of the most consistent characteristics of an emotionally abused woman is her inability to sexually respond to her husband. Loss of sexual desire for her partner is an inevitable consequence of the deterioration of trust and the lack of friendship and intimacy that result from long-term abuse. This loss is not voluntary on the woman's part. She hears messages from her own upbringing, her husband, or the church that accuse her of not being a good wife if she does not meet her husband's sexual needs. This causes her to experience feelings of guilt.

The wife in these situations experiences intercourse as an indignity, almost as rape, because the physical and the deeply personal, loving aspects of sex have been torn asunder. Intimacy and trust, which lay the necessary foundation for a woman to respond sexually, have been removed from the relationship. Yet, she is still expected to meet her husband's sexual needs.

In order to manage her emotions, the woman will often detach herself emotionally from what is going on, becoming more of an observer than a participant. The guilt over not being able to be more responsive can be overwhelming. Yet, no matter how hard she tries, she cannot respond. Her partner adds to her dilemma with statements such as "If you really loved me, you would do this for me," "A good wife is supposed to satisfy her husband," or "If I just wanted sex, I could get that anywhere, but I'm a faithful husband. You should take care of me or maybe I'll have to get my needs met elsewhere." She is left feeling guilty, inadequate, afraid, and helpless.

These feelings commonly result in depressive episodes alternating with reactive behavior. If a woman has no effective means for handling feelings of hurt, helplessness, fear, guilt, and anger, she may engage in self-mutilation or self-deprecating behavior, or she may find expression of her strong emotions in organic disease. At the extreme end of the continuum, a woman may plan, attempt, or commit suicide.

It cannot be emphasized enough that even if individual controlling and hurtful acts of the abuser are not extreme, the cumulative effect of his tactics is oppressive and destructive to the woman experiencing them.

Responses to Emotionally Abusive Marriages

What is the prognosis for an abusive marriage and what options are open to a woman who is a victim? When a woman begins to recognize manipulation and control and finds the resources to grow toward increasing independence, the marriage is brought to a crisis point. Most likely, when the woman is no longer able to be manipulated, the husband will escalate in his abusive patterns.

It may be extremely difficult for the wife to convey what she has experienced. The community will probably be unable to see past the charming ways of the husband. People will often respond in a scrutinizing or critical manner toward the wife or reject her altogether. Many may give the husband a supportive ear instead of holding him accountable. This behavior inadvertently encourages him to continue his abuse. Abusive men draw energy and self-justification from people who listen in silence. When the crowds disappear, the wife becomes the target of his increased anger.

With the escalation of abuse and/or the response of unsupportive friends, the wife may either sink back into a depressed, helpless state or move toward separation and divorce. At this point a husband may become desperate and be willing to work toward change because he knows he will no longer be able to sustain the marriage through control. If the husband is truly broken regarding his behavior, intensive individual and marital counseling are vital for the restoration of the marriage. Some men, however, refuse to change. If a man does refuse to change, what option remains for a woman who is the victim of emotional abuse? What about separation and divorce?

These questions can be answered properly by first understanding the biblical view of marriage. Marriage is, primarily, a covenant with God to love and honor one another, to participate in partnership and mutual submission. Submission is often greatly misunderstood.

Both men and women are called to submit to God first and then to each other (Eph. 5:21; James 4:7). This submission to God and one another constitutes the biblical basis of the marriage covenant. In evangelical circles, the neglect of this teaching, or the misinterpretation of it, has led to an erroneous view of submission. The submissive role is assigned to the wife, while the husband fails to submit to Christ in his role as the head of the home. Headship is then defined as the man being in a higher position in the home, apart from the teaching of Christ, and in practice gives him the authority to rule as he desires. When a woman is not seen as being equal to her husband in dignity and is not treated with love and respect, people have distorted the scriptural view of marriage.

Biblical submission, by contrast, symbolizes the relationship between Christ and his church. We are always to look to Christ as our role model. Christ submitted willingly, in a place of strength, and for a purpose. A victim of emotional abuse submits involuntarily, out of weakness, and such submission does not glorify God. Therefore, a woman is not submitting and suffering for the sake of righteousness. She suffers because an abusive man cannot control himself and victimizes her in order to elevate his own self-esteem and sense of security.

Some people respond by saying that in Christ all things are possible and the woman should trust God to bring healing and restoration. All things are possible with God, but God, while willing, able, and wanting to do his part, leaves man to do his. God can bring healing, but both persons must be willing to do what God has called them to do or healing will not take place. No matter what a woman is willing to do or does, the marriage cannot be healed unless an abusive man changes his beliefs and his behavior, brings significant resolution to emotional pain from his own life, and grows in character.

The marriage relationship is intended to be a permanent one in which both partners are to have mutual respect, love, and knowledge of one another. This kind of relationship and abuse are mutually exclusive. When abuse occurs in marriage, the relationship becomes a setting for oppression, personal disintegration, and pain rather than a context for promoting the well-being of the partners.

To suggest that women who are being abused remain in the relationship rejects Scripture on several counts. First, God places great value on those whom he has called (1 Chron. 16:34; Pss. 6:4; 139:13–18; John 3:16; Rom. 5:8). Abuse, therefore, is in direct contradiction to how God's children should be treated. Second, by allowing an abuser to continue in his destructive patterns, a woman is not loving him. She enables him, permits him, to continue in sin. Finally, abuse places a woman in a relationship in which she is unequal to her husband. She becomes an object to satisfy the abuser's dependency and his need to continually act out unresolved hurt and pain. The victim is a means to an end.

What constitutes grounds for divorce has been an issue of debate within the Christian community. The Westminster Confession of Faith acknowledges two grounds for divorce: adultery and abandonment. Abandonment is sometimes limited to physical desertion, but this interpretation holds to the letter of the law and neglects the spirit of the law. Let us pursue this concept by way of hypothetical examples.

What if a husband chains his wife to a basement wall, freeing her only to do household chores? Has he not abandoned her as his wife? Or, suppose a man moves away physically and sends his wife enough money to live on but has no emotional or physical contact with her. Has he not abandoned her as his wife? If, then, a man is emotionally abusive, creating a new definition of marriage quite inconsistent with what Christ intended, has he not abandoned a woman as his wife?

When abuse exists, and the abuser refuses to change his attitudes and behavior, he has in fact abandoned his wife. He has chosen to serve himself instead of carrying out his marital obligations to love, honor, and cherish her. When this occurs, the marriage covenant has been broken. He has in effect chosen divorce by defiantly neglecting his marriage vows, giving the woman the right to file a legal suit.

Some people appeal to 1 Corinthians 7, saying a woman has grounds for divorce in the case of abandonment only if her husband is an unbeliever. This forces the question, Can anyone secure protection by claiming to be a believer? If a person continues in sinful patterns, the church is to treat the person as an unbeliever and send him or her out of the community. If the person discontinues the sin, then he or she may return. If someone continues in destructive patterns, it is reasonable to question whether that person is a believer. If a husband is destroying his wife by his words and behavior and refuses to change, is his heart right with God? "For out of the abundance of the heart the mouth speaks" (Matt. 12:34 NRSV).

Although we cannot know a man's heart for certain, 1 John does give us a framework for discerning if someone is a Christian. One criterion is whether a person loves others according to the definition found in 1 Corinthians 13. A second criterion is whether he obeys God's commandments. In ongoing abusive relationships, neither love nor obedience is carried out. There is reason to doubt that an abusive person who refuses to change is a Christian.

It seems that an emotionally abusive marriage can survive only if the woman breaks free from manipulative control and moves to a place of strength, thereby forcing the husband either to change or to lose the relationship. The husband is unlikely to change unless the cost of staying the same is too great.

Unless pastors and counselors can recognize the often subtle and always complex dynamics of emotional abuse, women will continue to be victimized first by their husbands and then by the church or the community. An abusive man who is not held accountable is indirectly supported and given license to continue his destructive patterns, and those around him become enablers. Women are not treated with dignity and respect, as God intended, and so God is not honored.

If the church is committed to saving marriages, understanding emotional abuse and applying proper counseling strategies are necessary conditions to make this happen. There is hope for victims and their abusers if the right steps are taken. If they are not, emotional abuse will continue to kill Christian marriages.

The Evangelical Family Is Sacred, but Is It Safe? 8

Nancy Nason-Clark

As evangelicals, we believe the family is an institution ordained by God. With the Bible on our side, we argue that God planned for men and women to choose lifelong partners and to share life's journey, for better, for worse. Through toil and celebration, we claim that fathers and mothers are commanded to love and nurture their children and to pass on the story of faith and obedience. From our pulpits and within our hearts, we cherish the message: The family is sacred.

As important and central as family values and family togetherness are to evangelical culture, there is a stark reality that we need to face. On a given Sunday morning in Canada and the United States, tens of thousands of evangelical women who have gathered for Christian worship leave the sacred sanctuary to return home to an abusive environment. The Sunday morning worship service, then, offers the Christian church an unprecedented opportunity to condemn violence in the home, to support abuse victims, and to model and encourage violence-free family living.

Let there be no doubt about it: Violence affects scores of church families, and many conservative religious men are batterers. While as evangelicals we teach that the family is sacred, we also need to recognize that sometimes it is not safe. It should alarm all of us, clergy and laity alike, that evangelical family life can be dangerous to one's physical or emotional health. And sounding the alarm should motivate us to action. But does it?

The Response of Christian Churches to Wife Abuse

The story of the response of contemporary Christianity to wife abuse is multifaceted. To respond pastorally to a battered woman is to support her as she begins the journey toward healing and wholeness. The journey is long and arduous. It is fraught with many obstacles to be overcome. And there are practical, emotional, and spiritual issues for the woman to face and resolve. Thus, the transformation of a woman's pain and suffering involves a myriad of relationships and resources. And for the woman of faith, the struggle for empowerment and safety has both temporal and spiritual overtones.

When women connected to evangelical faith communities experience violence in their intimate relationships, they tend to turn either to each other or the pastor for help. But what type of help is given? What advice is offered? Are battered women supported by their sisters in the faith when they disclose their personal pain? Or are they admonished to suffer in silence? And what about the advice or counsel of evangelical pastoral leaders? Do many clergy still tell women to "go home and pray" that the abuse will stop? Or do they offer spiritual and practical support for an abuse victim and thereby augment the healing journey?

These were some of the questions that led to the development of a research initiative exploring the role of congregations and clergy in responding to the issue of abuse. This research initiative was conducted through the Muriel McQueen Fergusson Centre for Family Violence Research at the University of New Brunswick in Canada. The multidisciplinary Religion and Violence Research Team, coordinated by this author, has conducted projects with the Anglican Church, the United Church, the Salvation Army, the United Baptist Church, and the Wesleyan Church.[1]

Throughout our research program, which involved almost 250 church women and more than 500 ordained clergy, we have learned that some abused Christian women receive the compassion, practical support, and spiritual counsel that assist them on the road to healing and recovery. Others do not. Some women feel that their faith community has been open and receptive to them, eager to assist in ways that would strengthen their resolve to live a life free from the abuse of the past; others feel betrayed, that their voices fell on deaf ears and that as a result the abuse continued.

The purpose of this chapter is to condense and summarize some of the research results to emerge from our exploration of how churches and their leaders respond to the pain and suffering created by the problem of violence in the family context. It will focus exclusively on the studies that have been conducted throughout Atlantic Canada among evangelical clergy within two specific denominations, United Baptists and Wesleyans, from whom we have received a 70 percent response rate. Some of these results have been published in scholarly journals (Nason-Clark, 1995, 1996), and more detailed analyses and description are available in *The Battered Wife: How Christians Confront Family Violence* (Nason-Clark, 1997).

This chapter, written with an evangelical audience in mind, is divided into three component parts: signs of church sensitivity to the suffering of abuse victims; challenges to seeing the church and its leaders as sensitive to the issue of abuse; and creating a safe environment within the church so that victims can find help.

Evangelical Churches and Abuse: Signs of Sensitivity

When the issue of wife abuse began to surface in the 1970s and the 1980s, it was hard for many laypeople and professionals alike to understand the pervasiveness and severity of the problem. In the intervening years, the secular community has started to acknowledge the extent and nature of abuse directed toward women, but faith communities have been slow to recognize the issue, to respond compassionately to the pain, and to be proactive so that violence in the family context can be eliminated. The picture of how evangelical Christianity in the 1990s is dealing with the issue is complex. There are signs of church sensitivity to the suffering, but there are some signs suggesting otherwise. From our fieldwork among pastors and church people, I have concluded that there are three major indicators of compassion as it relates to victims of violence: pastoral counseling with victimized women; the informal support network of faith communities; and the linkages between church women and the transition house movement.

The Experience of Pastors in Counseling Abuse Victims

Our research program reveals that evangelical clergy report ongoing but limited experience in responding to the plethora of needs represented by violence perpetrated in the family context.

We asked clergy to indicate their level of experience in offering help to a series of possible counseling situations involving victims or perpetrators of violence or couples in violent relationships. We learned that the four counseling situations conservative clergy are called upon most frequently to deal with include "a woman with an abusive partner," "a woman who was abused in childhood by a parent," "a man who is abusive toward his wife or partner," and "a couple commonly experiencing violence in their relationship." To be more specific, approximately 10 percent of the more than 343 evangelical pastors who responded to our survey had counseled five or more cases of "women with abusive partners" within the last year, and another 34 percent reported between two and four such cases within the same time frame.

These data reveal that the majority of evangelical clergy in Atlantic Canada have some pastoral experience in counseling abused women, abusive men, and couples in conflict. Yet, very few (about 10 percent) have a lot of experience in this area. Certainly their experience in offering help is no match for the level of violence experienced by parishioners.

In a face-to-face interview study with 100 evangelical clergy, we learned that 98 of these ministers could recall at least one ongoing counseling case in which they were attempting to help a woman from their own congregation who was in intense arguments with her husband in which she was being blamed for all of their marital problems; 53 of these pastors could recall a counseling scenario that involved physical violence against the wife in a Christian couple involved in leadership in their church; and 29 of these pastors had counseled women from their congregation who had been repeatedly and consistently physically abused by their husbands over several years.

Translating the evangelical message of "happy family living" into practical and spiritual support for abused women, abusive men, and couples in conflict is a time-consuming and emotionally draining task. Moreover, battered Christian wives and conflict-ridden religious homes pose a direct challenge to the evangelical message of marital bliss and family values. And for many pastors, providing safety and support for a woman victim can at times seem at cross-purposes with their desire to keep the family unit together. With the demand for counseling services by pastors on the increase, with little formal training to assist them in this endeavor, and with very limited knowledge of what community resources are available, many pastors are caught between their desire and inability to help.

While ministers reported that their interpersonal skills or friendship ties bring people to them for counseling, our data reveal that the first point of contact between an abused woman and the pastor is often at the time of her wedding preparation. It is here that the pastor's credibility as a listener and an enabler is established, and later on, when conflict and abuse occur, that initial link with the minister is reestablished, most often by the woman victim.

In our research program, we have sought to understand the myriad of ways that pastoral counselors respond to the abused women who seek their help. While clergy differ markedly from one another in terms of their experience in counseling or the specific advice they offer, our data offer no evidence that clergy deliberately or directly dismiss a battered woman's call for help. Ironically, pastors appear to offer far more in the way of practical support or advice than they do spiritual counsel. But the major problem area is that clergy are quite optimistic that violent men want to and can change their abusive behavior. In their desire to bring reconciliation and healing to the life of an abused woman, many clergy offer premature forgiveness to a temporarily repentant abusive man and suggest that the woman victim do likewise. For those clergy who maintain contact over time with such couples, their initial pastoral optimism is often tempered by the unwillingness of such men to engage in the counseling that has been offered or to alter their behavior as a result of therapeutic intervention.

When the violence and the pain are clearly communicated to the pastoral counselor, it appears that ministers offer supportive counsel and practical help to the victim. In these cases, they desire to augment healing and to ensure safety. But often the pain and suffering of an abused woman are obscured by other presenting problems, and it is here that clergy appear to have marked difficulty understanding her situation and need for emotional and physical safety. Clergy themselves lament their lack of training in counseling (only 8 percent of our sample reported they were well prepared in this area of ministry), but the needs of parishioners take precedence over personal feelings of pastoral inadequacy. As a result, both the pastor and the abused woman may feel that the help given is too little, too late.

The Informal Support Network

The clearest demonstration of the commitment of evangelical churches to the needs of abused women and their children can be seen in the compassion and practical support offered within the informal support network of women helping women. From our focus group research, which included almost 250 women assembled in thirty different settings, we learned that the majority of church women have sought help from another woman in their own church for a family-related problem and at some point sought the assistance of another Christian woman in a church other than their own.

When women of faith need help or advice, they look to each other. They offer one another a form of sisterhood and support under the umbrella of their evangelical worldview. Such personal empowerment from women of like faith perspective attends to the practical and spiritual needs of the church community even as it reinforces the religious ideology that is shared between them. When a conservative churchwoman is abused, she may feel her options are more restricted than those of a woman outside a faith community. The support and advice, then, that a religious woman receives from other women of faith become an important component in thinking through her options and charting her future. As a result, it becomes a central ingredient in the journey from victim to survivor.

Our data reveal that churchwomen themselves are quite knowledgeable about the prevalence and severity of wife abuse and that their knowledge in large measure is gleaned from the experience of women they know who have been the victims of such abuse. As sisters with other women, they have learned about violence through the experience of being a listening ear to another woman who is suffering. As a result, they are far less likely to condemn or question a woman's motives in disclosing her pain or to suggest that she reconcile with her violent partner. In this way, conservative churchwomen are more progressive than the clergy who staff evangelical churches.

So what types of help or support do religious women offer one another? Fifty-eight percent of the women who participated in one of our focus groups reported that they had given some form of assistance to a woman who was being battered by her husband. Sometimes this support involved child care, overnight lodging, or monetary gifts. Often, though, it involved listening—listening to disclosures of the pain that had been suffered, listening to the hopelessness a battered religious woman felt, and listening to how difficult it was to be married to a believer who was violent. Contrary to contemporary notions that ignore or downplay the support religious women offer each other, our data demonstrate that evangelical women practice a form of empowerment that neither demands that a battered woman sever all ties with her abusive partner for the duration of her life nor that she remain indefinitely in an environment that threatens her safety and mental health.

Evangelical women, though they are reluctant to call themselves feminists, employ selected feminist principles in their understanding of the etiology and impact of wife abuse (Beaman-Hall & Nason-Clark, 1997). Eager to uphold family values and the sanctity of marriage, they offer hope that is clearly connected to their religious framework and culture. Yet, as women they are able to internalize to some degree the pain, terror, and vulnerability of the abused wife. As a result, they draw upon both the religious culture and the secular culture as they respond to the suffering they see in their own midst.

While conservative churchwomen who are victims of abuse stay married longer and work more vigorously to save the marriage than do women outside of an explicit religious community, the practical and emotional support these women victims receive from other women of like faith is an integral resource in the decision to leave the abusive husband, temporarily or forever (Horton, Wilkins, & Wright, 1988).

Churchwomen's Response to the Transition House Movement

While the most dramatic sign of the evangelical church's sensitivity to the pain of abused women comes from the informal support network of women helping women within a shared religious framework, it is noteworthy that there is evidence of some formal contact and collective action in support of the transition house movement by groups of churchwomen. The link between churchwomen's groups and local shelters for battered women offers exciting evidence of collective action on the part of conservative religious women. And its potential for growth and development cannot be overstated. Many groups of churchwomen have translated their Christian call for compassion into material and financial support for a local shelter.

What type of help do church women's groups offer to transition houses? The many ways reported in our research have included hosting a "shower" and donating the collected gifts, decorating and furnishing a room in the shelter, preparing "comfort kits" (of toiletry and related items) for women residents, and planning specific fundraising events such as an Easter pancake breakfast. The monetary donations were always rather modest in comparison to the annual budgets of most transition houses, but the most important point to be made is the consistency with which churchwomen offered such support and the creativity and diversity of their offerings.

While churchwomen talked in terms of the transition house as a ministry, a phrase that would no doubt shock most shelter workers or the feminists who lobby on behalf of the transition house movement, workers reported in our research that their primary contact with religious organizations involved churchwomen's groups, not clergy. Apparently clergy avoid contact with the transition houses, even when a woman parishioner has sought refuge there.[2] Only a minority of clergy in our research reported that they had ever been to the local transition house, either in terms of obtaining information, driving a woman there who was in need of shelter, or other ministry capacities. Those clergy who had been to a local transition house were much more inclined to work with secular caregivers in the fight to end violence against women or to make appropriate referrals of victimized women. For whatever reason, visiting a transition house appears to be a radical act on the part of an evangelical pastor.

When churchwomen themselves talked about their interaction with the shelter movement, they did so with a marked degree of compassion. Perhaps more completely than other church organizations, women's ministries understand the limitations of clergy-only advice and are consequently eager to support efforts to bring together secular and sacred resources for battered women. For whatever reason, the pastors of churches were not aware of the link between women's ministries in their local congregation and the transition house in the community, nor were they cognizant of the financial and material support that had been offered. Whether this was a deliberate strategy on the part of women's leadership is hard to say. Probably, though, these women volunteers were aware of the tenuous relationship between evangelical clergy and the subject of wife abuse.

Challenges to Seeing Church Sensitivity

Despite the continuing effort made by women's voluntary organizations within churches to support the transition house movement, and despite the strong informal social support network whereby women of faith support each other in times of pain and crisis, the evidence that church leaders care about this issue is rather weak. Most evangelical clergy have had some experience in their counseling ministry whereby they have assisted a woman who has been battered or have responded to a couple who was experiencing violence in their marital relationship. And many pastors have offered a warning about violence in their premarital counseling. But most pastors have never preached a sermon condemning wife abuse, most have never been to a local transition house, and most are reluctant to refer parishioners to outside sources of help, even while they admit they personally are poorly equipped to offer that help.

As a result, the challenge to the evangelical church leaders is to wake up, to recognize the prevalence and seriousness of abuse among families of faith, and to begin to take steps to close the chasm between the rhetoric of "happy family living" and the experience of families in crisis.

According to the results obtained from our research program, there are a number of reasons to be less than fully optimistic that the relationship between abuse victims and churches is characterized by sensitivity. In fact, some of these issues pose major obstacles in the path to support an abuse victim and her family. In this next section, we will identify and discuss five such obstacles: how to name the violence that occurs in evangelical households, the role of reconciliation in the healing process for a victim of abuse, the low rate of referrals between secular and sacred caregivers, the reluctance to condemn violence from the pulpit, and clergy understandings of abuse in Christian families as predominately a spiritual issue (Nason-Clark, 1996, 1997).

Giving the Violence a Name

Clergy in our research appeared to have an aversion to the term *wife abuse,* preferring instead the phrase *family violence* to denote a home in which the husband has used physical force against his wife. On the whole, conservative Protestant ministers regard abuse in marriage as a family issue, evidence that God's design for marital harmony is not fully operational. Evangelical clergy are very resistant to laying responsibility for abuse solely with the violent man, favoring instead to conceptualize the discord as a problem that both marital partners have contributed to and therefore must solve together. Within this framework, the solution to violence is clearly placed within the family unit.

The transition house movement, by contrast, is very reluctant to talk about violence in any way that obscures or downplays the role of the aggressive male partner. Within their framework, abusive men must be restrained from further violence, and victimized women need safety and support. Moreover, they hold that the violence perpetrated in the household of the abusive man is symptomatic of a broader gender power imbalance within mainstream society. In this way, they see the personal pain of one woman as a public issue of male violence. Clearly, how violence is named has important ramifications for the nature and process of support.

Reconciling Abuser and Abused

Another major obstacle to sensitivity for the suffering of abuse victims is the role of reconciliation in the process of healing. From our research we have learned that most evangelical clergy believe that reconciliation of abuser and abused is both desirable and attainable. Given their theological worldview, with its emphasis on conversion and change, this is not surprising. As a result, they are sometimes guilty of offering premature forgiveness to the abusive man and then suggesting that the victimized woman do likewise (see Fortune, 1988). From the point of view of transition house workers, the reality of revictimized women returning to the safe house for shelter tempers optimism of reformed relationships.

Yet, clergy are often called upon to minister to both aggressor and victim. While ministerial contact with abusive men may be one of the unique roles of the spiritual counselor, it also brings a plethora of challenges. Ensuring safety for the victim and resisting the manipulative efforts of the temporarily repentant abuser are but two examples of this challenge. Within our clerical sample, those ministers with the most experience in responding to wife abuse refrain from seeing both abuser and abused until there is solid evidence that the violence has stopped. Until that time, they work with either the abuser or the abused and refer the other person to someone else.

Making Few Referrals

A low rate of referrals is a further complicating factor in the response of the evangelical church to abuse. Many clergy are resistant or at least reluctant to refer parishioners who come to them for help to either specific secular professionals or the agencies that employ them. This occurs despite pastors' personal unease with their training or competence in pastoral counseling, particularly in cases involving abuse. Yet, through our interviews, we have learned that many pastors fear that secular counselors will advise women to leave both their husbands and their faith communities as they look for personal healing and wholeness. Moreover, many clergy are unclear about the unique gifts or roles they bring as pastoral counselors to a woman victim, a male abuser, or a couple in crisis. As a result, they see secular and sacred care as competing rather than complementing one another.

The referral issue is a bi-directional problem, for few secular counselors are willing to include clergy in the therapeutic team. The fear on the part of nonclerical counselors appears to be that clergy offer only spiritual guidance, that they oppose divorce under all conditions, and that their main response to an abused woman is to "go home and pray" that God will allow her to become a better wife and mother and that through her suffering God will be glorified and her husband changed.

Our data indicate that very few pastors explicitly tell women to return home to an unchanged abusive environment, but neither do they clearly and unequivocally condemn the abuse or hold the husband completely accountable for the use of force. Where the violence is less extreme, clergy are less likely to see the need for safety or the long-term implications of the suffering. Clergy are optimistic about reforming abusive men, and they are very enthusiastic to reunite abuser and abused. Most clergy in our research were willing to advise separation only when it was clear that the abusive man was not heeding pastoral advice or when he was unwilling to cooperate with any therapeutic intervention. Ultimately it was the speed with which the advice to separate from the abuser was given that most differentiates clerical from nonclerical counselors.

Among those evangelical pastors with rather extensive experience in responding to violence, there is a greater willingness to refer to outside sources of help, and often an established working relationship existed between those clergy and the secular agencies in their local regions. In essence, one could argue that where referrals are most urgent (among those pastoral counselors with limited training and little experience), they are least likely to happen. Where referral networks were established, it was most often the pastoral counselors who initiated contact with community agencies and then followed up the referrals that they sent to them.

Preaching Reluctantly against Wife Abuse

As we conducted focus groups throughout eastern Canada, in large and small churches and in rural and urban environments, we were struck with the consistency with which these churchwomen reported growing impatient with the silence of their clerical leaders on the issue of wife abuse. These women expected their leaders to recognize the abuse in church families and then take practical steps to respond to victims and denounce violence as a way to resolve family conflict.

A total of 31 percent of clergy in our research reported that at some point in their ministry, they have preached a specific message on wife or child abuse. Yet, few women parishioners reported ever hearing such a message condemning violence.[3] We should not be surprised that clergy are wary of condemning abuse, for in recent years most evangelical clergy have been preaching to a shrinking group of men, and there is strong pressure from outside groups, such as the Promise Keepers, to bring men back into the fold. While it may be understandable why ministers wish to avoid controversy in their Sunday sermon, it is one of the few tools in the pastoral repertoire with which they can challenge the abuser and support the abused. I suspect if pastors understood how therapeutic it is to victims to hear their religious leaders condemn the violence they have suffered, some would be led to reconsider their silence.

Interpreting Abuse in Families of Faith

The majority of ministers within our studies understand violence in evangelical families as a sign of unresolved spiritual issues. They also see the abusive Christian man as someone who is struggling with a life of faith. Members of the clergy do not hold these views because they are unaware of the nonspiritual forces contributing to the prevalence or persistence of violence in mainstream society, for when these same clergy were asked to explain aggressive acts in secular families, they pointed to social science findings in their responses: intergenerational transmission of violence, violence as a power issue, violence as learned behavior, to name but a few. But clergy were resistant to explain violence within families of faith in terms other than the spiritual. Moreover, while clergy estimated violence against women to be fairly prevalent in the communities in which their churches were located, by and large they claimed that violence is far less prevalent among church families.

There are two implications of this bifurcated vision of wife abuse. First, if the issue of abuse can be explained primarily in spiritual terms for evangelical families, then the cure for abuse in evangelical families must be spiritual in origin. This view, then, supports pastors' reluctance to work with secular professionals or to refer parishioners to community agencies. Second, it poses less of a threat to the "happy Christian family" motif if the families that are violent are regarded as spiritually thwarted. It may be too painful for many ministers to acknowledge that men who appear to be fine Christian leaders can be abusive at home.[4]

Making the Church a Safe Place

With calls for fiscal restraint in the public sphere commonplace in contemporary society, there may well be new and renewed opportunities for churches to cooperate and collaborate with community agencies in the fight to end violence and to respond compassionately to its victims. For churches and their leaders, this signals a unique opportunity to implement the Christian mission to bind up the wounds of the brokenhearted. But are churches safe places to disclose abuse? Are clergy sympathetic listeners? What assistance can one pastor or one congregation offer to a problem as prevalent and persistent as wife abuse?

In the closing paragraphs of this chapter, I want to acknowledge that there are many ways people of faith and their leaders can challenge and respond to the violence that permeates our homes, our churches, and our communities. For the sake of brevity, I have listed only five.

Recognize That Abuse Exists

Churchwomen are asking their clerical leaders to recognize that violence occurs in our communities and in families connected to our churches. A willingness to recognize abuse means that sometimes clergy need to ask women who are in distress whether it is safe for them to return home. A willingness to recognize abuse means that sometimes within the text of the sermon there is a mention of a Christian home in which the husband has been violent. A willingness to recognize abuse will have implications for programming, since youth leaders will need to talk about it occasionally with the young people, and Sunday school teachers will need to learn to listen to children's cries for help.

Identify the Unique Role of the Pastoral Counselor

Our research program makes it clear that many pastors are confused about what unique gifts or skills they can offer a victim or an abuser. Victims need practical and emotional support, but religious women also have spiritual needs as they journey toward wholeness. In a sense, the pastoral counselor plays a vital role in helping an abused religious woman realize that God does not condone the violent acts of her husband, nor does God take pleasure in her suffering. While some abused religious women may not want contact with their religious leaders during the initial days of their disclosure of abuse, for many the support of spiritual leaders is a central ingredient in their healing.

Ensure That Victimized Women Are Offered Choices

Every abused woman desires to live a life without the fear or reality of further battery. It is important to realize that since victimized women differ from one another and the contexts in which their battering has occurred are not identical, neither will the choices they make in the process of recovery be the same. Not all victims of wife abuse will want to reconcile with their abusive partners, and not all abused wives will desire to leave their violent husbands forever. Like other victims, abused Christian women will follow a variety of paths as they work through their healing journey. The task of the pastoral counselor, then, is to assist a woman as she explores the options open to her and as she seeks to restore her battered self-image and self-concept, and to enable her and support her as she strives to find a life for herself and her children free from the abuse of the past.

Support Violence-Free Family Living

Violence-free family living is not an accident. Faith communities have many opportunities to model and encourage healthy family relationships. Sunday school during the year, vacation Bible school in the summer, camps and retreats for specific age groups, and the activities and socials during the church calendar provide opportunities for families to encounter models of healthy family living and to discourage unhealthy familial patterns. Churches also have many opportunities for educating and informing the adults in their community. Perhaps the greatest opportunity for such training is the Sunday morning sermon, but there are also informal times when clergy come into contact with church families or visit them in the privacy of their homes.

Build Bridges to the Community

Bridges join together discrete bodies of land. In the contemporary religious landscape, there is a marked chasm between the steeple and the shelter, or the church and the community. Pastors with vision and skill can play a role in bridge building, forging links where there may have been misunderstandings, looking for opportunities to cooperate or collaborate on ventures that meet both church and community mission statements. The pastor who invites a transition house worker to make a short presentation during a service is engaged in bridge building, as is the pastor who calls the local shelter in town to see if a visit might be possible.[5] Others may wish to work together with other pastors in the local area to compile a list of resources that they could draw upon when the need arises. Still other ministers might organize an information event for local clergy, shelter workers, and secular professionals. Pamphlets, brochures, fundraising events, or meet-and-greet sessions are a few of the many ways that clergy can take the lead in bridge building. Not all efforts will meet with success, but it is interesting to note that while reluctance can be bi-directional, so can cooperation.

For the Christian believer, Jesus' experience in the Garden of Gethsemane can sensitize us to the consequences of intense physical and emotional pain. Like many victims of wife abuse, our Lord was betrayed by someone he knew, loved, and trusted. The garden that offered shade from the heat and respite from the crowds was the place of betrayal. Evangelicals around the world celebrate family life and family values. Yet, many churchwomen are violated within their own homes by partners they loved and trusted.

The contemporary evangelical church needs to realize that although the evangelical family may be sacred, it is not always safe. The challenge before us is to ensure that our churches are safe places: places of refuge, places of support, and most of all, places where violence will not be tolerated.

Notes

1. Nancy Nason-Clark is the coordinator of the Religion and Violence Research Team. Team members include Lori Beaman-Hall, Terry Atkinson, Sheila McCrea, and Lois Mitchell. I would like to gratefully acknowledge financial support for my research program and that of the Religion and Violence Research Team from the following sources: the Louisville Institute for the Study of Protestantism and American Culture, the Social Sciences and Humanities Research Council, the Department of the Solicitor General, the Lawson Foundation, the Constant Jacquet Award of the Religious Research Association, the Muriel McQueen Centre for Family Violence Research, and the University of New Brunswick Research Fund.

2. One woman reported that her minister refused to visit her in a transition house for fear he would be seen going into the shelter. There is also reluctance on the part of some shelter workers to initiate contact with clergy for fear that they will advise an abused woman to return home to her unchanged, violent husband.

3. In a smaller study of ninety-four evangelical women who had participated in our focus group research, only a couple of women remembered ever hearing a sermon in which wife abuse was directly condemned (Beaman-Hall & Nason-Clark, 1997).

4. In fact, some abused women reported that when their husbands held leadership positions in the church, clergy were far more reluctant to believe their disclosures of abuse. Many clergy themselves reported in our interviews with them that it created a challenge to their own faith to be faced with the reality that a prominent church leader was violent toward his wife and/or children.

5. Some transition houses have policies about working with male professionals, preferring where possible to work with women.

Part 2

And the Healing

Sexual Abuse Survivors in the Church

9

Diane Strong Nesheim

C hristian beliefs," states Sheila A. Redmond, "do not make it easy for children who have been sexually abused to heal. . . . To those who suffer from the victimization of child sexual assault . . . [Christian virtues] reinforce personal guilt and responsibility. Without frank and open discussion of the negative aspects of Christian doctrine, there will be great difficulty in resolving the lingering feelings of responsibility for a crime which has been perpetrated upon them" (Brown & Bohn, 1989, p. 80). This chapter will address the long-term affects of sexual abuse on Christian survivors and ask questions that are critical to the church community: In what ways do our images and teachings about God support or sustain the sexual abuse of women and children? How do survivors of abuse interpret these teachings? What beliefs are liberating? How can we transform our Christian communities to be inclusive of abused women and children?

In *Secret Scars*, Cynthia Tower states, "Researchers and therapists have found that rape victims, battered wives, mothers in families where there is father-daughter incest and wives of alcoholics often report having been sexually abused as children. Is there a connection between being abused as a child and being abused as an adult?" (1988, p. 78). I believe there is a definite connection, and I will attempt to demonstrate this.

My Story

When I look back over my life, I realize I am a strong person. I am a Christian, an educator, a therapist, and a student of theology. I am a friend, a mother, and a sweetheart. I am also an adult survivor of incest. When I was five or six years old, my brother, who was eight years older, was left to babysit me. I remember him coming into my bedroom and telling me we would play a game. But it was not a game. Afterward I blamed myself, thinking I must have done something to encourage him.

Desperate to end the abuse, I told my parents, but my brother vehemently denied my story and they believed him. I was punished for lying; my words were turned against me; they told me I was crazy. No one listened to my pain. All trust in adults was broken. I could no longer trust my parents, my brother, or the world. More importantly, I learned I could not trust my own reality. I knew that if I were to survive in my family, I would have to deny my own feelings and perceptions and adapt to the way others wanted me to be. I adapted so well that I became someone else and left the wounded child behind.

My strict Pentecostal upbringing reinforced my trauma by filling me with feelings of fear and a sense of helplessness and abandonment by God. The most important message I heard in church was "obedience." "Eve was disobedient and that's why sin came into the world." "A woman must keep silent." "She must love her neighbor and be self-sacrificing." I learned from the Bible that women are the property of men. "Men supposedly have irresistible desires, and women have to be careful not to put men in compromising situations." I was commanded to "love my enemies," "forgive those who hurt me," and "carry my cross." I further learned that "sometimes God asks people to suffer and to make sacrifices. It is part of his plan." I was being tested or chastised but only because God loved me. Maybe being raped was part of God's plan, or he would have intervened to help me. I remembered Paul's words, that people who had committed fornication were condemned to hell. I concluded that I had no rights, not even the right to be treated with dignity and respect.

Upon completion of high school, I married, but my husband, who promised to love and honor me, subtly and repeatedly attacked my sense of identity over a period of eighteen years. In 1972, I gave my life to God and attempted to become the submissive wife my church prescribed. The abuse escalated. I pursued counseling from my pastor and church. I was told to "stay in the marriage and pray; just have faith and believe God." Rather than leave, I prayed for change in my husband and the courage to endure. I questioned my faith and at times questioned my sanity. I spent many agonizing hours in prayer and Bible reading. I believed God was trying to teach me something, and when I learned this lesson my suffering would be over.

I experienced a crisis of meaning in my life. Simplistic answers were given to complex problems, and at times I felt my faith failing and felt abandoned by God. My pastor was determined to save my marriage; he did not realize I was slowly dying inside. I stayed in my marriage and called it faith; perhaps it was denial at best, delusion at worst. The constant criticism and abuse destroyed my spirit. By the time I sought help outside the church, I had lost all sense of self-esteem.

Many years later I had a dream of a mask on the wall, a mask of a woman with no eyes, no spirit, and a tear falling down her cheek. In my dream I kept trying to get to that mask and knew if I could, I would be safe once again. Later, as I prayed for discernment, the Holy Spirit showed me that I was the woman and that I had worn a mask since I was a little girl. In order to survive in my family, I had numbed myself to all feelings. As I grew to adulthood, I was so out of touch with my body and my spirit that I was unaware of this mask. I realized that when I became a Christian, I put on a Christian mask. I went through all the motions, I knew all the Christian rhetoric and prayers, but I did not feel real inside. I did not know how to feel precious to God.

As I look back over those years, I understand that while suffering from the devastating aftereffects of incest, I allowed others to abuse me, control me, and define my life. I did not believe I deserved respect, consideration, and good treatment from others. I realize that because of my unhealthy family legacy, I allowed Christian doctrines, beliefs, and people to control my life, even though many were dysfunctional. Although I tried to love my neighbor, I did not love myself. It was in my search for God that I found healing and eventually myself.

People are good at wearing masks when attending church. Most say they are fine when they are dying spiritually, emotionally, and physically. The sexually abused hide their hurts behind facades and remain silent in order to be acceptable to the Christian community. It is not safe to talk about sexual abuse in Christian circles, and many victims do not know whom to trust, so they wear their perfect masks. They also carry secret scars in their spirits that prevent them from experiencing all that God has for them. As long as there is silence about these traumas, God is not allowed to heal the hurts. Christians need to question how this silence in our churches is perpetuated. Why are people not allowed to show their pain, articulate their rage and vulnerability? Why must we wear Christian masks?

Theologian Walter Brueggemann explains why some churches remain silent about abuse: "If we are such a bourgeois church that we have to keep all our vengefulness under the table, not because God can't take it, but because we can't take each other's reality, then we are contributing to the rise of violence in our society" (1988, p. 304).

Incest, Sigmund Freud believed, is a universal taboo and is more often the hysterical fabrication of a neurotic woman than the true reporting of sexual assault. But according to recent statistics, at least one-third of women and one-fifth of men have been sexually abused as children. Incest is a betrayal of the most basic trust between a child and an adult. Young victims depend totally on adults and parents to protect them, so when a parent sexually uses a child, that child has nowhere to run, no one to run to. The child's reality becomes a prison of dirty secrets. Incest betrays the very heart of childhood—its innocence. Although much has been written about the psychological aftereffects of abuse, little has been discussed about the damage done to the soul. *From Pain to Hope* describes the spiritual aftereffects of abuse: "The damage done extends well beyond a deep psychological wound; it causes radical soul-searching about the meaning of life and the pertinence of all that has been taught about God and religion" (Canadian Conference of Catholic Bishops, 1992, p. 28). Spiritual questions surface: Why is this happening to me? What have I done to deserve this? Why did God let this happen to me and my family? Maybe there is no God and I am in hell. Although survivors are screaming inside, they scream silently.

Wolves in Sheep's Clothing

Who sexually abuses children? Many abusers are members of a child's own family, members who are supposed to love and protect them. Other children are sexually exploited by babysitters and friends of the family. For many others, abuse occurred at the hands of priests, ministers, choirmasters, and Sunday school teachers. Canada has been stunned in the last few years by a scandal involving more than two dozen priests and Christian brothers who physically and sexually abused boys in an orphanage in Newfoundland. Sexual abuse survivors in institutions in other parts of Canada, moved by the courage shown by Mount Cashel's victims, have now come forward with their own tales of abuse. Many of these institutions were church operated. In my own city of Kingston, a highly respected choirmaster sexually abused many boys in his care over a ten-year period, leaving untold scars and contributing to the suicide of two victims.

The adult survivors of sexual abuse who tell their stories today are legion. Research indicates that pedophiles do not target just one child. Where one molested child is discovered, there may be twenty, thirty, sixty, or even more than two hundred other victims of the same assailant.

Why do we remain silent in our churches about sexual abuse and incest? Do we think that God does not know? God obviously knows that incest and rape happen—the story of Tamar's rape is recorded in 2 Samuel. Do we think God does not care? Of course God cares, just as God cared about David's affair with Bathsheba. David tried to carry out his adultery in secret, but God brought his act into the open by sending a prophet to speak to David. The Book of 2 Samuel informs the reader of God's view on lust, adultery, and rape.

Do we remain silent because we think no one else knows? Although some incestuous abuse is hidden, other times the situation is like Tamar's. Lots of people knew—Jonadab knew, Amnon knew, Tamar knew, Absalom knew, and David knew. If so many people knew, why did Absalom tell Tamar to be quiet? Tamar is not allowed to speak on her own behalf. She wanted to scream, tear her clothes—she wanted people to know what had happened. But her screams were silenced. God knows this story about Tamar and he is trying to tell us about her suffering. Will we listen to her story? Will we break the silence in our churches and listen to the silent screams of survivors in our own church community?

It is important for ministers, pastors, and priests to know that adults who have been sexually abused as children have grown up in a dysfunctional family and "view life through smoked glass. Nothing is bright and clean" (Grayson & Johnson, 1991, p. 81). Often their perception of God is seen through the lens of abuse. Adults who were sexually abused as children still describe God as "a terrifying, all-powerful ruler who always keeps an eye on us and is always looking for something for which to punish us." "God is just like my father." "God has patience, but at some point he loses patience with us and judges us harshly. He then becomes a God of revenge." "God is in control of all things and could have intervened if he wanted but chose not to answer my cries for help." "The God of the Bible sides with men; women are to submit to men." "Even when men hurt you, you must forgive." "You must love your brother, even if he rapes you." We who are survivors hear God is love but do not feel it in our hearts. We do not know how to feel until we heal the hurts of our childhood.

Some adult survivors of abuse seek escape from their inner pain through the use of drugs, alcohol, sexual addictions, and prostitution. Others seek escape by becoming involved in extremely conservative denominations. Adult survivors may use God, a church, a preacher, a scriptural text, a television evangelist, a belief system, or a mystical vision as a means to avoid painful memories. They go from one religious evangelist to another, always seeking a spiritual high. They discover that a particular religion makes them feel good, accepted, or powerful. Fundamentalist churches typically preach the we-they dichotomy, adding to the feeling of specialness of these survivors.

Conservative congregations are encouraged to look to the church for answers; only their pastor has the truth. They are further encouraged to read only certain Christian books, listen to certain Christian music, travel only in certain Christian circles, and seek counseling only from Christian pastors. As a result, they are totally isolated within a church cocoon. Once they are isolated from the world, however, a major problem develops for these survivors. Women can become easily controlled by an authoritarian pastor who reinforces women's submission to men, even if the men are abusive.

Issues That Contribute to Abuse

Headship and Submission

Traditions perpetuated in fundamentalist churches may appear fine on the surface, but on a deeper level they can be harmful. Jim and Phyllis Alsdurf state, "Within fundamentalist circles the entire issue of roles has been elevated to a level of idolatry. Men in leadership give definitions very authoritatively as to just what a woman's role or a man's role is to be, without any consideration of cultural conditioning or without regard for the variety of gifts God has given irrespective of sex" (1989, p. 138). While not all men abuse, many will and do.

A theology that enables abuse emphasizes a hierarchy of human existence and authority. Authority flows from God to adult males to adult females and finally to children. A hierarchical view of human relationships sets women and children under the power of males and gives male authority the stamp of the divine. Most commonly, directives on marriage based on Scripture are given to women and not to men, and these directives state that wives must submit to their husbands. In a hierarchy, the worth of individuals is decided by focusing on certain identifiable characteristics such as sex and age. "Children and women are given less authority and thus are less able to challenge the abuse of power by men. . . . Both become the property of men who stand between them and God. Such a theology worships male authority rather than God and is idolatrous!" (Fortune, 1988, p. 5). Additionally, some ministers have sexually abused their own children. Strong belief in the primacy of the father as the patriarch of the family can set up the kind of authoritarian hierarchy that breeds incest.

Misinterpretation or Selective Use of Scripture

In dysfunctional or unhealthy homes, the selective use of Scripture and misinterpretations often used by abusers perpetuate abuse.

The misinterpretation of Bible teachings can warp parents whose literal belief impels them to view childish behavior as satanic and needing strong correction. Because Scripture is so important in their lives, evangelical women and children may be more susceptible to abuse than others. Margaret Rinck describes how a perpetrator may quote Scripture to justify his actions: "These men use it as a weapon to control and manipulate others" (1990, pp. 71–72). "Appealing to 'God's will,' 'God's best,' 'what God would want' . . . all become powerful motivators. No Christian wants to be 'out of God's will' . . . so compliant, dutiful wives [and children] fall into line when misogynists use these phrases whether or not it makes sense, feels right, or seems healthy" (1990, p. 73).

Abusive men manipulate Scripture to create doctrine and dogma designed to keep women and children in submission, fearful of error. They make the rules and say the rules are God's, so that questioning the teachings or the teacher equals questioning God. Abuse, therefore, continues in the name of God.

Obedience to Authority

"Besides having a deep respect for Scripture and for God, the Evangelical Christian respects authority. All authority figures are seen as receiving their authority from God. To question one's parents, the pastor, . . . is unthinkable in many Christian homes. The husband is seen as the 'head of the home.' . . . He has final authority, and what he says goes!" (Rinck, 1990, p. 74). Since all sexual abuse hinges on the unfair use of power against someone weaker or of lower status, this makes women and children more vulnerable in cultures in which religion promotes their subordination. This perceived headship of the male becomes a divinely appointed power that not only claims to speak for God but also insists that the submission of a woman is the way to God. From the cradle on, female children are trained to look to someone else to tell them what to do, when to do it, and what will happen if they do not.

There is danger in teaching children blind obedience. Teaching them never to question adult authority makes them vulnerable to abuse by adults—teachers, police officers, babysitters, coaches, and parents. Most children do not know they can say no to adults who make inappropriate requests. Rapists who have been interviewed by researchers report that they choose a specific type of victim, someone they feel is vulnerable and will not fight back. Factors that make a child unlikely to resist sexual assault are a poor self-image, fear of saying no, need for attention, lack of sex education, and fear of physical coercion. If we want to reduce the incidence of child abuse, we cannot continue to insist on unthinking obedience to authority.

Hindrances to Healing from Abuse

Faith or Magical Thinking?

Magical thinking, common in dysfunctional families, makes it possible to deny abuse. Many adult survivors of abuse, believing that they are always wrong, look for a fixer (that is, God) who is going to make everything right. If the fixer does not, then it is because they have not done something. Resigned to their victim role, they believe they have no choice but to keep shouldering their cross and going on. They wait for God to work a miracle; they wait to be good enough for God to fix their lives. Many abused Christian women cling desperately to the assurance that suffering in this life will be rewarded in the next life (Heb. 11). The promise of heavenly rewards as compensation for suffering now often keeps survivors in abusive situations and denying reality. Many, calling it faith, cling to magical thinking until their spirits are destroyed. They then feel abandoned by God.

Simplistic Answers

When adult survivors of abuse approach evangelical pastors because of chaos in their inner lives, they are frequently offered simplistic spiritual formulas that do not aid them in dealing with the trauma they are facing: "It's all under the blood"; "the slate has been washed clean"; "keep the commandments and everything will be fine"; "keep praying"; "accept Jesus Christ as your Lord and Savior and you will be happy"; "you must forgive seventy times seven"; "put it in the past and forget about it"; "pray harder." While these are all basic tenets of Christian faith, alone they are inadequate to deal with experiences of incest and sexual abuse. Furthermore, these teachings can reinforce the blame victims place on themselves for their suffering.

In *Creating a Safe Place,* Curt Grayson and Jan Johnson describe the agony of one Christian recovering from child abuse:

> I figured that I had some terrible sin in my life, so I asked forgiveness. I listened to Christian radio programs all the time so that I could be more spiritual. I followed people's advice to "claim the victory." I felt completely alone. It seemed that no one, including God, could reach inside me and calm the craziness there. I had no answers, only questions, and I was giving up hope that I would regain control again. I went through three years of soul searching—tears, fear, prayer, suicidal thoughts, failed relationships and advice from well-meaning friends. (1991, p. 120)

Loss of or Misplaced Trust

When a child's trust is shattered, the world becomes a fearful place. If trust is defined as a feeling of safety, comfort, or security with a person, then the incest survivor can be said to be incapable of experiencing trust. At the same time, however, because a survivor has learned not to trust her own perceptions or emotions, she may trust without properly evaluating a relationship and become involved with another abusive man. She has not learned the judgment necessary to decide who and when to trust. She may trust everyone in an attempt to have the relationship she never had. She may trust all the wrong people. Or she may trust no one. Many do not trust God.

Cynthia Tower articulates the words spoken by an incest survivor: "How can you trust when you know that around every turn there is a new betrayal? How can you love when your life is used for an adult's pleasure? How can you care about yourself when others see you as counting for no more than the several body parts they can use for their own gratification?" (1988, p. 141).

Guilt Reinforced

The belief that "it's all my fault" is never more intense than with an incest victim. This belief fosters strong feelings of self-loathing and shame. Because she feels guilty about the past, the survivor is often plagued with the belief that she does not deserve to be respected or loved and that she needs to suffer to atone for her sins. If she has rigidly religious parents, they may compound the problem by feeding her heavy doses of guilt and making her believe she is a sinner for not always obeying and honoring them.

Grayson and Johnson explain how survivors of dysfunctional families often interpret sermons on sin and guilt:

> We heap on ourselves inappropriate false guilt that we learned in our dysfunctional families. We judge ourselves too harshly and take ourselves too seriously. If we don't follow the letter of the law, we feel inadequate. We condemn ourselves in the same ways in which we were condemned in the past. . . . We ask forgiveness but we never feel forgiven. . . . We are damaged goods. This kind of shame grows out of shame-based childhood experiences, not guilt over recent sin. (1991, p. 98)

Denial of Feelings

There is a vital and relevant relationship between God's will, reality, and our mental health. To find God's will for our lives, we must be in touch with our inner selves, but this thought terrifies survivors of sexual abuse. The trauma to body and spirit was often so severe that survivors had to shut down their bodies to protect themselves. All senses become dulled. Some survivors have reported that they experienced a form of losing consciousness, dissociating themselves from their bodies and from their feelings. They mount a psychological cover-up, pushing these memories so far beneath conscious awareness that they may not surface for years, if ever. They become very skilled actors, wearing their masks to perfection. In their inner world there is so much terror, sadness, isolation, and loneliness that many develop a false self with which to relate to the outside world. In extreme cases of abuse, they may develop multiple personality defense. In some senses, they are the walking dead among us.

Dan Allender describes this numbing: "The heart aches, and there is no immediate recourse for relief, except the soul-numbing choice to abandon a sense of being alive. If the victim wants to be free of the pain, then she must choose to not be alive. . . . In most, if not all, cases, profound helplessness leads to deep scars and wounds. The internal damage follows the path of doubt, despair and deadness" (1990, p. 102). As adults, many survivors still function as if in a daze, going through the motions of being alive. These adults have become so good at dissociating themselves from life in order to avoid pain that they are seldom truly present when they are with others. Their state of slumber has become a nightmare, and the real self is hidden from everyone, including themselves. In order to recover, survivors must integrate their bodies with their minds and their emotions with their thoughts.

Virtue in Self-Denial

The Christian tradition has frequently been associated with denunciation of self. Reginald Bibby says, "Christianity . . . has not lacked for emphasis upon human sinfulness, the need to deny self, the importance of being poor in spirit, the acknowledgment of one's being capable of nothing apart from the grace of God. In the process, self has often been impoverished" (1987, p. 263). Jesus said "love thy neighbor as thyself," but survivors from unhealthy families and homes in which abuse takes place do not know how to love themselves, do not know how to find themselves, and do not know who they are. If we do not love ourselves, how can we love others? If we do not know what we need, how can we see others' needs?

Christians have been consistently exhorted to repent of pride and to imitate Christ's servanthood. But the church's emphasis on the sinfulness of pride and the virtue in self-denial does not help the spiritual state of abused persons and, in fact, often lowers their already battered self-esteem. Abused women typically reveal an underdevelopment or negation of the self, including dependence on others for self-definition. Virginia Mollenkott addresses the effect of these messages on women and children who are oppressed: "What any oppressed person needs to repent of is not pride but lack of it! . . . To preach Christlike servanthood to people who have never been in touch with power and autonomy is to commit an obscenity. . . . You cannot choose to give up power or use it to serve others until you have the power to choose!" (1989, p. 84). Adults who were abused as children need to reclaim the spirit that was stolen from them, to heal and become whole with the help of God and a loving community.

Suffering as Payment for Sin

When a person experiences suffering, the foremost question is, Why am I suffering? "If you are a good Christian girl, then God will protect you" is a common theme taught in Sunday school. This theme, combined with religious teachings that emphasize God's care and protection, often causes survivors to believe that bad things happen only to bad people. When something bad does happen to them, they believe they must have deserved it or it would not have happened. For the survivor, her victimization is then interpreted as a sign of her sinfulness, as Marie Fortune explains: "If one accepts this simple formula (which makes a theological assumption that God's love is conditional) then when one experiences any form of suffering, one feels punished or abandoned by God. . . . When people attempt to utilize the simple answer and it is insufficient, they feel that their faith has failed them or that God has abandoned them" (1988, p. 2). Survivors need to hear that when there is injustice among people, God is with those who suffer. The prophets constantly depict a God who is distraught at children's suffering and yearns for their restoration and happiness.

Virginity Upheld

Every adult who was molested as a child brings from childhood pervasive feelings of being hopelessly inadequate, worthless, and bad. No matter how different their lives may appear on the surface, until they are healed, all adult victims of incest share a legacy of tragic feelings. Many survivors believe that others can see scarlet letters on their foreheads saying, "different," "damaged," "dirty."

The damaged-goods syndrome is particularly prevalent in religious families, which stress the virginity of daughters. Daughters are frequently told by mothers, "Keep yourself pure for your wedding night," "No man wants damaged goods," "Sex without marriage is sin." These comments lay a terrible burden of guilt on children who have been sexually abused.

The Church's Role in the Healing Process

Allowing the Expression of Anger and Rage

The church is frequently referred to as the family of God. This image suggests positive parallels of trust, intimacy, caring commitment, and respect that should be the basis of church life. Using this model, the church has sought to build relationships among members of genuine love and care, providing in some cases a family for those who have no families. But if we truly are the family of God, we must become comfortable enough in our churches to hear stories of pain, anger, injustice, abuse, and suffering. Many churches talk about a religion that frees its participants—but we avoid discussing the topics that might actually free us (Noddings, 1989).

Sheila A. Redmond articulates the need for survivors to speak their anger and rage:

> Not only the abused person's rights but their very being has been violated and they need an opportunity to vent anger and rage. . . . It is clear from the therapies of women who have been sexually assaulted as children that a necessary component to resolving the trauma of the assault is through an articulation of rage, anger and hatred at being used, at the powerlessness of their position when they were children. Feelings must be accepted as they are exhibited and allowed to run their natural course. (1988, p. 127)

Offering Forgiveness

Adults who were sexually abused as children and have lived with the reality of violence in their family frequently feel like illegitimate worshipers. They are unable to have the loving, forgiving feelings that are expected of them and often find it difficult to affirm the faithfulness and goodness of God.

In *We Weep for Ourselves and Our Children,* the authors explain the importance of truth-telling: "Christlike forgiveness is based on a total commitment to telling the truth. While the biblical model opposes seeking personal vengeance, it does not exclude the expression of anger or even some appropriate name calling. True forgiveness is not at odds with pointing out who bears the responsibility for a sin" (Feldmeth & Finley, 1990, p. 135).

Real forgiveness comes at the final stage of a long process through which victims regain control of their lives. They no longer let the experience of violence dominate their lives and are ready to move on.

Seeing the Family as It Really Is

Christians affirm the dignity and worth of each person as God's creation. We recognize the necessity of just and loving relationships in support of each person's dignity, and we consistently lift up the family as being divinely ordained. But not all family relationships are liberating. Some are hostile and destructive. Biblical history speaks of jealousy and hate between brothers that result in the murder of Abel by Cain. Sarai turns against Hagar, the mother of her husband's child. Joseph's brothers are ready to kill him. Tamar is raped by her brother Amnon. The Levite's concubine is raped and tortured, and her master cuts her body into twelve pieces and sends them throughout Israel. Clearly a false idealism about family life must be tempered with the truth-telling of the biblical record.

We need to talk realistically about families in the Bible and emphasize their humanness. We cannot gloss over parts of the Bible that speak of brutality and violence. We can speak the truth about human relationships and failings, teach about the humanness of our saints, and point out God's mercy in the midst of failures. Before we can heal the world, we must begin to heal the church.

Using Alternate Images for God

Exclusive use of male imagery for God reinforces the idea of male superiority and authority and leaves people who have experienced violence at the hands of men, particularly those who have been abused by their fathers, without any satisfactory way of imaging God. If our images for God, such as Father-God or Lord and King are exclusively male, the child abused by a father or a father figure may have no means for perceiving God as loving and protective of the vulnerable. "A God with mother-like patience and compassion for fumbling children is a much less abuse-enabling image" (Bowman, 1988, p. 4).

The experience of being abused has forced many to ask if they can believe in God when the images for God are male and when a predominantly male church hierarchy seems to be inattentive to their needs. Joanne Feldmeth and Midge Finley state the position of many Christians:

> Unfortunately, many Christians are not very tolerant of anyone who finds God the Father a less-than-comforting picture. But if a little girl were mauled by a circus lion, few of us would insist that she think of God as a strong lion, although that is a biblical image of God used in Isaiah 31:4. We would understand that her picture of lion was associated with pain and damage. God is also called "My Rock" (Ps. 18, 28); the good Shepherd (Luke 15:4–7; Ps. 23); the fortress (Ps. 18:2); the eagle (Deut. 32:11); the celebrating hostess (Luke 15:8–10); the woman in childbirth (Isa. 42:14–16); the mother of an infant (Ps. 131:2); the nursing mother (Ps. 91:4); the lion (Isa. 31:4); the king of glory (Ps. 24:7–10) etc. Taking time out from the overused Father God images is not only valuable to survivors of sexual abuse, it is a way for all of us to broaden our understanding of who God is. (1990, p. 106)

Not all adults abused as children view a Father-God image negatively. For many survivors it is comforting to realize they have a kind and loving Father in heaven who replaces their cruel father on earth.

Transformed Christian Communities

Christian Education

To be effective agents of change in the Christian churches, we need to develop new models of ministry and reexamine existing models. Christian congregations can provide and encourage healthy role models for men and women. Children need to see men responding in warmth, tenderness, vulnerability, and tears to those around them; they need to see women in places of leadership. Midweek Bible study groups for men could explore the use or abuse of male privilege in the church and in the community. Women's groups might explore issues of child abuse and violence against women. Christian education in the church presents an ideal context for helping families learn how to shape caring, intimate relationships.

Through youth programs we can work toward developing a sexual ethic among young people that emphasizes mutuality and love rather than power and authority in intimate relationships. Teenagers need a strong and consistent message that runs counter to the often abusive and exploitive media messages that bombard their consciousness. We might establish training sessions and protocols for youth ministers and Sunday school teachers to assist them in identifying victims of abuse. Through youth ministries or youth camp we can reach out to many children who are suffering silently. Young people need information about sexual abuse so if someone attempts to take advantage of them, they will know where to go for help (Fortune, 1982).

We need to consistently teach our children in Sunday schools how Jesus welcomed and loved children. In our schools, the media, and even the church, children are admonished to act grown-up, an admonition that implies that acting like a child (even during childhood) is unacceptable. The stories of Jesus establish a view of children that is radically different from the one society reflects. In the Scriptures children are not regarded as lesser beings but as persons with special qualities and gifts to offer the community. Childlikeness is held up as an ideal in the Gospels as Jesus tells his disciples, "Truly I tell you, unless you change and become like children, you will never enter the kingdom of heaven" (Matt. 18:3 NRSV; see also Mark 9:33–37; Luke 9:46–48).

Churches must teach children that the biblical injunction to obey parents does not mean they must submit to sexual abuse. We also need to combat models of family structure that place fathers in positions of ultimate authority over women and children and require unilateral submission and obedience. We need to dispel the idea that what happens in our homes is private and no one else's business. We are called to care for each other, regardless of familial boundaries. When one of us is wounded, the entire church suffers.

Reinterpreting Scripture

"But the Bible says . . ." is frequently used to explain, excuse, or justify abuse between family members. Transforming our Scriptures means direct and radical criticism of misogyny and racism. The Anglican Task Force's report, *Violence against Women*, states, "The standard must be that no reference from Scripture can be used to justify the abuse of another human being" (Anglican Church of Canada, 1986, p. 41).

We need to incorporate an understanding of the Bible that contains both the apparently oppressive and the liberating stories, and emphasize the more liberating ones. Some biblical material that appears not to address women or appears hostile to them nonetheless contains liberating themes. Many survivors have received comfort from the Bible passages about Martha and Mary, the woman caught in adultery, the woman at the well, and twelve-year-old Jesus in the temple. Survivors need to hear frequently about the woman whose issue of blood made her an outcast but on whom Jesus had mercy. Evangelical churches that tend to overuse the teachings of Paul could instead emphasize the teachings of Jesus and how he always affirmed the personhood of women. In many passages we find hope; in others, courage; and in still others, signs of a God of justice and righteousness. We need to read our Bibles with new eyes.

Training for Clergy

Clergy, because of their positions, are entrusted with respect and authority and, as a result, have a sacred responsibility to their congregations. It is crucial that ministers who counsel and teach have adequate preparation and education. Education in psychology and spirituality are necessary to bring about true healing. The task of harmonizing the spiritual and the psychological is difficult, but there can be no spiritual healing without being in touch with the emotional; there can be no fullness of emotional healing without the spiritual. If clergy do not have this training, they must ensure that referrals are made to professionals who do.

Ezekiel's words of warning to the shepherds of Israel apply equally to the shepherds of today: "You have not strengthened the weak, you have not healed the sick, you have not bound up the injured . . . but with force and harshness you have ruled them." Because the shepherds ignored the plight and the pain of the sheep, God says: "I am against the shepherds; and I will demand my sheep at their hand, and put a stop to their feeding the sheep" (Ezek. 34:4, 10 NRSV).

Seeking Justice

There is much in our society we need to rethink and conventions that we need to upset, even as Jesus did with the Pharisees. While many do not abuse, many others will and do. Churches must acknowledge their part in the perpetuation of abuse by truth-telling, by naming abuse as sin, and by breaking the silence not only on an individual level but on a corporate level as well. The church must make clear that any form of violence against another is unacceptable and reinforce these pronouncements with action. The church is called to persist in advocating for the powerless and vulnerable— the victims of family violence. This persistence may involve advocating for individuals who need legal, medical, or social aid, or it may involve advocating on a larger scale to change unjust laws and practices that exacerbate the suffering of victims of family violence and deny help for the abusers, leaving them to repeat their past sins. The gospel mandate is clear: We as the church are called to bind up the wounds of the victims and to confront the destructive actions of the abusers. We are called to seek justice.

The church as sanctuary can no longer be only a refuge from fear but must become a prophetic space in which to speak truth. We must break through the suffocating silence that hurts all of us. Although we cannot undo all the wrongs of the past, as the people of God, we are called to action for the future. D. Morris articulates our call for a transformed Christian community:

> The greatest contribution the Christian church can make towards ending violence and abuse in families is to create a community of love and support where everyone's dignity is respected, where they

can gather, tell their stories and be healed from any injury incurred in their most intimate relationships. . . . Children are cherished and allowed to speak in such a community. They are no longer forced to keep secrets that can poison their lives. When we face the challenge of ending violence in families by hearing each other, by believing what is said or what is clear, yet unspoken, and when we respond appropriately in the context of a faithful community, our personal and collective healing begins. (1988, p. 164)

"God, I Hate You";
"Sally, I Love You"

10

Pamela C. Court

The psalms are replete with images of the psalmist working through distress in a direct and emotional dialogue with God. Consider Jeremiah 20:7–9. Convinced of his ultimate failure as a prophet, Jeremiah accused God of having wronged him and complained of the ignominy that had befallen him.

> O LORD, you deceived me, and I was deceived;
>   you overpowered me and prevailed.
> I am ridiculed all day long;
>   everyone mocks me.
> Whenever I speak, I cry out
>   proclaiming violence and destruction.
> So the word of the LORD has brought me
>   insult and reproach all day long.
> But if I say, "I will not mention him
>   or speak any more his name,"
> his word is in my heart like a fire,
>   a fire shut up in my bones.
> I am weary of holding it in;
>   indeed, I cannot.

When you read these words, do you hear the resonant voice of Gregory Peck or Charlton Heston soliloquizing? Or do you hear real, gut-wrenching, painful anger? Surely the latter is more realistic, yet

149

we often suppress our angry feelings. Anger is a normal, natural, neutral emotion that is creative when it is correctly channeled (Augsburger, 1986). When anger is denied, distorted, or displaced, it contaminates all relationships and situations.

According to William J. Gaultiere (1989), Christians often hide their anger from God because at both home and church we are told it is "unthinkable to get angry with God." Social and religious taboos in this area result in our feeling guilty and afraid to discuss anger toward God or others. This hidden anger, Gaultiere writes, further "distances the embittered individual from God and leaves him or her caught in an unsettled faith crisis" (p. 39).

Ephesians 4:26, "In your anger do not sin," is a biblical verse often quoted to highlight the dangers of anger, and the assumption is that we should deny our feelings.

Archibald D. Hart, by contrast, comments:

> My understanding of what Paul is saying here is that it is not the anger itself (as feeling) that is wrong, but that anger has the potential for leading you into sin. The point is that it is the translation or conversion of anger feelings into aggressive and hostile acts that leads us into sin. To feel anger, to tell someone that you feel angry, and to talk about your anger are both healthy and necessary. As long as you recognize the anger as your own and avoid hurting back the object of your anger, you are keeping it as a feeling—and all feelings are legitimate! What you *do* with your feeling may not be, and this is where you can fall into sin. (1979, p. 85)

John Court points out our need to differentiate between righteous anger and that which is selfishly induced. He discusses the outcome of the expression of human anger that is "commonly and typically intended to hurt, to destroy and to wreak vengeance. Godly anger is directed toward resolution and to correction of evil, even when expressed punitively" (Court, 1986, p. 44). P. W. Clement (1986) suggests the use of behavioral interventions, and David Augsburger (1986) recommends that therapists model a clear "I-Position," encouraging owning of responsibility in all dimensions. Gaultiere's (1989) modus operandi has been to encourage people to write their own imprecatory psalms in which they express their anger at God and others who have harmed them.

Clement writes:

> One of the potential problems with anger is that it can easily distract or focus the person in an unhelpful direction. The angrier a person is, the less likely s/he will be in thinking in terms of *positive goals* (e.g., "What do I want?"). Instead, the natural tendency when angry is to think in terms of what I don't want or want to get away from (i.e., *negative goals*). Unfortunately, negative goals can be achieved by moving in *any* direction but they can never be reached. This any-direction-will-do nature of negative goals seems to be the reason that persons who are caught up in chronic anger and negative goals are ambivalent, confused and bothered by meaninglessness in life. (1986, p. 44)

Sally was one such angry person pursuing negative goals.

The Case of Sally

Sally was a twenty-three-year-old, blond, blue-eyed woman. Small and muscular in appearance, she seemed to vibrate with energy and life. She had a beautiful, wide smile and projected an image of truly joyous living.

Her presenting problem was that she was constantly being sent off the court for aggressive behavior during her amateur basketball games and was in danger of being asked to leave her sports club.

In response to my question, "How have you already tried to solve this issue?" her hostile reply was, "I have been to five psychologists and psychiatrists and they are all airheads. You will be one too, so I won't come back again!" I unwittingly took the "air" out of her sails because I did not know what an airhead was and had to ask. The mood changed in the room as she taught me, and we laughed together and made images of what airheads could look like.

Toward the end of the session, I remarked that she had a wonderful smile, but it had been in place all the time she was with me and it made me concerned for her. I said I wondered if she ever stopped smiling. She said no and that it was because she was always happy. I ended the session early by saying I thought something was making her upset but that she had learned not to upset people by letting it show. She still smiled. I told her I had an appointment free at the same time next week but as she was not interested in coming back I would not bother to put her name down. I also told her how much I had enjoyed her humor. She made the appointment with the secretary and did not fail to appear for one appointment in the entire year of therapy. This was my only paradoxical intervention with Sally.

The next appointment was spent compiling a genogram. Again we used a lot of humor, and from this session I discovered that Sally had been reared as a Baptist and attended church most Sundays but as an adult had had to change churches often. Her bad language and violent behavior were not accepted and she was asked to leave. No one had tried to support her. The referrals to other therapists had been instigated by various churches she had attended.

During that session five other relevant areas were uncovered:

friction between mother and daughter from the time Sally was about nine; the friction increased in severity to the point that Sally rarely stayed home, preferring to live in a room provided by the children's home where she worked as a nurses' aide

increasing friction between Sally and her brother Sam each time she visited her family ("He is always telling me what to do")

friction in her social and work settings

perceived lack of support by the church

a background in Christian living and education (Sally's parents and brothers still regularly attended church)

It was evident early on that Sally was blocked developmentally at around nine years of age. In the office she often behaved in a child-like but endearing manner. She placed chairs in various positions before she made a final choice of which one to sit in. (The chair positions often indicated how she felt.) She was very short and would sit forward while swinging her legs back and forth, knees well apart. She always wore jeans, a T-shirt, sneakers, and a man's watch, but feminine earrings. Her hair was bobbed and her muscular appearance (she lifted weights) caused me to wonder as to her gender identity. She was always clean and tidy. For our first six sessions she was physically restless. Sally refused to have her family involved for six months.

Recognizing her need for autonomy, I encouraged Sally to control the content of her next few sessions. She chose to talk about her two friends, Becky and Cindy, and recognized grieving issues over both. Becky was leaving to work in another state, while Cindy was eight months pregnant and was moving to the country after the baby was born. Sally was about to lose her only strong supports in a brief spell. Her antisocial behavior had increased since she had discovered she would lose her friends, but this loss was not the underlying cause for her behavior. (The underlying cause was revealed after three months of therapy.) As we discussed her need to grieve her losses, it became apparent she had no conception of what grief felt like. Sally had no feelings and did not recognize anger as an emotion, though she was able to show her anger. For many months Sally was unable to verbalize her aggression constructively. It was some months before she began to accept that she should have feelings. She was self-blaming, self-punitive, and obnoxious to others, although she did not display these traits in therapy. A poem she wrote four months into therapy illustrates this:

> Unsure and afraid
> Two roads and confusion
> Not looking forward to another day!
> My heart and my mind don't agree
> Never ending battle
> That no one can see!
> All this effort to win
> Is it worth it all
> Or is it easier to sin?
> Look at my life
> What a mess
> All I cause is strife!
> Does God love me
> Who cares anyway
> He's not here to see!
> I'm angry, hurt, and afraid,
> I know I'm bad

Who knows why I was made?
A reject for sure
How can anyone love me
Lucky there was only one and no more!
I'm feeling very depressed
Hope I can find what I'm looking for,
Something that will put my life at rest!
I'm feeling very alone
I wish I had a friend at home!

We talked about anger, normalized it, and applied it to biblical knowledge—that it was how she expressed her anger that presented issues for her. Very briefly her smile relaxed and she said, "So I'm not all bad!" Sally refused to be drawn into what made her believe she was all bad, but later I was to discover it related to abuse and anger at God that had simmered for many years. At the end of this session I wrote out John 8:32, "You will know the truth, and the truth will set you free," and prayed with Sally that God would help us find out the truth that would free her. On her own initiative, she stuck this paper to her bathroom mirror and read the verse each time she looked in the mirror.

I was eager to discover what other supports she had in her life, especially as she had all but closed out her family of origin, was losing two friends, and was threatened with losing her position on the basketball team. She had no other supports. I asked her to teach me about basketball and discovered that she had no close friends on the team but needed the physical exertion. (Physical exertion was her way of reducing her anger and pain, a fact that she recognized later.) Her behavior on the court was physically abusive and her language foul. She said that at times she "lost it," which meant she was totally out of control of her emotions and behavior. Throughout therapy I modeled feeling language and gave her words to describe what most people would experience in the various situations Sally encountered.

When Sally commented that she had dizzy spells, I asked her to have a medical check to rule out pathology. She was well screened and the results were all negative.

At the eighth session Sally admitted that she drank heavily but did not know why and that she smoked heavily but had cut down since coming into therapy. She had experimented with drugs at school but did not use them. I began relaxation exercises using Christian symbolic imagery (e.g., being bathed in perfumed oil and cleansed internally and externally; reminding her that God loved her just as she was). We taped the first session and she took the tape with her. She used the recording twice a day for two weeks and then intermittently for three months. Four weeks later her dizzy spells had stopped, she was less aggressive on the court, and she had stayed away from her drinking friends for two weekends. I asked her to consider going to an Alcoholics Anonymous (AA) meeting and offered to go with her. She said she would go alone and was so appalled at the process she said, "I will do it on my own." (Four weeks later a new friend, Natalie, came into her life, and Natalie was able to verify Sally's abstinence and occasional failures.)

The Push to Religious Conformity

Church had provided Sally with no close friendships, but she liked the music and said, "I feel good when I am there." She refused to discuss God with me and said she did not feel she had to go to church but chose to go. Her unfeminine and aggressive behavior was unacceptable to several churches she had joined. It was obviously hurtful to her to be asked to leave these churches, but this hurt was displayed nonverbally and/or by putting on an exaggerated act of being happy and saying, "I don't care—they were airheads anyway." Her lack of gender conformity was unacceptable to the Christian community, and her five previous therapists ("all airheads") had apparently tried to encourage her to reform her outward, masculine aura by dressing and behaving in a more culturally acceptable manner.

Sally was rightly angry in that the source of her problem had not been revealed to these therapists. Three months after therapy began, Sally disclosed the genesis of her behavior. Her reason for hiding her femininity related to being sexually abused. From the time she was eight until her thirteenth birthday, she had been raped almost weekly by her best friend's brother, Stephen, who was sixteen at the time of the first rape. Her mother was "busy with church things" on Fridays, so she arranged for Sally to stay with her eight-year-old friend Tania. From age eight, Sally's behavior and grades deteriorated and she was labeled a behavior problem. Most days her mother would be angry because her daughter would not get out of bed in the morning but would cover her face with the sheet, "feeling dead." Her use of this feeling word was a major step in disclosing her inner state.

Gender Issues

Gender issues we had to address were

- abuse by the teenager, by society, by the church, and by therapists demanding gender appropriateness from her
- feelings about the abuser—the abuse itself; his male force in his sexual use of this little girl; the source of his belief that he was free to behave in this way; what society and his family may have contributed to this
- verbal abuse and dominion by her brother in the here and now
- lack of protection by her father (she had not previously recognized the importance of this) and her mother
- the maleness of God, who had allowed her to be abused when he was "supposed to protect children"

Over time Sally began to see that her issues were mostly related to her feelings of being controlled.

A breakthrough in therapy came five months into our work together. Sally sat smiling broadly and said, "Cindy's baby died three days ago." The two-month-old girl had died of Sudden Infant Death Syndrome (SIDS). Sally had been so excited when the baby was born and had spent a week visiting Cindy after she left the city. I took the mirror off the wall, asked Sally to look into it and think about the baby's death, and to see the change on her own face. The smile began to slip and a tear appeared. It was the start of the smile being controlled and emotions being acknowledged.

I helped Sally write a letter to Cindy and her husband. Then we talked about where the baby was now—"with God." Praying together through this for Cindy led Sally to risk telling me of her feelings about God after she related her troubled past.

Treatment initially took the form of revivification during deep relaxation (when Sally no longer smiled but experienced her pain) to access the feelings that we worked with (cognitively) for some months: the abuser's culpability, her right to feel angry and want restitution, her innocence of personal wrongdoing, and mentally cleansing her body during relaxation.

Anger at Her Family

Sally's anger toward her family had to be addressed in the following weeks. She felt intense anger at her mother, who was too busy "doing church things to see I was being hurt" and who was angry at her daughter for not wanting to go to school, for acting out at school, and for being an academic failure. A major gender issue was that Sally expected her mother to be the sole nurturer. Her father was completely exonerated from any blame regarding the lack of protection for Sally the child, but during therapy it occurred to Sally that her father had also been away from home on Fridays, a fact that contributed to her abuse.

During therapy Sally realized that she no longer returned home for visits because her brother Sam, who was twenty-five, kept demanding she give up smoking and drinking and dress like a girl.

Six months after therapy began, Sally felt ready to invite her parents to "one session" together. Treatment in this area was via family therapy. We started with prayer. The parents told Sam about Sally's past abuse, for he had been unaware of the situation. Sally was able to tell Sam that his attempts at controlling her present behavior were revivifying her lack of choices with her abuser and impinging upon her safety as a woman, in that her dress and behavior denied her femininity but protected her from male sexual interest. Sam's demands as a male were experienced as abuse and male control by Sally, a fact that reactivated her helplessness and degradation as a little girl. Sam cried throughout this session when he realized what she had experienced. Both parents were accused by their daughter of failing to protect her, and her mother especially for being too preoccupied to notice Sally's distress. The father also quietly cried from time to time. By the end of a long session, each family member had been able to forgive and accept forgiveness for their part in Sally's distress.

Sally's mother came alone for one consultation to confess her neg-
ligence as a mother. I pointed out that the Christian values she had
passed on to Sally had sustained her and brought her to healing, and
that she had done the best she could as a mother.

At a second family session instigated by Sally, she and her mother
spoke for the first time about the effects the abuse had had on them.
Only facts had been discussed before—nothing had been said since.
Both women spoke and shared information freely. The mother was
able to express her distress and feelings, but I pointed out to the family that Sally had not used one "feeling" word throughout the sessions
and that this was counted against her as a woman because she constantly discussed facts, not feelings—a masculine trait. They were
intrigued by this, recognizing that it profoundly affected how they
perceived her and responded to her. The father's lack of protection
was also discussed, and he recognized that the mother had taken the
full responsibility for Sally's plight when in fact he had failed also.

At a third and final family session, therapy with her family pro-
gressed well and, as they gave Sally space and recognized her needs,
they were all able to take part in a forgiveness service. Sally continues
to visit her family every week, and they are appreciative of the new
closer relationship. They are also helping her recognize and use feeling words.

Sally's Issue with God

Sally was not ready to deal with the issue of God until eight months
into therapy. When I discovered the abuse during deep relaxation, I
asked Sally if she could see Jesus in the room. She said, "Yes, he is on
the other side of the room, with his back to me." She would not let
Jesus comfort her, so I used the safety of the adult Sally to comfort
and empathize with the child Sally.

Later we discussed why God let the abuse happen. "Wasn't he supposed to protect and love children?" was her hurt and angry question.
Free choice for all people gave her rapist free choice to abuse or not to
abuse. We tried to imagine God's distress at his precious little child
being abused, and also his distress at the damage this would do to her
abuser's soul and later judgment. Sally also began to consider what

was going on in her abuser's life. She chose to forgive him, but not what he did, by recognizing God loves the person but hates the sin.

As she began to work through the abuse, Sally came to realize that she had loved and trusted God before her abuse but felt deep anger now. Her contention with God was stated when she said, still smiling (when she was relaxed there were no smiles but much pain), "Jesus is supposed to love children and protect them. He did not care about me. He is a liar." We read the creation story in Genesis and shared the dilemma God has. When he gave us free will, it meant he could not be a just God if he kept taking it back. Stephen had exercised his free will. He, not God, was the abuser. God was in the room each time she was abused. If God is omnipresent, omniscient, and omnipotent, he was with her, observed all that happened, and ultimately was in control. She tried to visualize God's anger at his "precious little child" being hurt, and then his anger toward Stephen who was causing her pain, and finally God's own pain that his gift of free will was being so abused. However, his just nature had to leave her abuser with his free will. Using Scripture, we talked and prayed through this difficult exegetical situation for weeks. Sally was able to recognize that one positive outcome of her abuse was that she had a deep desire to comfort the children in pain with whom she worked.

During this stage of therapy Sally formed a strong friendship with a Christian hospital nurse her age. She frequently attended sessions as they lived together and regarded themselves as "family." Natalie was a mature person who soon learned to protect her own boundaries and not accept Sally's faulty lifestyle.

Sally had been regularly reading daily Bible study notes I had given her from *Strong at the Broken Places* by Selwyn Hughes. The notes begin with a quotation from Ernest Hemingway: "Life breaks us all . . . but many are made strong at the broken places." These daily devotionals were especially healing for her, and most days she read her Bible and prayed.

The Use of Imprecatory Therapy

After nine months into therapy, being assured that she was in a closer relationship to God, I asked Sally to tell him how angry she was with him. She was not prepared to do so during therapy but said she would at home. I asked her to perform this ritual: She was to read her Bible and pray as usual, tell God how she felt toward him for not protecting her as a child, and then wait for him to speak with her. We fixed a time for the exercise and a time for her to call me to say she had completed it. She called to say she had, but when we met she confessed to completing only stages 1 and 2. She had written a poem afterward but would not share it.

The exercise was repeated the next day, and we met immediately after she called me. Natalie accompanied Sally and insisted that Sally should show me the poem she wrote after her first attempt. It was vitriolic, full of rage toward God for failing her, and so foul it was as though the page were covered in excrement. Natalie said it was distressing to hear Sally's violent vocal tone and disgusting language from the next room. I commended Sally for her strength and honesty and asked what happened the second time. "I said, 'I hate you, God' as loudly and angrily as I could, then stopped. I was so afraid but waited like you said."

I asked, "What happened?"

Her voice became very gentle, soft, and awed, and she said, "He said, 'Sally, I *love* you.'" It was an emotionally charged session during which we three women passed the tissue box to each other many times. Natalie asked Sally to show me the poem she wrote after the second experience. It was a paean of praise of such light and beauty that it was hard to believe the same person had written it. (Sally promised me copies of the poems but never gave them to me. Natalie said later that Sally was too ashamed to let me have the first one so I received neither. This was after we terminated.)

There was no spontaneous healing. Sally still had a lot of growing up and forgiving to work through. She recognized her fear of being controlled and worked through the issues in relation to her family, sports club, and her work supervisor. The latter was a big step for Sally in her maturing. She began to reach out to her supervisor and showed her caring behavior—her "Christlike bit," she called it. She discovered the woman who had caused her so much pain was in deep pain herself, and Sally became her confidante. As a result, her work became more rewarding.

After a year, Sally began to spend more time visiting her family, going to a different church where she could begin afresh, being accepted by her basketball team as a new person and welcomed back. She found new friends with Christian standards. She began to recognize when strong feelings should be present and to be able to put some feeling words to felt emotions. She stopped smoking and, except for two occasions that Natalie told me about, did not drink again—recognizing that she no longer needed to drown the pain of being abused and feeling abandoned by God and her mother. She eventually forgave Stephen, not for what he did but because he did not have the moral fiber to fight his weakness. She was able to release him to be healed in Jesus as she released herself into Jesus' healing.

Sally terminated therapy five years ago when I left the area. When I contacted her to ask permission to use her case, she said she was growing more and more mature, loved God in a way she had never done before, and was more spiritually alive than she could have imagined. She is still experiencing difficulty describing feelings and being assertive but is improving gradually. She sent me the following poem she recently wrote when she was depressed. Her emotions are now evident.

> God, at times I'm overcome
> With great anger.
> With this anger I feel
> A tremendous pain.
> My anger stems off
> Memories of hurt and fear
> And a feeling of unjustness.
> My memories will never leave me
> The loneliness and fear within.
> But, God, I pray each day
> That you help me believe in
> Your love and safety.
> God, when I run because
> Of disbelief of your love
> For me please be waiting
> To meet me when I get there.
> Please don't leave me
> Alone and afraid.

Give me wings to fly
And rise above, to overcome,
To keep my eyes on the
One who for me gave up
His only Son.

From Victim
to Survivor and Beyond

11

Anne Findlay Chamberlain

I did not intend to work primarily with survivors of abuse any more than I intended to be a survivor of abuse myself. There were no courses in graduate school on sexual abuse, I had not read any books on the topic, no one was talking about abuse. But in my years of practice as a mental-health counselor, I have seen more and more survivors of abuse. At any point, about 60 percent of my practice is made up of people who are abuse survivors.

This chapter begins with some of the facts about abuse. Next, I articulate a philosophy about the healing process and suggest helpful attitudes and ideas for survivors and other concerned individuals. I weave in not only some of the stories that I have heard professionally, but also some of my own story. Details of stories have been changed to protect individuals. My prayer is that the journey from victim to survivor becomes more real and that those concerned with sexual abuse will find hope for healing.

What Is Sexual Abuse?

In John 8:32 Jesus tells his disciples, "You will know the truth, and the truth will make you free" (NRSV). Jesus' reference to spiritual freedom applies to the study of abuse. I believe that it is important to know the truth about abuse so that the journey to freedom can begin.

163

All abuse is damaging, and the victims experience long-term effects that can affect their day-to-day living and functioning. Believing that one type of abuse is more damaging than another is a way for us to deny the fact that all abuse hurts.

Christine A. Courtois (1988) explains that sexual abuse occurs when a child of any age is exploited by an older person for the perpetrator's sexual stimulation. Sexual abuse is not limited to physical contact; it can include visual, verbal, and/or psychological interactions. Although some of the abuse that happened to me included physical interaction, one of my perpetrators was an older man in our neighborhood who exposed himself to me.

Sexual abuse can also take place by talking about a person's sexuality in a way that makes fun of it or is derogatory (Allender, 1990). One woman told me that her father regularly made derogatory comments about her developing breasts. She responded by believing she was ugly. One man tells of being the fourth son born to parents without a daughter. There was a strong feeling in the family that he should have been a girl. He remembers being at a church-sponsored skating party when he was six and being escorted onto the rink for a mother-daughter skate with his mother.

Sexual abuse is not limited to adult-child interactions. It can also include exploitation by a person in authority over the victim. One woman reported that during her divorce she went to her pastor for counseling. The pastor began to be affectionate with the woman, which surprised her, but she believed that since he was the professional, he knew how to help. When the affection turned sexual, she left.

Who Are the Victims of Abuse?

One out of three girls and one out of seven boys will be sexually abused by age eighteen (Courtois, 1988). At least one out of six girls are victims of incest, or sexual abuse within the family. Children of every race, culture, class, and religion are victims. Research shows us that even among the least severely abused persons, 74 percent of those people later admit they had some damage in life because of the abuse (Courtois, 1988).

In May 1993, I had the opportunity to travel in Central America, and I heard repeatedly the same stories of abuse that I hear in the United States. The issues people face, in terms of people not respecting gender, in terms of homes not being safe, in terms of sexuality not being safe, were the same. Abuse and incest are universal.

Christians wish to think that because we are part of the church, abuse does not happen to us or it happens less often to us, but that is not true. A study by a Canadian Anabaptist group found that rates of abuse within the church were equal to the rates of abuse outside the church (Block & Shantz, 1991). Being a Christian and being part of a church do not protect us.

Who Are the Abusers?

Most abuse happens within families or is initiated by people whom the victim knows. Ninety percent of offenders are known to the victim (Krall, 1994). Offenders may be a father, mother, stepfather, stepmother, aunt, uncle, brother, sister, cousin, neighbor, boyfriend, babysitter, teacher, or pastor. It is less usual for a stranger to perpetrate abuse.

As I was writing this chapter, I realized that the easiest type of abuse for me to talk about are the instances in which I was hurt by somebody who was removed from me. As I started to think about abuse that was closer to home, I could feel myself getting cold and my body going numb in a dissociative feeling of fear. It is much harder to talk about the abuse that is closer to home.

The Journey of Healing

We all know the saying "Even the longest journey starts with a step." Healing is a process, a journey rather than a destination. It is not easily defined by progressive steps. It is more like a tire on a wheel. In the center is the wheel, with the tire circling it. The wheel keeps going around, and at any place in time, only one part of the tire hits the ground. For the survivor of abuse, particular issues arising from the abuse will be where the rubber meets the road.

I heard a story about a woman who had lost a child through death. She reported at the end of the first week that she had gone through all the stages of grief: the denial, the anger, and the depression. Everything was fine, and she was going to get over it. That is not the way healing takes place. Survivors go through those stages and steps many, many times. Healing from abuse is a journey that lasts a lifetime.

The Effects of Abuse

Emotional Effects

A *Charlie* cartoon illustrates some of the emotional aftereffects of abuse. Charlie is at the customs gate at an airport. The caption reads, "Have you brought back any phobias, neuroses, psychoses, paranoias, delusions, or manias?" Survivors carry into adulthood emotional cargo resulting from abuse. There are a number of emotional ramifications of abuse.

Depression and anxiety. For me, the biggest ramification was depression. I ended up in a major depression and needed to be hospitalized and on medication to get better. The depression, born from keeping all those feelings inside, of not letting people know what was going on with me, was a result of the abuse.

People who are abused are often extremely anxious; they worry that people will find out. Survivors are often anxious about trying to be good and trying to be pleasing to people.

Dissociation. At my wedding, I could see the church full of people as I went down the aisle. I was shaking, terrified. I could not believe that I was making this permanent decision. Part of me watched me walk down the aisle. I saw myself going through the motions, but I did not feel that I was in my body. That is dissociation.

Everyone dissociates from time to time. Sometimes dissociation can be helpful, as when a person has a splinter in his or her hand and needs to pull it out. If he or she can dissociate and not think about the pain or feel it, that can be beneficial. Many people dissociate when driving down the highway. And I believe that many people dissociate in church. Early in life I learned how to look as if I am paying attention. I can sit with a pious look on my face while I com-

pose my grocery list or think about the rest of the day. So, dissociation is something that happens to many people in many situations.

Survivors of abuse dissociate in ways that they are not necessarily aware of. At times they are cut off from their feelings or their bodies. For a number of years, my body could be active when I was
involved sexually with my husband, but there was a way in which
my soul and my emotions were detached.

Guilt and shame. Guilt is feeling remorse about something that
we have done. It is important to distinguish between healthy and
unhealthy guilt. Healthy, biblical guilt is a consequence of sin, sig-
naling that we have broken one of God's commands. Unhealthy guilt,
or neurotic guilt, is feeling guilty for events and situations beyond
our control. Survivors of abuse often have much of this unhealthy
guilt.

Worse than guilt is shame. Whereas guilt is feeling bad for something we have done, shame is feeling bad for who we are. It is feeling horrible about our personhood. People who have been sexually
abused have a tremendous amount of shame because of the abuse.
I remind clients that the shame belongs to the perpetrator, not the
victim.

Self-contempt. Shame gives way to self-contempt (Allender, 1990).
Survivors often feel a great deal of contempt for themselves. They
may feel contempt that their body responded during the abuse. Others may feel self-contempt because of their need for affection.

Powerlessness and betrayal. Survivors also have a sense of powerlessness. When a little child is being hurt by someone who is bigger and stronger, the child has no power. That overwhelming sense
of powerlessness is often carried into adulthood. When the perpetrator is a mother, a father, or a caretaker, the betrayal of trust ampli-
fies feelings of powerlessness.

Ambivalence and feeling crazy. Survivors also may suffer from a
sense of ambivalence. A perpetrator may be somebody whom the
victim loves very much, but at the same time, the victim may feel
intense anger about the abuse. The conflicting feelings can be con-
fusing and can cause the survivor to feel crazy. Additionally, others
often deny the abuse. When what is seen or experienced as true in
oneself is contradicted by others, feelings of craziness result.

Physical Effects

Sometimes survivors of abuse (for example, young children who are raped) experience physiological injury. Or, survivors may have too high a pain threshold. Sometimes the clients that I work with will suddenly discover that they have an ulcer or another physical problem. Their use of dissociation and their physical numbing may mean that serious physical symptoms go unrecognized.

Survivors may tend to ignore their bodies and avoid going to the doctor. One of my clients needed to go on an antidepressant medication, and I had referred her to a psychiatrist. She stated that she did not want to go to this psychiatrist forever. I said, "That's no problem. You can just be referred back to your family physician." She looked sheepish and confessed that she did not have a family doctor. She avoided going to the doctor because she feared gynecological examinations. Avoidance of physicians can create a lack of preventative care.

Some of my abuse involved my mouth, so I cannot bear to go to the dentist. And, as a child, I had a dentist who could have played in *Little Shop of Horrors*. Those were pre-fluoride days and I had numerous cavities. This dentist did not believe in administering Novocain, so I experienced much pain getting cavities filled. To this day, going to the dentist can elicit memories of abuse.

Sexual Effects

Survivors may experience sexual dysfunction. People who have been sexually abused often have mixed feelings about sex: Some parts feel all right and other parts feel extremely scary. Survivors sometimes go through periods during which they do not feel sexual at all, and they may feel bad about themselves. They may believe that something is wrong with them. Sometimes survivors of abuse may act out sexually and be more sexually involved than they want to be. A client described this dilemma as feeling like either a virgin or a vamp, never able to strike a healthy balance of sexuality.

Another result of abuse can be the sexualization of intimacy and touch. Nurturance and affection became tinged with sexual feelings and overtones for the survivor. Touch that is safe can feel sexual, and so the survivor avoids it.

Relational Effects

Boundaries. Some survivors have few or no personal boundaries, which is also called codependence. Codependence involves worrying about and taking on another person's feelings. It is waking up in the morning, turning to one's spouse, and saying, "How do I feel this morning, honey?" For the survivor of abuse, codependence is an important coping mechanism. Being aware of another person's feelings and trying to test and measure the environment to keep safe is a way to cope. Taking care of other people can, however, lead to poor self-care. Other victims of sexual abuse may keep rigid boundaries and suffer from a lack of intimacy. I use a metaphor of a castle with a moat around it. People who are codependent always have the drawbridge open, so that what is inside can flow out and what is outside can flow in. People who have rigid boundaries have the drawbridge up, and they never open it. A healthy person learns to be able to move the drawbridge up and down, based on whom they are with.

Trust. Problems with trust can arise from abuse. Some survivors respond by being too trusting. More frequently, survivors have a great deal of difficulty trusting anyone. A child who is abused by a trusted family member or a caretaker often feels a powerful sense of betrayal. To avoid further abuse and betrayal, the survivor may not trust anyone. Even persons who may be safe need to earn the survivor's trust.

People pleasing and perfectionism. Survivors may become people pleasers. I picture them as Velcro—all the comments, feelings, and opinions of others cling to them as burrs cling to wool socks. Life is one long struggle of removing one sticky set of feelings before the next comes along. It is important to please others, and trying to please people leads to a pattern of perfectionism.

Families in which abuse takes place often present a perfect facade to the outside world. One survivor told of attending church on Sunday mornings dressed in her finest, while her abuser, her father, brought the sermon from the pulpit. I refer to such families as "fan families." In our church we have fans that are kept in the pews for the summer. On each fan there is always a picture of a mother, a father, a son, and a daughter. All are Caucasians with blond hair and blue eyes. The children have rosy cheeks and are dressed beautifully. They sit perfectly still with incredibly devout expressions on their faces, looking up toward God, who resides somewhere beyond the stained-glass window in the background. Survivors of abuse sometimes adhere to the rule that "if I can just do everything right, maybe I can keep myself and my secret safe."

Spiritual Effects

Survivors of abuse often raise spiritual questions: Where was God when this happened? Why did God let it happen? A woman who survived satanic ritualistic abuse (SRA) would call out to God as a seven- and eight-year-old, "God, kill me! Let me die! Don't let this continue." She is alive, filled with many questions about God.

Another effect of abuse is fear of God. Taught to be afraid of God and to be afraid to be honest with God, survivors have a real fear that they were responsible for the abuse and will be punished.

A tremendous amount of anger at God is another thing that comes out of abuse. Survivors may be angry that God, who is omnipotent and omniscient, allowed the abuse to happen.

Some survivors feel abandoned by God and utterly alone. When I think about that kind of abandonment, I think about what Jesus said when he was on the cross: "My God, my God, why have you forsaken me?" (Matt. 27:46 NRSV). Any boy or girl who is being abused probably feels the same way. Christ identified with that.

Finally, survivors may feel a great sense of distance from God. One survivor decided that since God did not answer her prayers by stopping the abuse, God must not exist.

Guidelines for Survivors

The Choice to Heal

The survivor must make a choice to heal. That choice is often a daily one rather than a once-and-for-all decision. It is important to make the choice, given what has happened, to work on this and choose to get better. That means coming out of denial and admitting what happened, to own what happened, to remember what happened.

The first memory I had of abuse was in a dream that was unlike most of my dreams. Dreams are usually symbolic. For example, if I am having a fight with my husband, I may dream of a tornado, or if I am worried about my children, I will dream about a flock of sheep. But this was an incredibly realistic dream, just like a memory. I had been praying that God would help me know what I needed to know about myself, and then I had the dream. As I talked about the dream with some family members, they confirmed that what I was remembering had happened.

Memories can have three different foci (Kaufman, 1992). One focus is that we remember things in our body. If you go into an old elementary school building, the scent will cause you to be suddenly flooded with memories. In a similar way, some survivors have body memories. They do not have pictures or words or scenes to go with the memory, but they have strange body feelings. One woman reported that when she is thinking about a particular age, she will have a pain in the middle of her chest even though she is perfectly healthy. Sometimes the body memories take the form of a sexual feeling. The survivor might be in the context of a conversation or an experience and suddenly have a feeling that is sexual. It is not based on anything pleasurable, nor is it a normal sexual fantasy or feeling.

Memories can also take the form of a picture. A scene of abuse might be remembered without accompanying words or emotions or feelings in the body. One woman, dealing with food-related issues, was trying to explore why she eats even when she does not want to eat. In some areas of her life she is very disciplined, yet she has an emptiness that she keeps feeding. Suddenly she had a mental picture of a clock on a wall above a counter. She remembered that it was the clock on the kitchen wall when she was a child.

A third way that memories can occur is in words. A survivor might hear in his or her mind, "Don't tell. No one will believe you." The person might hear those words but does not have a scene, a particular set of pictures, or feelings to go with it.

Paradigm Shift

A paradigm is a global way of looking at something. Stephen R. Covey (1989) tells a story about a man who was riding on a New York subway at about ten o'clock on a Sunday morning. At one station, a man and three young children got on the subway. The original passenger was reading a Sunday paper, trying to relax. The three children, who began running up and down the aisles, bumped into him, and ripped his paper. He thought, "Boy, these kids are incredibly obnoxious. I can't believe this father is letting them run wild." They all got off at the next station, and the man noticed that the father had tears in his eyes. The man said, "Excuse me, is something wrong?" The father said, "I'm sorry about how my kids are acting, but we just left the hospital. Their mother just died." The difference in how the passenger then viewed the children's behavior describes a paradigm shift.

Making the choice to begin to heal causes a crisis. The old way of viewing reality will shift.

Regaining a Voice

Believing means telling someone. It means regaining a voice. I occasionally have a weak voice when I talk. I tend to get asthma and bronchitis, which is one of the reasons I lose my voice. When I started dealing with my abuse, I was hoarse most of the time for about three months. I literally lost my voice, which had been silent about the abuse for decades. When I tried to talk about the abuse, I could not. One of the reasons I choose to write and speak about abuse is to regain my voice.

Get Safe

A survivor must get away from abusive situations and from abusive actions. Sometimes this means stopping self-inflicted abuse. It is helpful to have other people assist in providing safety. Get help and support from an objective person. Getting help can mean talking to a pastor or a counselor or a friend. Abuse happened in the presence of another person, and it usually takes the presence of another person to heal it.

A story is told about an insane asylum. A man was going to visit a locked ward in which there were twenty violent people. Only three orderlies worked in this ward. The visitor asked one of the orderlies, "Aren't you afraid that with just three of you these people are going to gang up on you and get out of control?" The orderly said, "Insane people never work together." That principle applies to healing. Talking to other people helps survivors not to feel crazy and provides some support.

We are told in Scripture that God is the person who forgives, but in James 5:16 we are also told to "confess your sins to one another . . . so that you may be healed" (NRSV). I am not implying that a survivor of abuse is guilty of sin. But if we look at the process advocated by the verse in terms of healing, I think God is telling us that healing comes in community and not individually.

Trust Your Intuition

Survivors need to learn to trust their intuition and instincts, to believe themselves, especially about abuse. From the moment one client stepped into my office, I felt I was being violated, and yet the client's words were not necessarily bad. I thought, "This is because I'm a survivor of abuse. I'm feeling this but it really isn't going on; this is my stuff." So I saw him again, and I felt worse. I talked to a supervisor and realized that this client was a sex addict who was violating a number of my boundaries.

It is important to pay attention to intuition. A number of years ago I observed an interaction among a grandmother, a mother, and two grandchildren. The older son was complaining about his younger brother to his grandmother and mother. He said, "Sometimes I just hate Andy." The grandmother replied, "We don't hate people." This comment was teaching the boy not to trust his intuition. His mother, however, was able to say, "Brian, it's okay that you feel like you hate your brother, but you can choose how you act toward your brother."

Learn to Love Yourself

Paul writes in Romans 12:3, "I say to everyone among you not to think of yourself more highly than you ought to think, but to think with sober judgment" (NRSV). Many Christians interpret that verse to mean we need to be humble and not feel good about ourselves; I think it means we need to love ourselves realistically. Paul is telling us to know the truth about ourselves. The truth is that we are children of God and that God loves us. Survivors of abuse, however, may have a difficult time seeing any positive traits in themselves. One client was unable to list a single positive trait about herself.

Learn to Love Your Body

To love your body in our culture is incredibly difficult. If a woman is not five foot eight and a hundred and fifteen pounds and does not look like Barbie, she does not qualify as attractive. Survivors have even greater difficulty since they associate their body with abuse.

I had to start small with loving myself because I felt awful about who I was and how I looked. At a workshop the presenter said, "Start with one little thing that you feel is okay about your body, and concentrate on that." So I picked my feet, which are exceptionally small. I have always been upset with my feet because I cannot easily find dress shoes. I started thinking, "I appreciate these feet. They are small and they work hard. These feet have carried around my body and they have carried around two babies and laundry and wood and groceries." Instead of being angry at my feet because I cannot get shoes, I am trying to treat them in a loving way. If you can start with an earlobe, do that. Write to that part of your body, or look in a mirror and talk to it, or treat it kindly, perhaps by putting cream on it. Work up to the parts that are hardest. For many survivors of abuse, the sexual parts and the genital parts are the hardest parts to love.

Learn to Love the Inner Child

I find the inner child to be a helpful metaphor. There is evidence in Scripture that Jesus loves children. I believe that since God is timeless, there is a way in which God can love the little-child part of survivors even as he is loving the adult.

Take Time

A survivor needs to take time to think through confrontation and forgiveness (Dalton, 1993). A woman's husband abused their daughter, and she forgave him within a week. It is now ten years later, and they are on the verge of a divorce. This woman did not deal with her feelings but forgave her husband much too quickly. Inside of her was a seed of anger and rage and distrust that was never dealt with. Please allow as much time as is necessary to heal.

Find Healing Communities and Rituals

One woman, as part of her healing from childhood sexual abuse, held a ceremony to dedicate her inner child. She invited people who were special and close to her. The survivor needs to find a healing community in which healthy rituals can occur.

When Jesus raised Lazarus, he said to the people who were looking on, "Unbind him, and let him go" (John 11:44 NRSV). It took other people to help loose Lazarus's burial cloths. Survivors need to find safe people to remove what binds them.

Learn Balance

Create balance in your life. Learn to give yourself a break. My mother says that all work and no play makes Jack a dull boy. It is important in the healing process to learn to have fun and to learn to play and to learn to laugh. Part of balance is finding healing activities and nurturing activities. These activities can include bubble baths, a walk in the country, or listening to music.

How Others Can Help Survivors

Spouses

Learn to listen. Men and women communicate differently, and it is important for the spouse of a survivor to try to be bilingual. It is important to listen and to speak in your partner's language. When I listen to my husband, I need to be linear and logical and sequential in my thinking, and then he feels understood. When he listens to me, he needs to be abstract and emotional and empathic, and then I feel understood.

Get perspective. It is important to know that the reactions the survivor has are not always the partner's fault. There have been times when my husband would come up to me and give me a kiss, and I was ready to push him away. It was not his fault that I was dealing with a particular memory that was upsetting to me.

It is also important to know that sometimes things that were okay for a long time may suddenly change. Before I started remembering the abuse and dealing with it, I was able to be sexual and to be dissociated emotionally from it. There were a variety of activities we could participate in. Once I started dealing with the abuse, the repertoire of things that were safe for me became extremely narrow, which was very upsetting for my husband. For example, he could not walk up behind me and put his arms around me and give me a hug because I would turn and face him, ready to defend myself.

Understand abuse. It is important to try to understand the abuse as best as possible. For several years I tried to explain to my husband how bad the abuse felt. It was hard for him to put abuse in the context of my being a two- or three-year-old. Finally, I said, "If I called you from the hospital instead of coming home and reported to you that I had been raped, what would you say? How would you feel?" Those questions gave him a completely different context in which to understand the abuse. It is important to learn as much as possible about abuse. My husband found a chapter in *The Courage to Heal*

(Bass & Davis, 1988) helpful. Another helpful chapter is in *Women's Sexuality after Childhood Incest* (Westerlund, 1992).

Family and Friends

Learn to listen. The most important thing is to listen in a non-judgmental way. Survivors need to talk to someone who will acknowledge the experience. The listener can reflect the survivor's thoughts and feelings. Statements such as "I hear you saying . . ." or "That must have been awful" let the person know he or she has been heard.

Avoid easy answers. There are no easy answers for the emotional or psychological effects that survivors of abuse experience. When I was hospitalized for depression, a well-wisher sent me a letter and suggested that there was a relationship between the hole in the ozone and depression. What was I to do about the ozone hole?

There are no easy answers to spiritual difficulties either. I absolutely believe that God is with survivors. He loves them and he is going to walk with them through recovery. A woman reported that a well-meaning deacon told her, "God will take care of this. Just pray." To the survivor, that response sounded trite.

Give spiritual grace. Allow survivors to be angry at God, or to question their religion, or even for a while to decide that they do not want to be part of a church or go to church. If God can give grace for all our sins and for who we are, then surely we can give grace to people who have been hurt.

Remove unhealthy guilt. Let the person know that he or she was not responsible for the abuse. Let survivors know that their responsibility now is to take the time they need to heal.

Encourage. Be available. Sometimes that means taking a phone call in the middle of the night, or going for a fifteen-minute walk, or making time for a cup of coffee. Encourage healthy behaviors, such as eating balanced meals, taking vacations, and playing. When I was depressed, a friend used to come and take me to various activities. I would have stayed home by myself otherwise.

Have hope. Survivors need someone to hold hope for them. They need someone to pray for them when they do not feel that they can pray. When I went through a major depression, a friend gave me a wonderful gift. She offered to take my prayer concerns and to pray for the things I would normally pray about. In the middle of my depression, I felt as if God were a million miles away and that there was a solid lead shield between us. I felt my prayers were ineffective, and so my friend prayed for me.

Respect defenses. Learn to love and respect defenses and coping mechanisms (Friesen, 1991). Rather than criticizing the survivor for how he or she coped, give credit for what was done to cope. For example, one person refers to Multiple Personality Disorder (MPD) as "Multiple Personality Technique." Honor the techniques that the person used to survive.

The Church

Acknowledge abuse. Acknowledge that abuse occurs and support interventions, conferences, and counseling. Our church has a fund for people to tap into if they need counseling and do not have adequate insurance coverage. Talk about abuse at meetings. Talk about it informally. Talk about it in sermons. Let people know that it happens. Let them know that it is healthy to break the silence.

Teach about abuse. Sunday school curriculums, even for junior high and elementary-school children, need to teach about safe and unsafe touching. High school students need to know about date rape. Our children need to know that sexuality is not supposed to mean that a person wants sex even if he or she says no. Our children need to learn how to say no. Have classes and workshops on abuse.

Be sensitive. Although it is important to talk about spiritual disciplines, on any given Sunday, survivors in the congregation may feel a million miles away from God and need some grace. If appropriate, tell the survivor, "I want you to know that this is not for you to have one more thing to feel guilty about."

Be open about sexuality. Gain practice and comfort in talking about sexuality. Model to others, particularly children, that it is all right to talk about sex. The more comfortable adults become at talking about sexuality in appropriate ways, the safer children will feel talking about their concerns. Use anatomically correct terms for sexual organs so that children have a vocabulary to talk about abuse.

Remember that Christ understands. We are told,

> Since, then, we have a great high priest who has passed through the heavens, Jesus, the Son of God, let us hold fast to our confession. For we do not have a high priest who is unable to sympathize with our weaknesses, but we have one who in every respect has been tested as we are, yet without sin. Let us therefore approach the throne of grace with boldness, so that we may receive mercy and find grace to help in time of need.
>
> Hebrews 4:14–16 NRSV

I am so thankful that I have a God that understands and is with me. God is Immanuel—God with us—through all the events of our lives. God is a God not of prevention but of redemption. I have seen survivors choose to heal and to redeem the abuse. I hope that the suggestions given in this chapter can help others recover from the many effects of abuse.

Group Work with Evangelical Abused Wives

12

Mary Williams

With all the exposure on television and in newspapers about domestic violence, one would think evangelical Christians would be trying to help abused women. This is not the case. In the extensive traveling around the United States that my husband and I did during our furloughs from the mission field, as well as in my reading of Christian literature, I never heard any mention of the kind of atmosphere I experienced at home: constantly "walking on eggshells" and terrible psychological tension. This I lived with for twenty-five years of my married life.

I could not afford to go to a counselor, for financial control was my husband's strongest tactic. He also caused me constant emotional stress, treating me as a servant and a possession, using intimidating glares as well as "Christian" physical violence—pushing, shoving, and blocking my exit from a room while haranguing me, or sticking his foot in the way of the bathroom door to stop my escape to my only place of shelter.

Six years ago I went into John's Book Shop in Wheaton, Illinois, crying out to God for his leading to a book with an answer for the oppression and craziness that filled my days. God heard me in my desperation and led me to one of Norman Wright's counseling books with a chapter titled "Women Haters." I was shocked by the heading; I realized that this was the way my husband reacted to his recent boss's wife and also our former coworker's wife. I did not yet see that

181

it also applied to me. I skimmed the chapter, since I couldn't afford the book, and then bought the secular paperback that Wright recommended: *Men Who Hate Women and the Women Who Love Them.* I wept with relief as I read the first five chapters, for at last there was an explanation for the insanity I had experienced all my married life.

For the past six years I've been working on my mental, emotional, and spiritual growth with the support of friends, counseling, and God, while still cohabiting with my husband. My choice—to stay with my husband—has not been given enough consideration by counselors, who talk only of two options: restoration, which is not possible until both parties admit their part of the problem and desire to change, or divorce, which is often not in the wife's best interest. Statistics show that the wife's income often decreases and the husband's increases. This leaves her to fend for herself financially, in addition to being physically and emotionally depleted. Meanwhile, her husband continues to live free of responsibility, never having to confront his own sin.

It was not until three years ago, while I was studying for my master's degree in social work and beginning an internship, that I learned the label for my household situation: domestic violence. Why hadn't I ever been told about it before? An article in the *Journal of Marriage and Family Therapy*, "Counseling Battered Women from Fundamentalist Churches," suggests several reasons: the church's "exclusiveness" and its views on submission, headship, and divorce (Whipple, 1987).

Since that internship and my training as a domestic violence worker, I have felt called to work with abused Christian wives. I feel this conviction not only because of my own experience but also because in the entire year I worked in Wheaton, not once did an abused evangelical wife come to the center for help. Yet I knew they were in Wheaton because I talked with them at my child's school and went to church with them. My experiences led me to the conclusion that group work is the most effective way to reach them. I had seen more progress in the women I counseled in group work than those counseled individually. Besides, group therapy allowed for more women to be helped at one time. Also, since there was a growing acceptance of church-oriented support groups among evangelicals (Grayson & Johnson, 1991), it seemed to be the best and perhaps only way to get into the church community. So I got approval to use my idea of developing a church-oriented support group program as my graduate research project.

The Literature

When I began my review of the literature for the research portion of this project, I found that domestic violence came to public attention in books published during the mid-1970s. Terry Davidson wrote about her abusive father, a Protestant minister, in *Conjugal Crimes: Understanding and Changing the Wife Beating Pattern*, but this had no impact on the evangelical community.

The first evangelical books on domestic violence came out fifteen years later. When I was at the Christian Booksellers' Association convention in 1989, I was again searching for a book to help me in my growth, and I found Accent's book *Lovestruck* by Catherine Scott. (It was revised and reprinted in 1992 by David C. Cook as *Breaking the Cycle of Abuse,* a fact that may indicate increased awareness among evangelicals.) The author worked in a Denver domestic violence center and stated in her introduction that although there are plenty of books about marriage, she could not find any about wife abuse among Christians.

Another publisher, Zondervan, published *Turning Fear to Hope* in the same year. It was written by a nurse and a college instructor, Holly Wagner Green, who gathered information from the Indianapolis Salvation Army domestic violence center. Their records for the first six months of 1983 showed that one-fourth of their clients were "professing Christians affiliated with evangelical churches" (Green, 1989). In 1990, Zondervan published a second book, *Christian Men Who Hate Women.* Its author, Margaret Rinck, looked at the situation from a clinical perspective, using the word *misogynist* (woman-hater) instead of *abuser.* She pointed out that "Christian men who hate women are in some ways even more dangerous and destructive in their relationships than their non-Christian counterparts. Non-Christian misogynists do not have the additional arsenal of church doctrines, God-talk, and the 'sanctioning' of male authority, which comes in a Christian marriage. Their wives are not taught from childhood to 'submit' to men 'no matter what' because it is God's will" (Rinck, 1990, pp. 19–20).

A third publisher, InterVarsity, brought out *Battered into Submission* (1989), which contained research on wife abuse in churches. James Alsdurf, a clinical and forensic psychologist, and his wife, Phyllis, a writer, called attention to an earlier study of six hundred church women. That study estimated that ten out of every sixty women suffered emotional and psychological abuse from their husbands and two or three would also be physically abused (Alsdurf & Alsdurf, 1989, pp. 32–33). Many of the one hundred abused women they interviewed were married to pastors, deacons, and church leaders, and "almost without exception . . . [said that] their pastors focused on getting them—not their abusive husbands—to change" (Alsdurf & Alsdurf, 1989, p. 23). This same attitude was confirmed by the authors' other study, a sample of 263 Protestant pastors, one-third of whom were from three clearly evangelical denominations and two-thirds of whom were from other Protestant denominations (Alsdurf & Alsdurf, 1989, pp. 153–55). This study also included data from the Indianapolis Salvation Army center, where the supervisor of their batterers' program stated that the problem of wife abuse in the church is "tremendous" and that "the more fundamental a church is, the higher the probability that abuse is happening" (Alsdurf & Alsdurf, 1989, p. 47).

Hindrances to Stopping Abuse

Not all churches have patriarchal systems, but women in such churches encounter many hindrances to stopping abuse (Whipple, 1987). Also, according to British authorities on domestic violence, research consistently indicates that the persistence of the patriarchal system in church and state structures causes much violence toward women. The first marriage law, written by the Romans in 753 B.C., stated that married women were "to conform themselves entirely to the temper of their husbands and the husbands [were] to rule their wives as necessary and inseparable possessions" (Dobash & Dobash,

1978, p. 427). Any changes in the Roman law would have been illegal, and the small religious sect called Christianity, which was struggling to maintain itself, had to embrace the patriarchal system to survive and to maintain family structure. From that early Roman period,
both the church and the state systems have supported the subordination of women and their husbands' control of them. Legal systems
continued to follow the view until the early nineteenth century, when
laws began to be challenged (Dobash & Dobash, 1978). But religious
systems have remained more resistant. Church leaders "departing
from or ignoring the feminist teachings of Jesus" (Hendrick, 1985, p.
137) have perpetuated the domination of men.

Rinck agreed that the patriarchal church system perpetuates the
abuse of women. "Many conservative Christians dismiss the idea of
sexism as non-Christian, silly, feminist, or irrelevant. . . . It is time
for the church to examine its role in maintaining prejudice against
women" (1990, pp. 79–81). The Alsdurfs' church-based research continually showed results of sexism and patriarchal influences. More
than two-thirds of the women "felt it was their Christian responsibility to endure their husband's violence." More than one-third "felt
pressure from their churches to submit to their husbands despite
the violence," and 55 percent said that their husbands told them that
"the violence would stop if they would be more submissive" (Alsdurf & Alsdurf, 1989, p. 84). The authors concluded that teaching in
the churches made the women believe their ability to suffer reflected
their "Christian commitment," which in turn made the women
"more susceptible to violence" (1989, p. 82).

Vicky Whipple's statement—that the fundamentalist view of
divorce puts the abused woman "in a double bind: Stay and be
beaten or leave and risk the wrath of God, or at least the wrath of the
church" (1987, p. 255)—was confirmed by the Alsdurfs' research.
The results of the surveys about pastors' attitudes showed that

> one-third felt that the "unwillingness of some wives to be submis-
> sive to their husbands" was the reason for the husbands' violence
> one-fourth held that by "submitting to her violent husband" a
> wife could be assured that the violence would stop or that she
> would be able to endure it

one-third questioned the woman's truthfulness about who was
actually responsible for the violence

almost one-half believed that the violence should not be "overem-
phasized and used as 'justification' for breaking the marriage
commitment"

one-third said that the "abuse would have to be life-threatening"
before the woman was justified in leaving home

one-fifth felt "that no amount of abuse would justify a woman
leaving" (Alsdurf & Alsdurf, 1989, pp. 156–58)

The Alsdurfs concluded that "most pastors in this study indicated
that they would be more than willing to accept a marriage in which
some wife abuse is present, even though it is 'not God's perfect will'—
than they would be to advise separation, which could end in divorce"
(1989, p. 158).

Lack of Awareness

With these hindrances of twisted beliefs and insensitive attitudes,
it is difficult for abused women in churches even to become aware
that they are being abused. Several women I have worked with have
had mental breakdowns or were committed to hospital psychiatric
units, only to find out later that they were not the "sick" one in the
household. A woman in a southern state was told by her church to
never mind her husband's abuse of her, and ten years later child welfare workers were called in because he abused their children. Still
another wife told me that her abusive husband, an elder in a large
evangelical church, had also sexually abused their daughter. This
woman was heartbroken as she realized that the daughter had married an abuser. The saddest thing is that other abused women, rather
than someone in the women's churches, had helped them. Denial
grips the church, and as Rinck states, instead of the church "being
a place where people feel safe to expose their painful problems, the
church is often a 'holier than thou' social club where everyone tries
to appear more sanctified than everyone else" (1990, p. 76).

Because of this lack of insight about domestic violence in evangelical churches, abuse is also found in the households of their mission organizations overseas. I know several wives who have lived in such households. One former missionary showed her bruises to the mission board, whose members did not believe her! Another wife said that their board knew of her husband's sexual abuse of a neighborhood girl but never dealt with it. Instead, the board moved them to another country. The wife now realizes that she has been living with domestic abuse all her married life. But when one is in Christian work, violence in the home can be so covered with a flurry of activities for the Lord that one becomes almost dizzy, and the truth about what is happening gets buried.

I gave four Christian books about domestic violence to one abused wife I knew. She told me that they were "too depressing to read" because she did not know of any help available to her. Note that she was living in Wheaton, Illinois, the mecca of evangelicalism. As Catherine Scott says, not many evangelical counselors are educated in domestic violence, nor have they had experience in it. I have found that many counselors still believe the husband first—male privilege, as it is called in domestic violence terms—even when there is evidence of wife abuse, pornography, child sexual abuse, and sexual affairs. Instead, the wives are considered "crazy" and not "real Christians."

After hearing all this from Christian wives, I became convinced of the need for stronger intervention in evangelical circles. Public education through books on domestic violence is not enough. Wives need support groups to make them aware of their home situation and allow them to receive help and support as they deal with it.

Group Work

It has been well documented that there is real psychological value in group work with abused women: The women finally encounter people who listen to them and believe them. They arrive at a better view of themselves and their situations. They learn how to problem solve. They begin to feel empowered as they realize they can make changes in their situations and be more in control of themselves. They learn that they can take care of themselves rather than being a victim of their abusers. Their self-esteem and self-confidence begin to grow again (Swift, 1988; Williams-White, 1989). Moreover, the isolation tactic of an abuser is stopped, as the wife is no longer kept from having friendships and going places on her own. The women begin to grow in trust and hope as they share and learn from women who have had similar experiences and have dealt with their problems. The group method allows the women to choose their own way to get involved: to listen, talk, vent, give and receive help, or observe. All of this is empowering, as they do not have to ask permission or be dependent on someone else to tell them what to do (Hartman, 1983). A group is also nonpatriarchal, so the women can be both "giver and taker, healer and healed, teacher and student . . . [of] their past, present, or future . . . from their logical or intuitive strength" (Hartman, 1987, p. 80).

According to *Talking It Out: A Guide to Groups for Abused Women*, "the presence of leaders to provide structure and guidance enhances a sense of safety and enables each woman to take as much responsibility for the group as she is willing or able" (NiCarthy, Merriam, & Coffman, 1984). My experience of leading groups verified these findings. My heart's desire was to see more of my sisters in Christ experience this opportunity for healing. I also felt that the Christian women would be comfortable with this form of meeting, especially if they were from patriarchal churches. I envisioned that all the group work could be done in a modified twelve-step study.

I realized that some domestic violence workers object to the terms *recovery* and *codependency* being applied to abused wives because such terminology undermines the fact that abused wives are victims. Yet there is some dysfunctional behavior in the lives of the women, as any abused woman knows too well. In *Abused No More: Recovery for Women from Abusive or Co-dependent Relationships*, an authority on codependency defines it as "an emotional, psychological, and behavioral condition that develops as a result of an individual's prolonged exposure to, and practice of, a set of oppressive rules—rules which prevent the open expression of feelings or other direct discussion of personal and interpersonal problems" (Ackerman & Pickering, 1989).

Problems

During my review of the literature on abuse, I could not find any materials about support groups on domestic violence that had been developed by a church, so I had to experiment with different materials. For the first cycle we used *The Search for Significance* (McGee, 1990) developed by Rapha, a Christian mental health organization that operates twenty-five centers at hospitals in the United States and trains church-oriented support group leaders. I combined this text with domestic violence information. For the second cycle we used *Breakout! A Twelve Step Adventure to Spiritual Maturity—and Wholeness* (Bryson, 1992), a discussion manual used with the Serenity Bible and corresponding audiotapes. For the third cycle we used *A Hunger for Healing: The Twelve Steps as a Classic Model for Christian Spiritual Growth* (1991) by J. Keith Miller and his corresponding videotapes developed by NavPress.

More problematic than a lack of materials was my difficulty in finding an evangelical church where we could meet. A pastor at one of the larger churches in Wheaton told me he didn't want me to use *Battered into Submission* as a supplement because, although he believed the first and last parts of it, he did not agree with the Alsdurfs' writing on submission. The director of Wheaton Youth Outreach, a local Christian social work agency, allowed us to meet in their building. Later, after a canvass of Wheaton pastors, the second cycle of meetings was held at Creekside Free Methodist Church, where the pastor and the board were very supportive. The third cycle was held at one of the wives' homes. Her children were too young for her to be away from them and she was separated from her husband, so she was free to have us meet there.

The Format

The meetings run in a fourteen- to sixteen-week cycle and are held once a week. The format is psychoeducational and includes a cognitive exercise at the beginning of each meeting, giving each person opportunity to briefly tell of a positive experience that she has had during the week. The women review their responses to the past week's material, discuss the present week's topic or step, have a time of sharing, and close with prayer.

Procedures for evaluating the group process include a pre- and post-test using Hudson's *Generalized Contentment* (for depression, with which abused wives have a problem); observations of the members' progress; a closing survey to be filled out by the group members; and follow-up individual visits with the leader. For my research project, I was required to write the bias of the study, namely, that "the group was composed only of women from the Wheaton area." But I decided that this could become an asset, because once the program begins operating well, the fact that it comes out of Wheaton will likely make it more acceptable to evangelicals in all areas of the United States.

The ground rules are kept at a minimum to prevent the wives from feeling they are being controlled again. The only two rules are "confidentiality" and "consideration." Abused wives have applied these principles to their dealings with their husbands and children for all their married lives, so the challenge for these women is to apply the principles to themselves. The meetings are kept open, since the women do not always know if they can attend regularly. The wives also try to keep in contact with each other during the week by phone calls or short visits, so as to support each other. Literature is always available, so they can continue to educate themselves; they know their sanity depends on their growing awareness and knowledge.

The first meeting was well attended. Only a couple of wives dropped out after the introductory night, and with no apparent reason, another stopped coming halfway through the program. These patterns are not uncommon in groups whose members move in and out of denial. Often these women will begin to attend again at a later time (another important reason for keeping the meetings open). The women ranged in age from twenty-seven to late fifties; one had been divorced five years ago, one was in the process of divorce, and the rest were still in abusive marriages.

Of the women who completed the sessions, two were also in private therapy, and the others, as well as the woman who dropped out, had stated that they "couldn't afford it." The women bonded almost immediately, and, in fact, met at another time to celebrate a member's birthday. One of the older women contacted a younger one about a good employment opportunity at her office.

The use of the cognitive opening exercise helped to set the tone for the meetings, keeping the focus on the women themselves and preventing gripe sessions. The material on dysfunction helped to develop self-awareness in such a healing manner that everyone was excited about the meetings from the beginning. By the fourth meeting, one member said she had told her therapist she wouldn't have made as much progress as she had, if not for the group meetings. The women supported each other as they discussed their progress and shared their needs and problems. For example, they coached the younger woman through her divorce process and encouraged another member in asserting herself with her husband. At the closing meeting, everyone commented that the rapport and support were the best part of the group. The women also said the materials were "terrific" and "very helpful."

For two reasons the group considered changing its name from "Women Dealing with a Difficult Marriage" to "Evangelical Women from Domestic Violent Homes." First, they felt the church community needs to be alerted and educated to the fact that there is domestic violence in church homes. Second, several college girls realized they too were from this type of home and had requested a support group. With the change in name, the students could be included along with the wives. The wives hoped that if the college students joined the group, they might be able to work through their own problems earlier than the wives had, thus breaking the abusive generational cycle before they too ended up in abusive marriages.

Conclusions

When I wrote my research project, I concluded that the findings from the first group's cycle of meetings suggested that it is possible to use group intervention to educate, support, and help abused wives from evangelical homes. The wives in the group were able to develop self-awareness, grow in their self-esteem, and form supportive, deep friendships. They also became enthusiastic about starting new groups, as well as repeating the present group for their own growth and progress. There were marked changes in the depressed states of several of the wives, as shown by the pre- and post-tests and their behavior. Their home situations changed as a result of the changes in their own self-awareness, confidence, and conduct.

These findings also indicate that there is a need, as well as potential, for the development of local domestic violence support groups. Not only counselors, church staff, and church workers but also lay-workers can be trained by reading the Christian books I have already mentioned, along with others in the reference list and in the public library. Courses about domestic violence are offered at local junior colleges and are open to anyone. Another resource is the local domestic violence shelter, which offers speakers, information, and, perhaps, training.

After a couple of layworkers are trained and comfortable with the subject, the beginning of a support group can be announced at any church-sponsored function that women attend. Once women know who the layworkers are, they will slowly begin to approach the workers. Expect progress to be slow at first, since the women will feel that no one knows or believes that a Christian marriage can be difficult. But once a couple of women contact the workers and discover that they do understand, those women will spread the news and a group can be formed. As a Rapha female counselor said to me when she heard of my idea for a support group, "Once they learn that you understand them, they'll start coming out of the church woodwork!"

Developing support groups for abused wives from evangelical homes solves only half the problem. If lasting results are to be attained, there also need to be interventions for the husbands. In *Battered into Submission,* the Alsdurfs write of a program developed by a pastor and former abuser, Paul Hegstrom. He worked through his own abusive behavior by attending a domestic violence program and remarried the woman he had abused and finally divorced. In 1985 he developed a domestic violence learning center, now called Family Life Skills Learning Center, where behavior modification and education are used with both spouses. In 1988 the center was featured on Focus on the Family for two days, with the program titled "Battered Families: Help and Hope" (Alsdurf & Alsdurf, 1989). One of their pamphlets states that "the Learning Center provides tools in helping its clients learn to rebuild their lives and improve their self-image. The goal is to help clients increase their capacity to function in relationships and, where possible, to offer hope of reconciliation [in] the family. . . . Skills to change behavior are taught in classes that are separate for men and women." According to information from its office headquarters, Life Skills International in Aurora, Colorado, any church or professional group can call for a package that gives information about starting a local center.

I hope that evangelical churches will see that they need to start providing support groups for abused wives in their congregations. Until churches begin such groups, I think the initiative will have to come from evangelical women who learn all they can about "Christian" domestic violence and then do all they can to help each other. Perhaps the greatest hope lies in the idea of developing Family Life Skills programs in evangelical churches. I suspect such programs will be easier for churches to accept, since the principles of Family Life Skills centers support preservation of families and the sanctity of marriage. This program does not confront couples on their theological views and systems. Yet it will help couples correct their patterns of relating to each other. The vision is that the couples will then change not only themselves but also the church, providing support groups for other recovering couples.

A Theological Analysis of Hierarchicalism

13

Joan Tyvoll

Elizabeth, hugging herself and rocking back and forth, huddled in a chair. Recounting childhood memories of her abuse was always a difficult prospect for Elizabeth, who is a Satanic Ritualistic Abuse (SRA) survivor. "Telling" was strictly forbidden, and the punishment was severe.[1] Telling is frightening, because if you tell, you can no longer deny the reality of the abuse. Telling is part of the healing process, however, and this day marked another step forward for Elizabeth, who suffers from Multiple Personality Disorder (MPD) as a result of her severe abuse.

Elizabeth's support team includes her pastor and an elder from her church, another pastor from the community, her counselor, and me. We all sat with her as she began remembering specific details about the hierarchical structure within the cult that abused her. This was a male-dominated cult whose principal strong-man (demon) was male.[2]

The picture that unfolded that day added to the story of gross abuse and perversion that Elizabeth had been revealing to us for more than two years. Extreme physical, emotional, sexual, and spiritual abuse kept women and children under the domination of several men. Many of these men were prominent members of their community who lived double lives and succeeded in keeping the cult activities secret.[3]

Today Elizabeth remembered the demon second in charge, a woman. Among other things, this demon's job was to teach the women

195

and girls in the group how to "service" the men. I could hear in Elizabeth's words the women's hatred for the men who controlled them. Theirs was not an easy domination.

I heard something else too. The women despised themselves and each other for being weak, for being used, for being women. The abusive structure of the cult and the abusive power that upheld that structure bred hatred, jealousy, and contempt among the women.

In a flash of insight I realized that this was as close as I would ever get to seeing the origin of abuse. Although Elizabeth's case was a worst-case scenario, I had heard this story before. It is usually told in milder forms, but it is the same story. Physical, sexual, emotional, or spiritual abuse results in the victim hating the abuser and then hating himself or herself.

That day I finally got it. I understood that there is a system that creates the atmosphere or the excuse for abuse to happen. That day God named the system for me: hierarchicalism. Hierarchicalism places one group of people over another on the basis of unjust and arbitrary criteria such as gender, race, ethnic origin, and material wealth. The apostle Paul says it is energized by the three influences of evil—the world, the flesh, and the devil (Eph. 2:1–3). This system breeds abuse at every level of human relationships. For several years I have had a personal conviction that hierarchicalism is bad, but I know many good people who believe it is right. They structure their homes and churches according to it. I have been unwilling to judge them, because for some it seems to work. Until this counseling session with Elizabeth, I was willing to live and let live. If they can stand it, I thought, it is their affair, not mine.

God has changed my mind to such an extent that I can no longer use that apathetic approach. During Elizabeth's counseling session, the mask was torn off hierarchicalism, and I saw the face beneath it. Abuse is evil, whether it occurs in a satanic cult or in a Christian home. The type of structure that supports abuse is also evil whether it is found in a satanic cult or in a Christian home. I am convinced that hierarchicalism is an inherently evil, counterfeit structure that is superimposed on God's good plan for the structures of society that govern his good creation.

The tragedy is that instead of modeling a better way, the church subscribes to this evil system and labels it as God's ideal for his church, for marriages, and for families. I believe there is a more just and biblical way to uphold the authentic structures of existence that God has put in place to do us good.

Writing this chapter has been a powerful exercise for me, because God has given me still another evidence that the message of equality is true. It is bound up in who he is and who we should be as well. I hope to give a comprehensive picture of the origins of hierarchicalism and place it in the context of God's dealings with people throughout history. I hope to make it clear that God's way is the way of true equality and justice.

Made in the Image of God

Any theology of equality begins at the beginning with God, who by the power of his divine word created the heavens and the earth. He made something out of nothing, putting his creative genius to work to form a beautiful ordered world. The climax of this marvelous creative enterprise came when God said:

"Let us make humankind in our image, according to our likeness; and let them have dominion over the fish of the sea, and over the birds of the air, and over the cattle, and over all the wild animals of the earth, and over every creeping thing that creeps upon the earth."
So God created humankind in his image,
in the image of God he created them;
male and female he created them.

Genesis 1:26–27 NRSV

Because all humankind is created in the image of God, dignity and respect are due to all. An individual's worth comes not from what he or she can offer to the world or to God, but from the inherent image of God residing in each person.

What is the image of God? Any orthodox answer to that question begins with the three-in-one God. Julia Castle sums up the historical teaching of the church on the image of the trinitarian God in this way: "The doctrine of the Trinity can be stated in three propositions about God: 1) God is One. 2) God is one substance (or essence) subsisting eternally in the three Persons of the Father, the Son, and the Holy Spirit. 3) These Three are coequal, coeternal, and possess fully every divine attribute" (1991, p. 3).

A Social Theory of the Trinity

Many theologians believe that a social theory of the Trinity best explains this crucial concept. Cornelius Plantinga expands our picture of the relationship of these three-in-one, coequal, coeternal, consubstantial persons by stating that true trinitarian Christianity affirms "God as a society or community of three persons in the richest sense of 'persons.' Each of Father, Son, and Spirit is a vibrant center of act, knowledge, and loving relation" (1988, p. 24). The reality of the three persons of the Godhead can be found in the trinitarian formulas in the New Testament. In these formulas, the names of the Father, Son, and Holy Spirit appear in close association. An example is found in 2 Corinthians 13:13, where we read, "The grace of the Lord Jesus Christ, the love of God, and the communion of the Holy Spirit be with all of you" (NRSV).

In the Gospels, and especially John's Gospel, we see the picture of a Trinity wherein each member has distinction and differentiation yet is unified in the Trinity. This climaxes in Jesus' astounding prayer found in John 17. His wish was that his disciples would be one, "as we are one" (John 17:11 NRSV). Our model for unity and love as a community is to be found in the Trinity. In that self-sacrificing, giving, agape love, we learn to love. Race and gender should be accepted and appreciated for the glory of God. "As you, Father, are in me and I am in you, may they also be in us, so that the world may believe that you have sent me" (John 17:21 NRSV).

Social Trinity and Creation

If we were created to be in the image of God from the beginning, what does a social theory of the Trinity do to our understanding of the account of the creation of man and woman (Gen. 1:26–27)? These verses, with the switches between singular and plural pronouns, mean God wants us to pay attention. He is doing something significant, and the way it is written says clearly "this is an important concept to grasp." Jurgen Moltmann explains it in this way:

> [T]he image of God (singular) is supposed to correspond to the "internal" plural of God, and yet be a single image. In the next verse the singular and plural are distributed in the opposite way: God (singular) created the human being (singular), as man and woman (plural) he created them (plural). Here the human plural is supposed to correspond to the divine singular. Whereas the self-resolving God is plural in the singular, his image on earth—the human being—is apparently supposed to be a singular in the plural. The one god, who is differentiated in himself and is at one with himself, then finds his correspondence in a community of human beings, male and female, who unite with one another and are one. (1985, p. 218)

The relatedness of the three persons of the Trinity to each other is the basis of our being made in the image of God. We are relational social beings, as God is related to each member of the Trinity.

What distinguishes humanity from the rest of creation is not something we do. That starts from the wrong end of the question. Before people do something (i.e., exercise dominion), they are something. They are, first of all, in relationship with God. After that, humanity's image bearing is not merely in possessing certain characteristics or in relating only to the triune God. It is bound up in a person's whole existence: "The whole person, not merely his soul, the true human community, not only the individual; humanity as it is bound up with nature, not simply human beings in their confrontation with nature—it is these which are the image of God and his glory. This does away with the question about particular phenomena constituting the image of God" (Moltmann, 1985, p. 221).

The social theory of the Trinity provides the intellectual means to harmonize personality and sociality in the community of men and women without sacrificing the one to the other (Moltmann, 1985, p. 199). We are all in the image of God, equal in worth and responsibility, but we are complementary as is the Trinity within itself. Both men and women share the qualities that distinguish us from the rest of creation.

Paul Jewett offers this definition of the image of God: "There should be no striving to transcend the distinction between male and female for to be in the image of God is to be male and female. The fellowship as male and female is what it means to be in the image of God" (1975, 23). This is not talking about the sexual union of male and female. It is clearly wrong to say we are truly human only when we experience the bonds of marriage. Marriage is not the most basic form of human fellowship. But "to talk about Man as such is precisely to talk about Man as man and woman" (1975, p. 24). To be in the image of God means to be male and female. It is in this interplay, this dance of complementary humanity, that we reflect the Trinity to the world (John 17).

A social Trinity is a great leveler of all society, not just male and female. There is no hierarchy within the Trinity that can be used as an excuse to dominate women, other races, or other countries or peoples. As there is perfect equality between the persons of the Trinity, so God created humankind with perfect equality. The social Trinity gives us the true pattern of unity for men and women made in the image of God.

God created men and women equal, with a joint blessing and a joint charge: "God blessed them, and God said to them, 'Be fruitful and multiply, and fill the earth and subdue it; and have dominion over the fish of the sea and over the birds of the air and over every living thing that moves upon the earth.' . . . God saw everything that he had made, and indeed, it was very good" (Gen. 1:28, 31 NRSV).

Hierarchicalism Enters with the Fall

God had a good plan for structures of society to govern his good creation. One can only speculate about what structures would have been instituted had there been no fall, but it is reasonable to assume that there would have been governing authorities to organize and regulate everyday interactions among peoples. Paul defines these "good servants" for us (albeit in light of the fall) in Romans 13:1–7. The point is that God has put something good in place for the orderly regulation of society.

What then has happened to this good thing? Throughout history the structures of society have done great harm to millions of people they were intended to protect. Every Christian knows the answer to that is sin. Into God's beautifully created, ordered, and balanced world stepped sin. The warm and open relationship between God and his creatures was destroyed, as was the equality and open communion between all people.

Authentic Power and Secular Power

Until Genesis 3, humankind had seen and experienced only God's authentic power. Authentic power is creative and redemptive. The serpent offered a different kind of power outside the will of God. Cloaked in deceit, this power sounded useful, attractive—wholly desirable. What Adam and Eve did not see, or perhaps did not want to see, was that this other power was a counterfeit. The evil power of darkness is not able to create anything, it is only able to distort what already exists. "Goodness is, so to speak, itself: badness is only spoiled goodness. And there must be something good before it can be spoiled. . . . Evil is a parasite, not an original thing" (Lewis, 1943, pp. 49–50).

A new definition of power entered into the consciousness of man and woman, but it was only a distortion of the truth. The definition of power became "the prerogative to determine what happens, and the coercive force to make others yield to your wishes—even against their will" (Campolo, 1983, p. 11). The advent of this power is the reason for the break that exists between God and humanity and also explains

man's alienation from himself, from his neighbor, and from nature. Hate, greed, violence, war, immorality, drunkenness, jealousy, rivalry, strife, selfishness, and all the other disorders that plague man's existence are rooted in his break from God. Man's attempt to rule and harness nature without respect to its order, rhythm, and cycles are acts of aggression against the creation, ultimately rooted in his rebellion against God. Further, man now enters into a struggle, a wrestling not "against flesh and blood, but against the principalities, against the powers, against the world rulers of this present darkness, against the spiritual hosts of wickedness in heavenly places" (Ephesians 6:12). (Webber, 1979, p. 40)

Secular power became the way for people to force others or their environment to serve them apart from the will of God through spiritual power (witchcraft and pagan religions that manipulate spiritual forces), military might, personal charisma, or positions or offices in the world system.

Hierarchicalism as the Secular Power Structure

Genesis 3:16 predicts the new power structure that would support this distortion of true power: "Your desire shall be for your husband, and he shall rule over you" (NRSV).

At the fall we see a counterfeit structure superimposed on God's good order. It is hierarchicalism, not God, that places one group of people over others.

We can learn the difference between good power and evil power, between God's good structures and hierarchicalism, by looking at God's dealings with people in the Old and New Testaments. The New Testament gives us a picture of what relationships could have been like and can be again because of Christ's redemptive work on the cross.

God and Hierarchicalism in the Old and New Testaments

God never endorses the hierarchical system adopted by his fallen people. He never allows himself to be put in a theological box, and he does not allow himself to be subject to societal norms acceptable to his fallen people. Time and again we see him breaking into the established hierarchical power structures as a way of reminding us of its imperfections. God used, and still uses, whomever he pleases to accomplish his purpose for humankind: to bring himself glory (Isa. 43:7).

Old Testament Examples

The Old Testament is replete with examples of God's egalitarian attitude toward his people. He used women: Deborah, Huldah, and Esther. He blessed second borns: David and Gideon. He chose Israel, not because they were a numerous or mighty people, but because . . . well, just because he chose them.

His choice of David as king of Israel sums up his philosophy of who is chosen, who is fit for the great task of glorifying himself. David was the youngest, his seven brothers surpassing him in stature and ability. "But the LORD said to Samuel, 'Do not consider [Eliab's] appearance or his height, for I have rejected him. The LORD does not look at the things man looks at. Man looks at the outward appearance, but the LORD looks at the heart'" (1 Sam. 16:7).

New Testament Examples

It is no surprise then to see the way Jesus also treated individuals. The poor, the mighty, the righteous, the unrighteous—all were recipients of his notice and mercy. He looked at the heart of Nicodemus and said, "You must be born again" (John 3). He looked at the heart of the leper and declared him well because of his faith (Luke 17). He looked at the heart of the sinful woman who anointed him and wiped his feet with her hair and said, "Your faith has saved you; go in peace" (Luke 7:50). He looked at the hearts of the woman at the well and of the woman caught in adultery, compassionately called them to purity, and saved them (John 4; 8).

Jesus called men to follow him, and he called women. The New Testament contains numerous examples of men and women working side by side for the cause of the gospel (Mark 15:41; Luke 8:1–3; 10:38–42; Rom. 16:1–16; Phil. 4:3; Col. 4:15; 2 Tim. 4:21; Heb. 11; 1 Peter 5:13; 2 John 1).

The Body of Christ—
the Model for the Community

God has condemned the secular definitions of power and has
revealed the redeemed creation plan through the body of Christ:

> Consider your own call, brothers and sisters: not many of you were
> wise by human standards, not many were powerful, not many were
> of noble birth. But God chose what is foolish in the world to shame
> the wise; God chose what is weak in the world to shame the strong;
> God chose what is low and despised in the world, things that are not,
> to reduce to nothing things that are.
>
> 1 Corinthians 1:26–28 NRSV

Galatians 3:28 is the declaration of victory over the power of sin
predicted in Genesis 3:16: "There is no longer Jew or Greek, there is
no longer slave or free, there is no longer male and female; for all of
you are one in Christ Jesus" (NRSV). In our new relationship with God
through Jesus Christ, we can reverse the prescription found in Genesis 3:16. "From now on, therefore, we regard no one from a human
point of view; even though we once knew Christ from a human point
of view, we know him no longer in that way. So if anyone is in Christ,
there is a new creation: everything old has passed away; see, everything has become new!" (2 Cor. 5:16–17 NRSV).

The Trinity can again be reflected in the community of believers.
This truth is clearly taught in 1 Corinthians 12:12–27, where Paul
describes the complementarity of the unified yet diverse body of
Christ. This unified body can be a light in the darkness caused by
the distortions and misuse of the structures of existence. We can be
salt in a decaying society, agents of change who redeem the broken
structures of our society.

The church of Jesus Christ has failed to do that redemptive work
because it has failed to recognize that hierarchicalism is evil. Not
only that, it sanctions hierarchicalism as God's ideal. It embraces it
in church governments, in families, and in marriages.

Humans in an abusive structure perpetrate abuse on other
humans. If the church is made up of humans who live according to

this evil abusive structure, it becomes abusive. When that happens, God is also labeled as an abuser.

Exposing the Evil of Hierarchicalism

If Genesis 3:16 describes the structure of abuse, then Genesis 3:15 provides the key element that energizes this evil structure (Warner, 1991, p. 11):

> "I will put enmity between you and the woman,
>   and between your offspring and hers;
>   he will strike your head,
>   and you will strike his heel"(NRSV).

God is speaking to the serpent, and he is describing the spiritual conflict that has existed from that time until now.

The Bible makes it clear that we cannot blame Satan for all the evil influence in the world. Paul teaches us in Ephesians 2:1–3 that sinful behavior stems from three compelling influences to be seen as three strands combining to make a sturdy cable:

1. The world: "The ways of this world"
2. The devil: "The ruler of the kingdom of the air," "the spirit who is now at work in those who are disobedient"
3. The flesh: "The cravings of our sinful nature . . . its desires and thoughts" (Arnold, 1992, p. 124)

Clinton E. Arnold believes, however, that Paul regarded Satan as the chief opponent of Christ and his kingdom.

The demonic explanation for evil behavior needs to be seen as the thread that ties together all the evil influences. In practice Satan exploits the depraved tendencies of the flesh and exercises a measure of control over all levels of a social order. . . . The powerful supernatural work of the Devil and his powers sets itself against individual Christians and the Church as a whole. The fact that the powers exploit the flesh and exert their influence over the world systems makes the extent of their influence comprehensive. (1992, p. 127)

To fully understand the spiritual conflict that permeates the biblical record from Genesis 3 on, we must understand the enemy and the roots of the conflict.

The Roots of the Conflict

Many theologians believe that Satan was probably one of the angels closest to God's throne—a cherub. This is a majestic being, the Bible tells us, a guardian of the throne of God (Exod. 25:19; Ps. 18:10; Ezek. 28:16; Heb. 9:5). Satan, or Lucifer as he was called then, knew the glory of God as few others of God's creatures knew it (Warner, 1991, p. 15). Isaiah 14 reveals that Lucifer became jealous of God and his glory and tried to ascend God's throne and take God's place. God cast Lucifer out of heaven, along with one-third of the angelic host who sided with him.

Timothy Warner suggests that the issue underlying the conflict between God and Satan then and now is Satan's jealousy over the glory of God. What does the glory of God have to do with us?

There may be another element in Satan's fall which will help us to understand the conflict in which we are involved today. It may be that the fall of Satan did not occur until after the creation of man. . . . It may be that when Lucifer saw this new order of beings created "in the image of God" (Gen. 1:26, 27), his jealousy was intensified. While these new persons were created lower than the angels for their time on earth, they were also created with the potential for glorification. Being "in the image of God," they had the capacity for likeness to God which Lucifer as an angel did not possess. . . . So if Lucifer was jealous of God over the issue of glory, he is also jealous of God's highest creation over the same issue. (1991, p. 17)

Satan's attempt to steal the glory of God by a direct attack on him failed miserably. Warner believes that Satan's strategy then shifted to an indirect, subtle attack on God's highest creation.

Satan's plan became one of using his angelic power to deceive God's children, and thus to divert them from reflecting God's glory here and from achieving the potential with which God made them for glorification after death.

The principal tactic of Satan in his conflict with God . . . has been to deceive God's children into believing the tremendous potential which resides within them can be realized by living life under their own control rather than under God's control and to believe that there is a legitimate source of power other than Yahweh. (1991, p. 18)

Although God in Genesis 1 and 2 gives us a picture of human relationships that can be described with the words "mutuality," "community," "codominion," and "equality," Satan has succeeded in distorting that picture.

A heresy that emerged early on in the history of the church tried to make a case for a structure of hierarchy within the Godhead. This heresy was firmly denied (Castle, 1991).[4] This idea has popped up again in recent years, mainly among groups who want to have an excuse for a chain-of-command structure in families and marriages. When humanity, and even the church, works within a hierarchical structure, we do not accurately reflect the image of God, and Satan wins. The glory of God has been dimmed.

Hierarchicalism Dims the Glory of God

Any human being has incredible potential. We are made in God's image and have access to the unfathomable riches of God's grace and power. God freely offers and supplies "more than all we can ask or imagine" (Eph. 3:20 NRSV). God's power empowers, which means to enable or permit. The purpose of the authentic power structures of existence is to do the same. The just, merciful, and empowering God invites "whosoever may come" to be blessed, restored, and made new.

Hierarchicalism, in direct contrast, takes away people's power. It uses secular power to coerce or force one's will on another. On the basis of unjust and arbitrary criteria, it limits and restricts the right of individuals or groups to realize the potential to reflect the glory of God. Using reasons such as gender, race, ethnic origin, or material wealth to oppress or dominate people is wrong, but such dominion occurs even in the church of Jesus Christ.

Hierarchicalism and Women

Self-esteem. Women learn that they are inferior when they grow up in a system that puts men in power over them. Women are not believed to be as smart or as capable as the men who control them. Traditional Christianity has even supported the idea that there is an inherent flaw in the very being or character of women that men must compensate for.[5]

It is an accepted fact that women struggle with low self-esteem and that some women's self-esteem decreases throughout their married lives. Is marriage the culprit we should blame for low self-esteem in women? Did God make a mistake when he instituted marriage as a foundation stone of society (Gen. 2)? I do not believe so. It is hierarchicalism, the counterfeit structure superimposed on God's good marriage plan, that breeds inferiority.

Evangelical Christianity places the blame for problems within a marriage on people not adhering strongly enough to a hierarchical structure. If the man would take stronger command, if the woman would submit better, if we would all accept our God-given place in the chain of command, our problems would be solved, so the rationale goes.

I have heard hierarchicalism presented by many of its advocates in terms of a benevolent dictatorship. Why think of it in negative terms, they ask, when the structure is only for the protection and benefit of women? The answer is that a benevolent dictatorship is still a dictatorship, and a dictatorship is morally wrong because it takes away the personhood of the individual. All human beings have a responsibility to learn, grow, and rule over their own lives and destiny. Each of us must be allowed to bear the full weight of life, to experience the good and bad consequences of our choices. In doing so, our characters are developed and molded.

A dictatorship takes away that chance for growth. If a woman's destiny rests in the hands of another, she never has to grow up or test the limits of her gifts and abilities. When she is not in control of her own life, she lacks creativity and spontaneity. She does not have the initiative to engage in life. That woman never becomes the person God intended her to be. The glory of God is never fully reflected in her, and Satan wins. The glory of God in his world is dimmed.

Abuse. A more serious charge to level is naming abuse as a consequence of the hierarchical system. The permission hierarchicalism gives for one person to dominate another, or for a group to dominate another, creates an atmosphere in which abuse can occur.

A man grows up believing it is his right to expect obedience and compliance to his wishes, whether a woman agrees or not. Her inferior position proves she is not fit for any position of authority or responsibility. She cannot control herself; therefore, for her own good, she must be controlled. Women and children are owned and become objects to be manipulated and used to the master's own ends. Objects can be used and abused, but persons never should be.

This man is a victim of the same dominating system. His power, his sense of worth and value, is perhaps being taken away every day at work by his boss or by an oppressive government or society. This powerlessness then sparks abuse at home. This man must look to less powerful people than himself to fill the emptiness inside himself. The less powerful people are, of course, his wife and children.

The frightening truth is that Christian men have an even bigger stick to shake at women than do men outside the church. God, say some Christian men, instituted this chain of command. Rebel against your place in the hierarchy, your role in this weighty structure, and you rebel against God himself. Women have a choice: lose themselves, or lose God. Is it any wonder radical feminists are reformulating Christianity?

A Better Way

Christians who are able to see hierarchicalism for what it is and are convinced that Jesus is calling us to a new life of equality and justice will be part of the healing in the church and in society.

For some people the challenge will be to model a better family structure in everyday life. Counselors will educate and heal victims and perpetrators as they come for help. Pastors and teachers will proclaim the truth through the written and spoken word.

I am a pastor. My calling is not to be an advocate for women's rights but to be a shepherd to a flock of God's sheep, men and women alike. In the process of that ministry, however, God is using me to bring truth, balance, and healing to these people. In my teaching I can address the issue directly. Through my leadership I can encourage men and women to fill positions they have stereotyped in the past. By my example they will see that women can do what they once thought only men could do.

Recently a twelve-year-old girl who attends a Christian school came to me with a question. During a discussion her teacher had explained that on the basis of 1 Timothy 3, women should not be deacons, elders, or pastors. The girl said to me, "Well, I knew *that* wasn't right, but I didn't know what to say to her either."

Why was this girl certain that the teacher was not right? Because she saw me functioning in the role of assistant pastor every time she came to church. To her, there was no reason to question my right to hold that position or my ability to do so. A woman in a place of leadership was so natural to her that it was her teacher's position that sounded odd and unnatural.

I went home that night praising God because he was using me to model a better way to that young woman. Girls and boys must grow up in an environment that gives them a healthy respect for the rights of all peoples. They must have healthy role models of men and women to aspire to, and they must be challenged to be what God calls them to be without the artificial boundaries of hierarchicalism dimming the glory of God in them. There is not one answer to the problem but many. We all must understand the gravity of the problem and be committed to be part of the solution.

Notes

1. The punishment was death. Elizabeth still struggles against the programming that taught her how to commit suicide if she disappointed the high priest or violated his cult rules. She also has good reason to believe her life is in danger from cult members who know she is talking.

2. This cult was male-dominated, but I have talked to another SRA survivor who was abused by a female-dominated cult.

3. Elizabeth remembers a doctor, a pastor, and a policeman being among those in the cult.

4. The Nicene Creed in A.D. 325 and the Athanasian Creed of A.D. 430 to 500 speak directly against any teaching that would advocate a hierarchy within the Godhead.

5. Material from the early church does not reflect this attitude, but by the second century, writings begin to reflect a deepening suspicion toward women. By the time of John Chrysostom, who was Bishop of Constantinople from 398 to 404, we see the restriction on the ministries of women to be taken for granted. Chrysostom writes that woman is inferior to man not only because of the fall, but also because she was inferior at the point of creation. Sources that track the deterioration of the high view that Jesus and the early church held toward women include Elizabeth A. Clark, *Women in the Early Church* (Wilmington, DE: Glazier, 1984); Roger Gryson, *The Ministry of Women in the Early Church* (Collegeville, MN: Liturgical, 1976); Ben Witherington, *Women in the Earliest Churches* (Cambridge: Cambridge University Press, 1988).

Disputing the Excuse for Abuse

14

Andrew C. Perriman

In the endeavor to construct a viable, biblical defense of the egalitarian position, and thus remove any final sanction for the abuse of women in church and home, evangelical scholarship has had to deal with two main areas of New Testament teaching that have traditionally been invoked as evidence for the proper subordination of women. One has to do with the restrictions, found principally in 1 Corinthians 14:34–35 and 1 Timothy 2:12, that are imposed upon the participation of women in certain areas of the church's public life. The other relates to those passages that speak of the man as "head" of the woman and correspondingly of the woman as being subordinate to the man. This is the more fundamental issue, particularly for understanding the Christian family, and is the subject of this chapter (for 1 Tim. 2:12, see Perriman, 1993).

Considerable progress has already been made toward a rebuttal of the subordinationist view of the relation between man and woman. The egalitarian case has rested on three basic lines of argument, but each of these suffers from certain drawbacks or limitations. First, a number of scholars have undertaken to show by exhaustive lexicological analysis that prior to Paul, *kephale*, when used metaphorically, does not naturally designate one who has "authority over" another. However, I am not persuaded that the alternative meaning generally proposed, that *kephale* means "source" or "source of life," has any better lexical or exegetical credentials, or that the relevant passages have yet been correctly understood. Second, although it is often said by way of mitigation that Paul sets the submission of the woman to the man in a context of mutual submission ("being submitted to one another in fear of Christ"[1]), it seems that this interpretation of Ephesians 5:21 is difficult to sustain. Third, an enormous amount of research has been done into the social condition of women in the ancient Mediterranean world, on the basis of which the case has been variously made that the subordinate status imposed on women in the teaching of the apostles was contingent upon cultural factors—the prevalence of patriarchy, for example, or the dubious reputations of women's religions—and therefore open to revision as society evolves. This has proved a highly illuminating project, but it has hardly been shown on textual grounds that Paul himself might have understood things in this way. While it remains essentially a hermeneutical assumption, we will always face the simple objection that Scripture plainly teaches the subordination of women within the order of marriage.

It is possible to address these shortcomings and to show that in speaking of the headship of the man and the subordination of the woman Paul did not mean to ordain the universal authority of the man over the woman. This will involve first a reconsideration of the meaning of headship. The more significant evidence comes from an analysis of Paul's manner of argumentation in 1 Corinthians 11:3–9 and Ephesians 5:21–24, from which will emerge a rather different reading of these crucial texts.

The Metaphorical Sense of *Kephale*

The debate over the metaphorical sense of *kephale* has become polarized around two interpretations: that "head" as it is used in Paul's letters signifies one who has "authority over" (Fitzmyer, 1989, 1993; Grudem, 1990) or that at least in the passages that speak of the man as head of the woman the word has some meaning such as "source" or "source of life" (Evans, 1983, pp. 65–66; Fiorenza, 1983, p. 229; Fee, 1987, p. 503; Witherington, 1988, pp. 84–85; Jervis, 1993, p. 240). My view is that neither of these interpretations properly describes the basic metaphorical sense of *kephale* for the New Testament and that we should understand the word in terms much closer to its obvious physical meaning. I would argue that in the Hellenistic Greek, *kephale*, when used metaphorically, almost always signifies only that which is foremost, uppermost, most prominent, preeminent. No doubt other connotations accrue to it according to context: the "head" of a river is associated with the idea of "source," but it can also be the mouth (Herodotus, 4.91; Callimachus, *Aetia* P. Oxy., XVII, 2080, 48); likewise, to speak of the "head" of a city or a nation is only to identify its most prominent figure ("the head of Aram is Damascus, and the head of Damascus Rasim" [Isa. 7:8]), but generally this will also be the one who governs it. It is a mistake, however, to confuse these contextually determined nuances with the conventional metaphorical sense of the term. The lexicological evidence for this interpretation cannot be reviewed here; it is a position that has been entertained by one or two scholars, although not as consistently as it merits (see Perriman, 1994; Liefeld, 1986, p. 139; Cervin, 1989).[2] We should, however, give some thought to the immediate exegetical implications.

1 Corinthians 11:3

It has been natural to suppose that when Paul writes in 1 Corinthians 11:3 that "the head of every man is Christ, the head of the woman is the man, the head of the Christ is God," he means the statement to stand as the logical premise of the ensuing argument, as though he were saying: *given that* the head of the woman is the man, she should veil her head when praying or prophesying. This assumption, however, is doubtful. The use of *kephale* to describe the relation of one individual to another, rather than to a group, is rare in Hellenistic literature. The only nonbiblical occurrence of such a usage with which I am familiar is in Artemidorus (II AD), where a man's father is compared to his head because he was the cause of his living (Artemidorus, *Oneirocriticum* 1.2; 3.66). But even in this instance the use of the metaphor is determined by a particular literal circumstance: The man had dreamed of being beheaded. The same is true in 1 Corinthians 11, where Paul's concern is primarily with the head in its literal sense, as that which is either veiled or unveiled in worship, rather than with the head as the locus of shame or glory, an idiomatic usage common in the Old Testament (shame and dishonor, for example: Num. 5:18; Deut. 21:12; Jer. 14:4; Ep. Jer. 31). The description of man as head of the woman and of the Christ as head of the man is, rhetorically speaking, a further extension of these ideas and formally determined by them. When Paul describes the man as head of the woman, he is not stating a premise but in effect anticipating and restating, in an elaborate play on the meaning of *kephale,* the later but logically prior argument that the woman is the glory of the man and that unseemly behavior on her part may bring dishonor on him (vv. 4–7). Behind this whole argument lies the traditional theme of the righteous wife, which is found, for example, in Proverbs 11:16 (LXX): "A gracious wife brings glory to her husband, but a woman hating righteousness is a throne of dishonor (*atimias,* cf. 1 Cor. 11:14)."[3]

The use of *kephale* in this passage, therefore, to describe the relation of the man to the woman is governed by two literary factors. The first is the conventional understanding of *kephale* as meaning "most prominent," and on that basis perhaps most representative. This accords much better with the theme of glory and shame than would an interpretation along the lines of either "authority over" or "source": It is because man holds the preeminent position in the patriarchal family that he is susceptible to dishonor brought on him by his wife's behavior. The metaphor naturally defines the visible or public aspect of the relationship: The whole passage has to do with appearance and attire, not with inner relations of authority or origination. The second factor is the significance of *kephale* for Paul's argument. This is both practical, in that he is concerned with headwear, and symbolic, in view of the common Jewish idiom that associates moral and religious qualities with the head. The real premise of the argument, however, is not that man is head of the woman but that woman is the glory of man, and this assertion is supported by the appeal to the creation story in verses 8–9: Woman is from man and was created for the sake of the man *(dia ton andra).* The allusion here is evidently to the creation of woman as a "helper like or equal to him" (*boethos homoios auto,* Gen. 2:22 LXX; cf. 2:18).[4] But it is introduced only in order to explain the asymmetry in the relationship with regard to the conferment of "glory"—that woman is the glory of man while man is the glory of God—and may in fact mean no more than that the woman

brings glory to the man.[5] Exactly what Paul understood by this in practical and moral terms is not easy to ascertain, but it undoubtedly had
something to do with the perception and management of sexuality
within the community. The words of Ben Sirach probably express the
sort of concern that motivated these instructions: "Turn away your
eyes from a beautiful woman, and do not consider another's beauty;
many have been deceived by the beauty of a woman, and herewith
love is kindled as a fire" (Sir. 9:8; cf. 25:21; 42:12; 1 Esd. 4:18–19).

The question of the man's authority has no bearing on this issue,
and the theme of origination ("woman from man") is introduced
only as a supporting argument or *approbatio* (woman is the glory
of the man *because* she was created from man), not as an interpretation of the idea of headship. In describing man as head of the
woman in this passage, Paul has in mind the disgrace that might be
brought upon the most prominent figure in the household by the
woman's unseemly behavior in worship (cf. Liefeld, 1986, pp. 139–43;
Keener, 1992, p. 35). The only absolute, creational component in this
argument is that the woman was created from the man and for the
sake of the man. This is made the basis for the view that woman is
the glory of the man, which should be understood in terms of non-
hierarchical sexual distinctions and the complementarity of man
and woman. But exactly what constitutes seemly behavior in worship and in what sense the woman brings glory to the man may be
recognized as culturally determined issues without thereby distorting Paul's argumentation. The scriptural objection is to the disgrace,
not to the particular actions that give rise to it.

Ephesians 5:23

The same figure in Ephesians 5:23 has no connection with literal
usage but is juxtaposed instead with the description of Christ as head
of the church: "a husband is head of the wife as indeed Christ is head
of the church, he himself being the savior of the body." It can be
argued—somewhat against the grain of scholarly opinion—that when
Paul speaks of Christ as "head" in Ephesians and Colossians, he has
in mind not any conception of him as having "authority over" or as
being the "source" of things but fundamentally his prominence and

primacy. In particular, there is a close connection between the thought of Christ as "head" and the theme of resurrection and exaltation.

This connection emerges most clearly in Colossians 1:18: Christ as head of the church "is the beginning, firstborn from the dead, so that he might become in all things preeminent." But it is also apparent in Ephesians 1:20–23, where it is said that God raised Christ from the dead, made him sit at his right hand in the heavens, and gave him as head above all things for the church (Barth, 1974, pp. 183–92). At first sight the assertion that Christ has been set "far above every rule and authority and power and lordship" and that "all things have been put under his feet" would seem to imply that intrinsic to the idea of headship is the exercise of authority. But a number of considerations count against such an interpretation.

There is no reason to suppose that in verse 22 the subordination *(hypetaxen)* of all things under Christ's feet is intended to interpret his headship "above all things for the church." In Psalm 8:6 (LXX) the statement "you appointed him over the works of your hands," to which the words "he gave him as head above all things" in Ephesians 1:22 apparently correspond, is linked more closely to the exaltation motif of verse 5 ("crowned him with glory and honor") than to the thought of subjugation that follows. Second, the proposition *hyper* used here with *kephale* means "over and above, beyond, more than,"[6] that a thing excels or surpasses some other thing. It is not used to define a relationship of "authority over," for which we should normally expect *epi*.[7] This is also true of *hyperano* in verse 21: The preposition indicates only that Christ has been exalted above "every rule and authority and power," not that he has authority over them.[8] Similarly, in Colossians 2:10 the description of Christ as "the head of all rule and authority" does not mean that he has "authority over": He is "head of," not "head over." The idea is only that he is foremost or preeminent in relation to all rule and authority. Third, it can be argued that Christ's session at the right hand of God (v. 20) signifies not the investiture of authority over others but only his exaltation to a position of honor. Although Psalm 110:2–3 (109:2–3 LXX), to which Ephesians 1:20 is an allusion, certainly describes the exercise of dominion over enemies, it is not necessarily to be inferred that the words "sit at my right hand" in verse 1 signify the assumption of authority. It is even less likely elsewhere in the Old Testament, where

the idea appears rather to be one of acceptance or approval, the conferment of honor (e.g., 1 Kings 2:19; Ps. 45:9; in a number of instances
it is the Lord who is at man's right hand to help him: Pss. 16:8; 109:31).

The New Testament picture is more complex, but the general
emphasis is the same. In the majority of the cases the motif marks
either the culmination of the process of Christ's exaltation or the close
association of Christ with God in heaven (Matt. 26:64 and parallels;
Mark 16:19; Acts 7:55–56; Rom. 8:34; Col. 3:1; Heb. 1:3; 8:1; 10:12; 12:2).
In none of these passages is there any explicit indication that the
phrase denotes Christ's authority or rule over other powers[9]; and it
is surely of significance, too, that in none of these passages do we find
the words "till I make your enemies your footstool" (Ps. 110:1). This
clause, which might be taken to suggest that the session at God's right
hand denotes authority, is included only at Matthew 22:44 and parallels, where there is no mention of resurrection or exaltation; at Acts
2:34–35, where it is explicitly quoted from the psalm and only indirectly applied to Christ; and at Hebrews 1:13, where the intention is
to differentiate Christ from the angels. In other words, where Christ's
exaltation is described in terms of the session at God's right hand,
the New Testament apparently prefers to avoid the connection, natural in view of Psalm 110:1, with the theme of subjugation and rule.
This makes it unlikely that the reader is meant to recall the words "till
I make your enemies your footstool" at verse 20 or, consequently, to
interpret the verse as a statement about the attribution to Christ of
a particular "authority over."

A rather different situation holds in the case of Ephesians 4:15–16,
which speaks of believers growing "towards him in every way who is
the head, [the] Christ, from whom the whole body . . . makes the
growth of the body," and only a digest of the arguments can be presented. These verses have often been taken as evidence for an interpretation of *kephale* as "source," but since it is explicitly Christ "from
whom the whole body. . . ," we can make better sense of the passage
as a whole if we understand verse 16 as a compressed recapitulation
of the preceding argument. That the growth of the church is from
Christ, therefore, would not mean that Christ is the source of its growth
in some vital or organic sense but would be a restatement of the idea,
set out at length in verses 7–12, that Christ gave gifts to the church for
its upbuilding. Correspondingly, the expression "according to the

working in measure of each individual part" should be read as a specific reference to the collaboration of the apostles, prophets, evangelists, and others in the work of building up the body of Christ (vv. 11–12). In the light of this it becomes appropriate to interpret the headship of Christ in terms of what has gone before rather than of what follows. Christ the head is the perfect and full Christ, the measure of Christian maturity, the exalted son of God (v. 13), who has "ascended far above all the heavens, that he might fill all things" (v. 10). The corresponding statement in Colossians 2:19 ("not holding fast to the head, from whom the whole body ... grows with the growth of God"), though belonging to a rather different context, admits a similar interpretation: Christ as head is the one in whom "all the fullness of the deity dwells bodily," the "head of all sovereignty and authority" (2:9–10), with whom we have been raised (2:12–13; 3:1), who is seated at the right hand of God, and who will appear in glory (3:1, 4).

It seems, therefore, that when Paul speaks of Christ as "head" in these letters, he has in mind two basic thoughts. First, by his resurrection Christ has been exalted to a position of preeminence above all things. Second, Christ is "head" in relation to the church because he is, in the words of Colossians 1:18, "the beginning, firstborn from the dead"; in his resurrection and exaltation Christ has preceded those who eventually will be raised in him. Paul does not make use of the metaphor of headship in 1 Corinthians 15:22–23, but the idea is the same: "in Christ shall all be made alive, but each under his own order: Christ the first fruits, then those of Christ at his coming." There is thus an important temporal aspect underlying the idea of Christ's headship in Ephesians and Colossians, which in the context of Ephesians 4:11–15 (and Colossians 2:18–19) has been modified only to the extent that Christ who in his resurrection is the perfect forerunner has also become the measure of the church's maturity. If we now turn to Ephesians 5:23, it should be apparent that the description of Christ as "head of the church" is in the first place a recollection of this double theme of exaltation and precedence in the order of resurrection, though the point of the statement will become clear only as we consider the development of Paul's argument in these verses.

Such an understanding of the headship of Christ obviously has implications for how we interpret the headship of the man in this passage. One of the central convictions about the relationship between man and woman that Paul explicitly draws from the creation narrative is the fact that man was created first (1 Cor. 11:8; 1 Tim. 2:13). In 1 Corinthians 11 this theme is closely connected with the statement that "the head of the woman is the man," and it is at least conceivable that the creational priority of the man provides part of the rationale for Paul's description of the man as head in Ephesians 5:23.[10] Since, however, the temporal aspect has no particular significance for the current argument and is in any case less pronounced in Ephesians than in Colossians, we should probably take the emphasis to be primarily on the socially perceived prominence of the man in relation to the woman. Indeed, it seems likely, bearing in mind both that *kephale* is not usually used to describe the relation between two individuals and that the broader focus is the household code, that the headship of the man with respect to the woman is in part an inference from his headship over the patriarchal household.[11] Therefore, as far as can be deduced both from the normal metaphorical usage of the word and from its particular application to Christ, I would say that *kephale* here defines not the authority of the man but his position or status within the order of society. We will consider in the next section whether this judgment needs to be amended in view of the close association of *kephale* with the argument for subordination in those verses.

The Argument about Submission in Ephesians 5:21–24

It seems rather unlikely that when Paul urges the Ephesians to be "subordinated to one another in fear of Christ" (v. 21), he is thinking of mutual subordination (as against Evans, 1983, p. 74; Bruce, 1984, pp. 382–83; Mickelson and Mickelson, 1986, p. 108; Lincoln, 1990, p. 365; Keener, 1992, pp. 168–72). The emphasis in the statement appears to be on the words "in fear of Christ" rather than "to one another," suggesting that we should not give the participle too strong an imperative force. Paul's point is almost, "Inasmuch as you are necessarily subordinated to one another, be so in fear of Christ."[12] Expressions such as "in fear of Christ" and "as to the Lord" (v. 22) seem inappropriate if the appeal is for mutual subordination. It makes more sense, surely, to regard them as a reinforcement of a type of behavior which, though necessary for apologetic reasons, was felt to contradict the unity and respect that believers experienced in the Spirit.[13] Although *allelois* would normally indicate reciprocal action of some sort (cf. 4:2, 23), such an idea is hardly evident in the formal injunctions that follow, and it seems best to attribute any awkwardness in the manner of expressions to stylistic constraints. The problem arises because Paul wants to designate relationships within the fellowship, rather than toward outsiders, for which he could have used *allois*.[14] More importantly, the idea of mutual submission is contrary to the basic meaning of the verb *hypotasso*, which presupposes an accepted order of things, whether established by force or by convention, within which there is submission and submissiveness. As with the metaphor of headship, Paul's language does not draw attention so much either to lines of authority and obedience (as is the case with children and slaves) or to the inner attitude of the subordinate party (submissiveness); it brings into view instead the structure or organization of things within the appropriate social context.[15] To some extent this conflicts with the earlier, more personal and egalitarian exhortations that they should "bear with one another in love" (4:2) and "be kind towards one another, compassionate, forgiving each other" (4:32), but this only reflects the inevitable tensions faced by believers in a highly stratified society.

The particular emphasis of verse 21 extends into verse 22, where the omission of the verb indicates quite strongly that subordination within the household is more an accepted fact than a deliberate objective, and that it is rather the indirect object ("to their own husbands") and in particular the manner of subordination ("as to the Lord") that are of primary concern to Paul. So his argument is not, "Be subordinate rather than equal or independent" but "Be subordinate as to the Lord, rather than from some less worthy motive." He is not teaching them to be subordinate but how to be subordinate. The logical force of the *idiois* ("their own") is difficult to ascertain; the word may have little more than a conventional or perhaps an intensive significance. But it is possible to demonstrate a quite consistent contrastive use of *idios* in Paul's letters, and there is perhaps the implication here that women should be subordinate to their own husbands or perhaps even directly to the Lord rather than to other men in the church (see Barth, 1974, p. 611).[16]

It is usually assumed that *idiois* in Ephesians 5:22 has no proper contrastive value (see, e.g., Bruce, 1984, p. 384, who regards the "exhausted" use of the pronoun as characteristic of the household code). J. A. Robinson argues from the absence of the word in Colossians 3:18 that its insertion in such a context was a matter of indifference. But the passage in Colossians is brief and it is in any case possible that the distinction was of less importance. Robinson also observes that *idiais* is added to *chersin* in 1 Corinthians 4:12 but is omitted in Ephesians 4:28 (according to the best text) and 1 Thessalonians 4:11 (Robinson, 1904, p. 204). But 1 Corinthians 4:12 has a polemical background (with our own hands, rather than being supported by others; cf. 1 Cor. 9:3–18) that is missing from the other two passages. The word is never included in the instructions to children, presumably because they would have had no such choice. In 1 Corinthians 7:2, where the issue is sexual immorality, the same pronouns are used as in Ephesians 5: *eautou* with *gynaika* and *idion* with *andra*.

If this is the case, then the injunction may reflect the sort of concern for the maintenance of good order that is voiced in 1 Corinthians 14:34–35: "Let the women keep silence in the churches; for it is not permitted to them to speak, but let them be submitted, as also the law says. If they wish to know something, let them ask their own husbands *[tous idious andras]* at home; for it is shameful for a woman to speak in church." In Titus 2:5, on the other hand, it is said that younger women should be "subordinate to *their own* husbands *[tois idiois andrasin]*, so that the word of God might not be blasphemed."[17] Likewise, Peter speaks of the women as "being subordinate to their own husbands *[tois idiois andrasin]*, that indeed, if some disobey the word, they will be won without a word through the conduct of the women" (1 Peter 3:1). As in Ephesians 5:21 the use of the participle suggests that subordination is as much an accepted state of affairs as an explicit requirement, and that the chief interest in the argument is in the person to whom women are subordinate. It is interesting to note that the exhortation to the men also has the participle form (1 Peter 3:7), but it is clear that *sunoikountes* ("living together") describes how things are, not how they should be. It is the manner of living together, just as it is the manner of subordination, not the fact, that is at issue. But whatever Paul's exact reasons for the inclusion of *idiois* in Ephesians 5:22, I would suggest that this emphasis on "their own men" is not redundant and has a significant bearing on how we evaluate the argumentative force of these verses inasmuch as it underlines the perception that the subordinate condition of the woman is more an accepted social reality than an express apostolic requirement.

The stipulation that women should be submitted to their husbands is supported by a chiastic argument in verses 23–24, in which the relationship between the husband and wife is set alongside that between Christ and the church:

> because a husband is head of the wife
> as also the Christ is head of the church,
> he himself being savior of the body;
> but as the church is subordinate to the Christ,
> so also the wives to the husbands in all things.

The development of this argument, however, has not generally been well understood and needs careful definition.

I have suggested that the specific proposition of verse 22 ("wives to their own husbands as to the Lord") has to do more with the indirect object of subordination than with the action itself. Even the words "as to the Lord" reinforce this emphasis. In view of this, the first line of the chiasmus ("because a husband is head of the wife") functions as an argument not for submission but for submission to the husband, whether or not there is an intended distinction from other men. Both for lexical and for logical reasons, therefore, I would say that the idea of the man's headship is not introduced as the premise for the subordination for the woman. On the one hand, *kephale* as a metaphor does not naturally denote one who has authority over another. On the other, the ideas of headship and subordination are carefully dissociated in the development of Paul's thought and we misread the passage if we suppose that *kephale* is to be interpreted by the verb *hypotassesthai*. That the man is head is not in itself an argument for the subordination of the woman. Paul is saying only that since the woman is subordinate, she should first of all respect the status and dignity of the man in the household. The fear might be, for example, that a woman's subordination to the leadership of the church (cf. 1 Cor. 16:16) might conflict with her responsibilities toward her husband.

The statement about the headship of the man is correlated with a parallel statement about the headship of Christ ("as indeed the Christ [is] head of the church"), but this correlation should not be construed analogically. That is, contrary to the usual interpretation of the verse, Paul does not put forward the headship of Christ as a model or an analogy for the headship of the man. In both the New Testament and the Septuagint, the simple comparative phrase *os kai*, which links the two statements in verse 23, is used only to assert the existence of a similarity; it is not used predicatively to present, in the manner of analogy or metaphor, one situation in the light of another (see, e.g., 1 Cor. 7:7; 9:5; Eph. 2:3; 2 Tim. 3:9). By way of illustration, consider the following statement, which says only that two things are similar: "Airplanes have the ability to fly, as indeed birds have the ability to fly." This is quite different from "Just as birds need wings to fly, so too airplanes need wings to fly," where the analogy is used to say something, or explain something, about airplanes.

No inference, therefore, about either the logical status or the character of the man's headship is drawn directly from the headship of Christ (cf. Ridderbos, 1975, p. 381; Fiorenza, 1983, p. 270; Witherington, 1988, p. 59). The argument is not, for example, that a man is head of the woman because Christ is head of the church, or that Christ's headship is a model for, or an endorsement of, the man's.[18] The man as head remains in the context of the passage an unsupported assertion that is arguably only descriptive in function rather than normative, a statement of how things are rather than of how they ought to be according to some theological or scriptural principle.

It is in verse 24 that a direct inference is made concerning the relationship between the man and the woman. The correlation now has a clearly predicative and analogical function, signaled not by the simple *os kai* but by the correlative pair *os . . . outos kai* ("as . . . so also").[19] The point of comparison has also shifted, from headship in the first pair of parallel statements to subordination in the second, a change of emphasis that is appropriately highlighted by the *alla* that introduces verse 24: "But as the church is subordinated to Christ."[20] Paul's argument is that if Christ's headship with respect to the church—

understood not in terms of authority but of either priority or promi-nence—is accompanied by the subordination of the church, then it is fitting that as long as the man has the sort of prominence that a patriarchal society attributes to him, the woman should be submit-ted to him. Whether or not Paul consistently thought of the headship of the man as provisional, we can at least maintain that his argument requires neither that the headship of the man be understood in absolute terms, nor that the subordination of the woman ought to be regarded as essential to the husband-wife relationship.

Other Passages That Address Subordination

A few other passages that speak of the subordination of the woman need brief examination. In Colossians 3:18 the subordination of the wife to the husband is couched in simple, less circumspect terms: "Wives, be subordinate to the husbands as is fitting in the Lord." This encapsulates the basic practical stipulation of Ephesians 5:21–24 without the subtleties of argumentation that appear to acknowledge the determinative influence of the social context. The two statements do not contradict each other: It is only that in Colossians 3:18 the contingent character of the paraenesis has not been made visible. Even taken on its own, it is not certain that the verse requires an inter-pretation in absolute terms. The expression "as is fitting" *(os aneken)* logically presupposes a frame of reference by which the suitability of the prescribed behavior is to be judged. While this may be established in very general terms in the prepositional phrase "in the Lord," this is obviously not the function of the phrase. "In the Lord" defines the context of appropriateness rather than the specific standard of ref-erence.[21] It is likely, therefore, that Paul has in mind the appropri-ateness of submission to the accepted standards of marriage.

Certain considerations suggest that the requirement expressed in 1 Corinthians 14:34–35 (that women should be silent in church and subordinate) also has a contingent character. The expression *ou . . . epitrepetai* suggests not an absolute but a limited prohibition: It is consistently used in the New Testament in the sense of giving some-one permission to do something, and is in every case related to a specific and limited set of circumstances. Even the permission to divorce granted by Moses (Matt. 19:8; Mark 10:12), which comes closest to being the imposition of a theological principle, is implicitly restricted to the period of the law. Authority is clearly located in the person granting or denying permission rather than in a body of absolute truth. The use of *epitrepo* here, therefore, makes the restriction a matter of church governance, of practical rather than theological authority (cf. Kroeger & Kroeger, 1992, pp. 82–83; Perriman, 1993, p. 130). It is unlikely that the "command of the Lord" refers to the instructions given to the women: It is those who profess to be prophets or spiritual who are in view. In any case, there is no reason in principle why a command of the Lord should not have only contingent significance.

The judgment that "it is shameful *[aischron ... estin]* for a woman to speak in the assembly" is a direct appeal to the prevailing social ethos, not to any absolute principle.

The requirement that women should be submitted is attributed to the law, but in view of Paul's ambivalent attitude toward the law (cf. 1 Cor. 9:20), it is by no means certain that this is meant as a binding ramification of the command. It seems more likely that he refers to the law only in an illustrative or incidental fashion: "as even/also the law says."[22]

Finally, I have argued that submission to the teaching—or to the teaching authority—rather than to men is charged in 1 Timothy 2:11 ("let a woman learn in all quietness in all submission"; Perriman, 1993, p. 31). The ground for this is found in the chiastic correspondence of this verse to the statement of verse 14 that "the woman, having been deceived, has come into transgression *[en parabasei].*" In Paul's writings, *parabasis* refers invariably to transgression against the law (Rom. 2:23; 4:15; 5:14; Gal. 3:19; see also Heb. 2:2; 9:15); the essence of Eve's sin was that she did not submit to what God had taught them, not that she disregarded Adam's authority.

Conclusions

In 1 Corinthians 11:3, the headship of the man is not put forward as a given theological premise on the basis of which certain conclusions are drawn about the way in which women should worship. The basic premise of the argument is rather that woman is the glory of man, which, on the one hand, reflects a well-attested Jewish tradition that a virtuous wife brings glory to her husband, and, on the other, is supported by appeal to the priority of the man in creation and to the fact that the woman was created as a helper for him. What is said about the headship of the man is essentially a restatement of this idea in a figure that not only reinterprets the Jewish idea of glory in terms of social position but also involves a play on the practical significance of "head" for the argument and the idiomatic association of the head with certain moral and spiritual qualities.

The interpretation of *kephale* in terms of prominence rather than authority or source is also valid for Ephesians and Colossians, although the use of the term for Christ, who is the firstborn from the dead, has also brought into view the idea of temporal priority. Paul's argument in Ephesians 5:22–24 is formulated in such a way that the headship of the man is not in itself made the reason for the subordination of the woman. The conclusion is drawn indirectly: Because the church is subordinate to Christ, and since both Christ and the man are "head," the woman should be subordinate to the man. But as in 1 Corinthians 11:3, the headship of the man is not hereby presented as a theologically determined premise. Both the subordination of the woman and the headship of the man stand in the argument as accepted social realities that must somehow be reconciled with the inner reality of Christian fellowship and the headship of Christ over his church. Elsewhere, it is true, subordination is prescribed in less equivocal terms (1 Cor. 14:34; Col. 3:18; Titus 2:5), but in Ephesians 5:21–24 Paul has taken greater pains to argue his case and in doing so has revealed something of his underlying motivation and convictions.

The designation of the man as "head" of the woman in 1 Corinthians and Ephesians, therefore, has to do not with any abstract relation of authority or origination but with the prominence of the man as a sociological phenomenon and, underlying this, with certain fundamental differences between the sexes that I will not attempt to specify here. The distinction is admittedly a subtle one and, in a patriarchal context, headship will no doubt entail the exercise of authority, but we are concerned not with the practice of headship but the manner in which any authority is validated. My point is that for Paul this validation was contingent upon prevailing social norms and the need to preserve the credibility and the integrity of the gospel, not upon the creational reality of man and woman. Likewise, subordination is enjoined upon the woman not as a necessary inference from the marriage relationship but, pragmatically rather than theologically, for fear that rocking the boat too much might sink it.

The important point is that these conclusions emerge from an examination of Paul's choice of language and of his argumentation. They do not depend upon hermeneutical assumptions, however plausible, about the conformity of Paul's teaching to the beliefs and practices of the ancient Mediterranean world. The significance of this should be obvious. If these conclusions prove valid, then one of the last redoubts of the male-supremacist position has been breached: There is no longer any final biblical excuse for the subordination and, in that respect, for the abuse of women.[23] To the extent that the man is socially prominent and in some way receives "glory" from his wife, it may still be appropriate to describe him as "head"; but in many families this prominence is now divided between the husband and the wife, and in such circumstances the figure of headship should also be applied, if it is retained at all, in a shared sense.[24] None of this, however, contradicts the authority of Christ over the household; the creational fact of sexual differentiation and the complementarity of male and female; or the need for love and honor in the conduct of the marriage.

Notes

1. Unless otherwise indicated, Scripture translations are those of the author.

2. One example might be considered. In Jeremiah 38:7 (LXX) the returning "remnant of Israel" is described as the "head of the nations" *(kephalen ethnon)*, but under the circumstances this can hardly mean that Israel has authority over the nations. The sense must be something like "foremost" or "preeminent nation" in that Israel was God's chosen people (cf. v. 9: "for I became a father to Israel, and Ephraim is my firstborn").

3. Cf. Proverbs 12:4: "A virtuous woman *[gyne andreia]* is a crown to her husband"; 1 Esdras 4:17: women "bring glory to men, and without women men cannot be"; Gn. r., 47 (17:15): "Her husband was crowned through her, but she was not crowned through her husband." In the story of Esther, Queen Vashti is said to have dishonored King Artaxerxes because she contradicted or disobeyed *(anteipe)* him (Esther 1:16–22 LXX). The real offense, however, is the dishonor rather than the disobedience. In the Odes of Solomon we find the idea that "the Lord is on my head like a crown" (1:1; cf. 5:12). On this theme generally, see H. Moxnes, "Honor and Shame," *Biblical Theology Bulletin 23,* (4) (1993): 167–76.

4. The widespread use of *boethos* to describe God in the Septuagint suggests that the meaning is "helper" not in the sense of a subordinate "assistant" but as one who makes up a significant deficiency or weakness (often a need for salvation or rescue from enemies). The underlying idea of "running to answer a call for help" is still determinative for usage in the Septuagint, and for that matter in the New Testament (cf. Acts 21:28; see F. Büchsel, in *Theological Dictionary of the New Testament [TDNT]*, ed. G. Kittel [Grand Rapids: Eerdmans, 1964–76], 1:628–29).

5. We should not necessarily assume that in verse 7 Paul means to deny that the woman is also the glory of God; it may only be that to his mind the social and sexual relationship between the man and the woman overrides her direct relationship to God.

6. W. F. Arndt and F. W. Gingrich, *A Greek-English Lexicon of the New Testament and Other Early Christian Literature* (Chicago: University of Chicago Press, 1979), s.v. *hyper* 2. Note also Sirach 49:16: "Sem and Seth were in great honor *[edoxasthesan]* among men, and Adam above *[hyper]* every living thing in the creation"; cf. Bel. 2.

7. E.g., 2 Kingdoms 6:21: "Blessed be the Lord, who chose me . . . to make me ruler over *[hegoumenon epi]* his people"; and 3 Kingdoms 2:35: "And the king gave Banaeas . . . over the army *[epi ton strategian]*." The difference between *hyper* and *epi* is illustrated by Psalm 96:9 (LXX; Lord over, exalted above) and Daniel 6:4 (it is Daniel's excellent spirit that raises him above the other two governors; the king then sets him over the whole kingdom).

8. This is the consistent prepositional use of the word in the New Testament and the Septuagint: Ephesians 4:10 ("he who also ascended far above all *[hyperano]* the heavens") and Hebrews 9:5 ("above *[hyperano]* it [the ark of the covenant] were the cherubim of glory"; see also Ps. 148:4; Ezek. 43:15; Dan. 7:6; Jonah 4:6; Mal. 1:5); in a number of Old Testament passages *hyperano* is used, as in Ephesians 1:21, in connection with an exaltation motif, but in each case the idea is not one of "authority over" but of prominence and glory (Deut. 26:19; 28:1; Ps. 8:1; Isa. 2:2; Micah 4:1).

9. First Peter 3:22 is a possible exception, but even here *hos estin en dexia theou* is separated from *hypotagenton auto aggelon* by the participial clause *poreutheis eis ouranon*.

10. In verse 31 Paul quotes explicitly from Genesis 2:24 ("Therefore shall a man leave his father and mother and shall cleave to his wife; and the two shall become one flesh"), which stands as a direct consequence of the fact that the woman was created out of the man.

11. This may also be true of 1 Corinthians 11:3. The expression "head of the household" is found in Hermas *Sim.* 7.3; note also Aristotle *Pol.* 1254ab, 1255b (see Witherington, 1988, pp. 58–59).

12. We do not meet in these paraenetic statements about the subordination of women the reflexive formulation that is found in Plutarch (*hypotattosusai . . . heautas tois andrasin, Moralia* 142E), which lays the emphasis more firmly on the deliberate action of the woman. The significance of the passive appears to be that women should acquiesce in an existing state of affairs.

13. The same tension, more sharply articulated, is found in the address to slaves: "Slaves, obey your masters in the flesh with fear and trembling in singleness of heart as to Christ" (6:5).

14. For the use of *hypotassein* with *allois* see Epictetus 1.4.19; 4.4.1.

15. This is particularly clear in Romans 13:1, where Paul urges submission *(hypotasseotho)* to the authorities that already "have power over" *(hyperechousais)* and are "ordained" *(tetagmenai eisin)* by God. Note W. Grundmann in *TDNT*, 8:41: "In the N[ew] T[estament] the verb does not immediately carry with it the thought of obedience."

. . . To obey or to have to obey, with no emphasis, is a sign of subjection or subordination. The latter is decisive as regards the content of the word."

16. First Peter 3:1, where the same wording is found *(hypotassomenai tois idiois andrasin),* is also important because it refers to wives of unbelieving husbands. Alternatively, we might view the injunction in the context of what is said about sexual immorality in Ephesians 4:17–19; 5:3–12—the marriage relationship was under particular threat at Ephesus. Colossians, which has only an abbreviated code for husbands and wives, also has much less to say on the subject of *porneia.* This might give greater credibility to the argument that "savior of the body" reflects, for instance, Hosea 3:1–2 or Tobit 6:18. Although *autos* certainly refers to Christ, there may be allusion to the idea that the husband as head saves his wife from sexual immorality. It might also explain the lengthy description of the process of sanctification in verses 26–27.

17. In 1 Timothy 6:1 it is clear from what follows that *tous idious despotas* refers to unbelieving masters, which makes it highly likely that a contrast is meant between these and Christian slave owners or leaders.

18. This does not necessarily mean that the use of the word *kephale* to define the status of the man is not in any way determined by the description of Christ as "head": The logical rather than terminological independence of the first statement is at issue.

19. Paul appears to make use of a similar method of argument in respect of the man in the progression from *kathos kai* correlation in verse 25 to the *outos* of verse 28.

20. The insertion of *alla* at this point has generally caused difficulties for commentators. See T. K. Abbott, *The Epistles to the Ephesians and to the Colossians,* International Critical Commentary (Edinburgh: T & T Clark, 1985), 166–67; Robinson, 1922, p. 205; Lincoln, 1990, pp. 370, 372.

21. In the same way it could be argued that in the clause "as it is fitting *[kathos prepei]* for the saints" (Eph. 5:3) the standards with reference to which "fornication," etc., are considered inappropriate types of behavior are not defined by the words "for the saints," which determine instead the context of application, but are implicitly, and perhaps explicitly in verse 5, the standards of the kingdom of God.

22. Possibly Paul has in mind Proverbs 31:25: a virtuous woman "opens her mouth heedfully and with propriety *[ennomos,* "subject to the law"; cf. 1 Cor. 9:21] and sets order *[taxin]* on her tongue." The verbal links between Paul's teaching about women and Proverbs 31:21–31 are striking. Note also Sirach 26:14: "A silent *[sigera]* woman is a gift of the Lord."

23. In some cultures, of course, there may still be a pragmatic justification, in which case the sort of reinterpretation of headship in terms of sacrificial love that Paul sets out in Ephesians 5:23–30 retains its full force.

24. Recognition of this allows for a measure of adaptability in evangelical paraenesis, which is important because the changes that have taken place in the family (the decline of patriarchalism, the increasing involvement of women in the marketplace) are to some extent at least a necessary response to the changes that have taken place in society as a whole (the education of women, contraception, etc.). For the Christian family and congregation to be prevented from adapting to these changes by a misplaced adherence to the patriarchal order would be to isolate it from its environment in such a way that not only women but also the gospel would suffer.

Conclusion

What Can the Church Do?

James R. Beck

Abuse in all its forms is a blight on our society. And abuse is especially despicable when it occurs in Christian homes. Responsible Christian people will agree that abuse, incest, domestic violence, and sexual assault are all gross offenses against the person, repugnant to God, and sinful assaults on human dignity. Yet in spite of this clarity regarding what abuse is, the evangelical church sometimes seems confused regarding how to respond to it.

We can readily condemn abuse outside the church. We can even be quite certain about remedies and responses to it: arrest, imprisonment, probation, rehabilitation, treatment. But when the victims and/or perpetrators of abuse are church members, we seem to lack conviction and courage. What can the church do? How should we respond? The church can be faithful to its prophetic calling by vigorously pursuing five strategies.

Respond to Abuse as Jesus Would

The Gospels give us ample evidence regarding the response Jesus would make to abuse. He would display healing compassion toward victims and necessary confrontation toward perpetrators (Matt. 9:1–7;

Luke 13:10–17; John 5:1–14 [read vv. 1–30 for the full implications];
8:1–11). Jesus would never blame a victim or excuse a perpetrator.
Jesus would never abandon a victim or turn his back on her plight.
Jesus would never cover up the offense of a perpetrator or launch a
campaign to hush the shame the perpetrator brings to the church.
Jesus would never urge a victim to forgive and forget prematurely, nor
would he accept a hasty "confession" from a perpetrator. In other
words, Jesus would never do what we often do when abuse occurs
within our ranks.

Responding to abuse as Jesus would requires uncommon courage.
Taking necessary steps in response to abuse will nearly always be
difficult. People will misunderstand, pressure will come to look the
other way, and our favorite agendas may be set aside while we deal
with the heartache that oozes from abusive situations. But ultimately
God is greatly honored when we take the actions against abuse that
the example of Jesus calls us to emulate.

Root Out Abuse

In 1918, on the eleventh day of the eleventh month at the eleventh
hour, warring parties signed an armistice marking the end of World
War I. More than seventy-five years later, tour buses take countless
visitors through the battlefields that stretch along a line from Flan-
ders to Alsace. In addition to seeing the cemeteries, the war monu-
ments, and an occasional fort, tourists can observe the scars of war
that are still visible on the landscape of Europe. In the lands of Ver-
dun, the soil long resisted any attempts at cultivation. Almost acci-
dentally, farmers discovered that the Austrian black pine would grow
in the badly damaged soil of the battlefield. In the 1990s, those trees
matured and are being harvested. In their place will soon grow hard-
woods such as beeches. This second tree crop will mature in another
sixty years or so. More than 135 years after the war ended, the land
may have healed sufficiently to sustain farming operations once
again. If land so destroyed by war takes this long to heal, how long
will the church take to heal once we can contain the abuse within its
ranks?

The evangelical church in the United States can no longer hope that abuse will quietly go away. We must address the shameful presence of abuse among us and vigorously root out the problem. We can never eliminate all possibility of the occurrence of abuse in Christian homes and circles, but we can expect to see a church that responds appropriately to the occurrence of abuse, that takes the problem of abuse seriously, and that is committed to confronting abuse whenever and wherever it occurs. We will have safer homes only when all of us understand that abuse is not an acceptable human behavior and when we refuse to tolerate abuse among us. Yet, we must remember that even after we root out abuse in our midst, we still have to face a long period of healing.

Educate the Congregation

The church can ill afford to allow ignorance about abuse to persist any longer among Christians. Abuse does occur in Christian homes, and abuse is always wrong. Help is available and effective, and help can bring healing and hope to the most hopeless of circumstances. The Bible does not allow for any sexual or physical violence within the home or the church. Authority figures who ask women or children to keep abusive behavior secret or who claim that abusive behavior is based on biblical principles are always in error. Church members need reliable, biblical information about abuse. Educating congregations after the fact will always be inferior to educating them before the fact.

Education is especially valuable when it is aimed at adolescents. Teenagers who are dating need to understand and realize the exact nature of abuse and why it is wrong and sinful. Young women need to take seriously any signs of undue anger, tendencies toward violence, or sexual excess that they may observe in the young men they date. Many adult women who find themselves victimized report that they noticed some alarming signs when they were dating, but they overlooked these warning signals because they thought that marriage would magically change their future spouse's behavior.

Understand the Relationship between Abuse and Misuse of Authority

The chapters in this volume argue that there is a connection between authority and abuse. Perpetrators also tell us this is so. Christian males who abuse often report to their therapists, secular or Christian, that they have abused their wives because they were unsubmissive or that they had to abuse in order to achieve their deserved position of authority. Perpetrators frequently quote Bible passages to support their contentions. In this volume we label such use of God's Word as Scripture abuse.

We need to call attention to an ongoing problem in evangelical circles: the abuse of women buttressed by an unwise, inaccurate use of the Bible to justify the abuse. We challenge all segments of the evangelical church to address this travesty with equal vigor. The chapters in this volume demonstrate that abuse does occur in Christian homes, that the rates are alarmingly high, that the abuse has tragic consequences, that continued denial that a problem exists among us will not correct the situation, and that only a concerted effort by evangelical leaders (including pastors, therapists, shelter workers, theologians, seminary professors, and denominational leaders) will eradicate this blight from our midst.

Much of the information in this volume comes from therapists who work with victims as well as perpetrators of the abuse. These workers tell us with great clarity and forcefulness that benign neglect, our most characteristic response to the problem, has done nothing to stem the tide of abuse of women in evangelical circles. The time has come for our churches to generate a new and more effective set of responses to domestic violence, childhood sexual abuse, and incest.

Christians for Biblical Equality (CBE) was the sponsor for the 1994 consultation in which most of these chapters first appeared. CBE is an organization dedicated to pursuing equality in Christ between men and women in the home, the church, and society. We maintain that ridding ourselves of an unnecessary and unbiblical difference between men and women regarding authority will help us attack the abuse of authority that occurs in our churches and homes. We contend that the underpinnings of equality in Christ for both women and men will enable us to attack with effectiveness the problem of abuse against women.

Create a Healing Environment in the Church

When abuse occurs within a church congregation, the victim all too frequently faces a second wave of abuse: church members who turn away from the victim, who abandon the victim at a time of great need, and who quietly or not so quietly imply that the victim was somehow responsible for the abuse. These congregational responses do not foster a healing environment for either the victim or the perpetrator.

Those persons who get trapped in the cycles of abuse, either as a victim or as a perpetrator, can be helped. Healing, recovery, and change are all possible. The church is the most logical environment for this healing. Churches need to view the nurture and care of a single victim as being as important as the evangelism of hundreds of people. Jesus was concerned for the ninety-nine but was even more concerned with the one who was at risk.

Churches can make good use of community resources to buttress their own efforts to bring about healing. Support groups, shelters, therapists, and law enforcement services can all be helpful supplements to a church's efforts. Inside the church, concerned and caring individuals can surround hurting people with prayer, support, Bible study, mentoring, and rehabilitation services. God is honored when we respond to abuse appropriately, when we adopt a standard of zero tolerance for abuse, when we educate our congregations regarding abuse, when we understand how easily authority can be misused, and when we create healing environments in our congregations. Only then will we fully honor the Lord and Savior of the church.

Appendix

Some Biblical Thoughts
for Abused Women

The Believer's Body as the Temple
of the Holy Spirit

Every sin that a person commits is outside the body; but the fornicator sins against the body itself. Or do you not know that your body is a temple of the Holy Spirit within you, which you have from God?

1 Corinthians 6:18–19 NRSV

If anyone destroys God's temple, God will destroy that person. For God's temple is holy, and you are that temple.

1 Corinthians 3:17 NRSV

An Abused Woman's Feeling of Betrayal

My friends and companions avoid me because of my wounds;
my neighbors stay far away.

Psalm 38:11

Even my close friend, whom I trusted,
he who shared my bread,
has lifted up his heel against me.

Psalm 41:9

My companion attacks his friends;
he violates his covenant.
His speech is smooth as butter,

yet war is in his heart;
his words are more soothing than oil,
yet they are drawn swords.

Psalm 55:20–21

The Prayer of One in Danger

Rescue me, O LORD, from evil men;
protect me from men of violence,
who devise evil plans in their hearts
and stir up war every day.
They make their tongues as sharp as a serpent's;
the poison of vipers is on their lips.
Keep me, O LORD, from the hands of the wicked;
protect me from men of violence
who plan to trip my feet.
Proud men have hidden a snare for me;
they have spread out the cords of their net
and have set traps for me along my path.
O LORD, I say to you, "You are my God."
Hear, O LORD, my cry for mercy.

Psalm 140:1–6

God Hears the Cry of Abused Women

Your lovers despise you;
they seek your life.
For I heard a cry as of a woman in travail,
anguish as of one bringing forth her first child,
the cry of the daughter of Zion gasping for breath,
stretching out her hands,
"Woe is me! I am fainting before murderers."

Hark, the cry of the daughter of my people
from the length and breadth of the land:
"Is the LORD not in Zion?
Is her King not in her?"

For the wound of the daughter of my people is my heart wounded,
I mourn, and dismay has taken hold on me.
Is there no balm in Gilead?
Is there no physician there?
Why then has the health of the daughter of my people
not been restored?
O that my head were waters,
and my eyes a fountain of tears,
that I might weep day and night
for the slain of the daughter of my people!

Jeremiah 4:30–31; 8:19; 8:21–9:1 RSV

God Is with Abused Women

Out of my distress I called on the LORD;
the LORD answered and set me in a broad place.
With the LORD on my side I do not fear.
What can mortals do to me?
The LORD is on my side to help me;
I shall look in triumph on those who hate me.

Psalm 118:5–7

The LORD is righteous in all his ways
and loving toward all he has made.
The LORD is near to all who call on him,
to all who call on him in truth.
He fulfills the desires of those who fear him;
he hears their cry and saves them.

Psalm 145:17–19

He heals the brokenhearted
and binds up their wounds.

Psalm 147:3

Reference List

Ackerman, R. J., & Pickering, S. E. (1989). *Abused no more: Recovery for women from abusive or co-dependent relationships.* Blue Ridge Summit, PA: Tab.

Adams, D. (1989). Stages of anti-sexist awareness and change for men who batter. In L. Dickstein & C. Nadelson (Eds.), *Family violence: Emerging issues of a national crisis* (pp. 63–73). Washington DC: American Psychiatric Press.

Allender, D. B. (1990). *The wounded heart: Hope for adult survivors of childhood sexual abuse.* Colorado Springs, CO: NavPress.

Alsdurf, J., & Alsdurf, P. (1989). *Battered into submission: The tragedy of wife abuse in the Christian home.* Downers Grove, IL: InterVarsity.

Anglican Church of Canada. (1986). *Violence against women.* The Report to the General Synod 1986 of the Anglican Church of Canada. Toronto: Anglican Book Centre.

Arnold, C. E. (1992). *Powers of darkness.* Downers Grove, IL: InterVarsity.

Augsburger, D. (1986). An existential approach to anger management training. *Journal of Psychology and Christianity, 5* (4), 25–29.

Baron, L., & Straus, M. A. (1989). *Four theories of rape in American society.* New Haven, CT: Yale University Press.

Barth, M. (1974). *Ephesians 1–3, 4–6* (2 vols.). New York: Doubleday.

Bass, E., & Davis, L. (1988). *The courage to heal: A guide for women survivors of child sexual abuse.* New York: Harper and Row.

Bayer, E. (1985). *Rape within marriage: A moral analysis delayed.* Lanham, MD: University Press.

Beaman-Hall. L., & Nason-Clark, N. (1997). Partners or protagonists: Exploring the relationship between the transitional house movement and conservative churches. *Affilia: Journal of Women and Social Work 12* (2), 176–96.

Beavers, R. (1994, February). Assessment of family competence. Address to 1994 Tennessee Association for Marriage and Family Therapists Annual Conference, Nashville, TN.

Belenky, M., Clinchy, B. M., Goldberger, N. R., & Tarule, J. M. (1986). *Women's ways of knowing: The development of self, voice and mind.* New York: Basic.

Bibby, R. W. (1987). *Fragmented gods: The poverty and potential of religion in Canada.* Toronto: Irwin.

Block, H., & Shantz, K. (1991, October). *Domestic, sexual abuse also found in Mennonite churches.* (Available from Mennonite Central Committee Canada Women's Concerns, 50 Kent Ave., Kitchener, ON N2G 3R1.)

Bohn, C. R. (1989). Dominion to rule: The roots and consequences of a theology of ownership. In J. C. Brown & C. R. Bohn (Eds.), *Christianity, patriarchy and abuse: A feminist critique* (pp. 105–17). New York: Pilgrim.

Bowman, E. S. (1988). When theology leads to abuse. *Update 12* (4). Oakland, CA: Evangelical Women's Caucus Int.

Brown, J. C., & Bohn, C. R. (Eds.). (1989). *Christianity, patriarchy and abuse: A feminist critique.* New York: Pilgrim.

Bruce, F. F. (1984). *The epistles to the Colossians, to Philemon and to the Ephesians.* Grand Rapids: Eerdmans.

Brueggemann, W. (1988). On pain, fear, and anger. In *Family violence in a patriarchal culture: A challenge to our way of living.* The Church Council on Social Development, Health and Welfare Canada. (For assistance contact The Keith Press Ltd., Ottawa, Canada.)

Bryson, S. C. (1992). *Breakout! A twelve step adventure to spiritual maturity—and wholeness.* Indianapolis, IN: Light and Life.

Burkett, L. (1987). *Answers to your family's financial questions.* Pomona, CA: Focus on the Family.

Campolo, A., Jr. (1983). *The power delusion.* Wheaton, IL: Victor.

Canadian Conference of Catholic Bishops. (1992). *From pain to hope.* Pamphlet.

Castle, J. A. (1991). Subordination in the Trinity? *Journal of Biblical Equality, 3,* 31–41.

Cervin, R. S. (1989). Does *kephale* mean "source" or "authority over" in Greek literature? A rebuttal. *Trinity Journal, 10* (1), 85–112.

Clement, P. W. (1986). Behavioral approach to anger management training. *Journal of Psychology and Christianity, 5* (4), 41–49.

Court, J. (1986). On the expression of anger—a response. *Journal of Christian Education,* papers 86, 41–45.

Courtois, C. (1988). *Healing the incest wound: Adult survivors in treatment.* New York: Norton.

Covey, S. R. (1989). *The seven habits of highly effective people: Powerful lessons in change.* New York: Simon and Schuster.

Dalton, G. E. (1993, summer). On forgiving those who have abused you. *Shalom: A Journal for the Practice of Reconciliation, 13* (3), 3–4.

Davidson, T. (1978). *Conjugal crime: Understanding and changing the wife beating pattern.* New York: Hawthorn.

Dobash, R. E., & Dobash, R. P. (1978). *The strong-willed child: From birth to adolescence.* Wheaton, IL: Tyndale House.

Dobash, R. E., & Dobash, R. P. (1978). Wives: The "appropriate" victims of marital violence. *Victimology: An International Journal, 2* (3/4), 426–42.

Dobash, R. E., & Dobash, R. P. (1979). *Violence against wives.* New York: Free Press.

Dobson, J. C. (1970). *Dare to discipline.* Wheaton, IL: Tyndale House.

Douglas, J. D. (Ed.). (1962). *The new Bible dictionary.* London: Inter-Varsity Fellowship.

Dutton, M. A. (1992). *Empowering and healing the battered woman.* New York: Springer.

Enns, C. (1988). Dilemmas of power and equality in marital and family counseling: Proposal for a feminist perspective. *Journal of Counseling and Development, 67,* 242–48.

Evans, M. J. (1983). *Woman in the Bible.* Carlisle: Paternoster.

Evans, P. (1992). *The verbally abusive relationship: How to recognize it and how to respond.* Holbrook, MA: Bob Adams.

Farley, M. (1976). Sources of inequality in the history of Christian thought. *Journal of Religion, 56,* 162.

Farrell, W. (1993). *The myth of male power: Why men are the disposable sex.* New York: Simon and Schuster.

Fee, G. D. (1987). *The first epistle to the Corinthians.* Grand Rapids: Eerdmans.

Feldmeth, J. R., & Finley, M. W. (1990). *We weep for ourselves and our children: A Christian guide for survivors of childhood sexual abuse.* San Francisco: Harper.

Finkelhor, D. (1983). Common features of family abuse. In D. Finkelhor, R. J. Gelles, G. Hotaling, & M. A. Straus (Eds.), *The dark side of families: Current family violence research* (pp. 17–28). Beverly Hills, CA: Sage.

Finkelhor, D., & Yllo, K. (1983). Rape in marriage. In D. Finkelhor, R. J. Gelles, G. Hotaling, & M. A. Straus (Eds.), *The dark side of families: Current family violence research* (pp. 119–34). Beverly Hills, CA: Sage.

Finkelhor, D., & Yllo, K. (1985). *License to rape: Sexual abuse of wives.* New York: Holt, Rinehart and Winston.

Fiorenza, E. S. (1983). *In memory of her: A feminist theological reconstruction of Christian origins.* London: SCM.

Fiorenza, E. S. (1993). Feminist hermeneutics. In D. N. Freedman (Ed.), *Anchor Bible dictionary* (pp. 783–89). Garden City, NY: Doubleday.

Fitzmeyer, J. A. (1989). Another look at *kephale* in 1 Corinthians 11:3. *New Testament Studies, 35,* 503–11.

Fitzmeyer, J. A. (1993). *Kephale* in 1 Corinthians 11:3. *Interpretation, 47* (1), 52–59.

Fortune, M. M. (1982, June). The church and domestic violence. *Theology, News and Notes*. (*Theology, News and Notes* is published by Fuller Theological Seminary. The article is available in resources produced by Mennonite Central Committee Domestic Violence Task Force, 21 South 12th Street, Box M, Akron, PA 17501.)

Fortune, M. M. (1988). Forgiveness the last step. In A. Horton & J. Williamson (Eds.), *Abuse and religion: When praying isn't enough* (pp. 215–20). New York: D. C. Heath.

Fortune, M. M. (1988). *Hands to end violence against women: A resource for theological education.* Toronto: Women's Inter-Church Council of Canada. (Available from the council, 77 Charles Street W., Toronto, Canada M4Y 1R4.)

Franklin, C. W. (1984). *The changing definition of masculinity.* New York: Plenum.

Freedman, D. N. (Ed.). (1993). *Anchor Bible dictionary.* Garden City, NY: Doubleday.

Friesen, J. (1991). *Uncovering the mystery of multiple personality disorder.* San Bernardino, CA: Here's Life.

Frieze, I. H. (1979). Perceptions of battered wives. In I. H. Frieze, D. Bar-Tel, & J. Carroll (Eds.), *New approaches to social problems: Applications of attribution theory* (pp. 79–108). San Francisco: Jossey-Bass.

Fugate, R. J. (1980). *What the Bible says about . . . child training.* Garland, TX: Aletheia.

Gaultiere, W. J. (1989). A biblical perspective on therapeutic treatment of client anger against God. *Journal of Psychology and Christianity, 8* (3), 38–46.

Gelles, R. J. (1979). *The violent home: A study of physical aggression between husbands and wives.* Beverly Hills, CA: Sage.

Gelles, R. J., & Cornell, C. P. (1985). *Intimate violence in families.* New York: Sage.

Gelles, R. J., & Straus, M. A. (1988). *Intimate violence: The causes and consequences of abuse in the American family.* New York: Simon and Schuster.

Gilligan, C. (1982). *In a different voice: Psychological theory and women's development.* Cambridge, MA: Harvard University Press.

Glazer, M., & Moessner, J. S. (1991). *Women in travail and transition.* Minneapolis: Fortress.

Gothard, B. (1978). *Supplementary alumni book* (Vol. 5). Institute in Basic Youth Conflicts.

Gray, E. D. (1992). Beauty and the beast. In K. Hagen (Ed.), *Women respond to the men's movement: A feminist collection* (pp. 159–68). San Francisco: Pandora.

Grayson, C., & Johnson, J. (1991). *Creating a safe place: Christians healing from the hurt of dysfunctional families.* San Francisco: Harper.

Green, H. W. (1989). *Turning fear into hope: Women who have been hurt for love.* Grand Rapids, MI: Zondervan.

Greenblat, C. (1983). A hit is a hit is a hit . . . or is it? In D. Finkelhor, R. J. Gelles, G. Hotaling, & M. A. Straus (Eds.), *The dark side of families: Current family violence research* (pp. 235–60). Beverly Hills, CA: Sage.

Grudem, W. (1990). The meaning of *kephale* ('head'): A response to recent studies. *Trinity Journal, 11,* 17–18.

Hampton, R., & Coner-Edwards, A. F. W. (1993). Physical and sexual violence in marriage. In R. Hampton, et al. (Eds.), *Family violence: Prevention and treatment* (pp. 113–41). Newbury Park, CA: Sage.

Harrison, B. (1976). The power of anger in the work of love: Christian ethics for women and other strangers. *Union Seminary Quarterly Review, 36,* 41–58.

Hart, A. D. (1979). *Feeling free.* Old Tappan, NJ: Revell.

Hartman, S. (1983). A self-help group for women in abusive relationships. *Social Work with groups, 6* (3/4), 133–46.

Hartman, S. (1987). Therapeutic self-help group: A process of empowerment for women in abusive relationships. In C. M. Brody (Ed.), *Women's therapy groups: Paradigms of feminist treatment* (pp. 67–81). New York: Springer.

Hauser, W. (1982). *Differences in relative resources: Familial power and spouse abuse.* Palo Alto, CA: R & E Research Associates.

Hendrick, M. C. (1985). Feminist spirituality in Jewish and Christian traditions. In L. B. Rosewater & L. E. A. Walker (Eds.), *Handbook of feminist therapy* (pp. 135–46). New York: Springer.

Hendricks, H. G. (1973). *Heaven help the home.* Wheaton, IL: Victor.

Herbert, T. B., Silver, R. C., & Ellard, J. H. (1991). Coping with an abusive relationship: How and why do women stay? *Journal of Marriage and the Family, 53,* 325.

Hilliard, P. A. (1988, October). Physical abuse and pregnancy. *Medical Aspects of Human Sexuality,* 20–33.

Hofeller, K. (1982). *Social, psychological and situational factors in wife abuse.* Palo Alto, CA: R & E Research Associates.

Horton, A., Wilkins, M., & Wright, W. (1988). Women who ended abuse: What religious leaders and religion did for these victims. In A. Horton & J. Williamson (Eds.), *Abuse and religion: When praying isn't enough* (pp. 235–46). New York: D. C. Heath.

Hubbard, M. G. (1992a). The mother goose syndrome: Myths which support hierarchical relationships. *Journal of Biblical Equality, 4,* 26–33.

Hubbard, M. G. (1992b). *Women: The misunderstood majority.* Irving, TX: Word.

Hubbard, M. G., & Hubbard, J. (1990). Psychological resistance to egalitarianism. *Journal of Biblical Equality, 2,* 26–52.

Hyles, J. (1972). *How to rear children.* Hammond, IN: Hyles-Anderson.

Jacobs, J. (1984). The economy of love in religious commitment: The deconversion of women from nontraditional religious movements. *Journal for the Scientific Study of Religion, 23* (2), 155.

Jaffe, P. G., Wolfe, D. A., & Wilson, S. K. (1990). *Children of battered women.* Newbury Park, CA: Sage.

Jeffords, C. (1984). The impact of sex role and religious attitudes upon forced marital intercourse norms. *Sex Roles, 11* (5, 6), 755.

Jeffords, C., & Dull, T. (1982). Demographic variations in attitudes towards marital rape immunity. *Journal of Marriage and the Family, 44,* 755–62.

Jervis, L. A. (1993). "But I want you to know . . .": Paul's midrashic intertextual response to the Corinthian worshipers (1 Cor 11:2–16). *Journal of Biblical Literature, 112* (2), 231–46.

Jewett, P. R. (1975). *Man as male and female.* Grand Rapids, MI: Eerdmans.

Jobling, M. (1974). Battered wives: A survey. *Social Service Quarterly, 47,* 82.

Kaufman, G. (1992). *Shame: The power of caring.* Rochester, VT: Schenkman.

Keener, C. S. (1992). *Paul, women and wives: Marriage and women's ministry in the letters of Paul.* Peabody, MA: Hendrickson.

Ketterman, G. H. (1993). Sticks and stones may break my bones, but words . . . ? *Christian Counseling Today, 1* (2), 20–24.

Klein, J. (1994, February 28). Crime bill garbage barge. *Newsweek,* 35.

Krall, R. (1994, March). The presence and incidence of abuse in society and the church. Plenary presentation at breaking silence, bringing hope: Facing family brokenness and abuse within the Christian community, Chambersburg, PA.

Kroeger, R. C., & Kroeger, C. C. (1992). *I Suffer Not a Woman.* Grand Rapids, MI: Baker.

LaHaye, T. (1968). *How to be happy though married.* Wheaton, IL: Tyndale House.

Lerner, G. (1986). *The creation of patriarchy* (Vol. 1). New York: Oxford University Press.

Lewis, C. S. (1943). *Mere Christianity.* New York: Macmillan.

Lewis, C. S. (1966). *The weight of glory and other addresses.* Grand Rapids, MI: Eerdmans.

Liefeld, W. L. (1986). Women, submission and ministry in 1 Corinthians. In A. Mickelson (Ed.), *Women, Authority and the Bible* (pp. 134–54). Downers Grove, IL: InterVarsity Press.

Lincoln, A. T. (1990). *Ephesians*. Dallas: Word.

MacArthur, J. (1982). *The family*. Chicago: Moody.

MacFarquhar, E., Seter, J., Lawrence, S., Knight, R., & Schrof, J. (1994, March 28). The war against women. *U.S. News and World Report*, 42–48.

Making sense of the men's movement. (1992, June). *Focus on the Family, 16* (6), 4.

McCann, L., & Pearlman, A. (1990). Vicarious traumatization: A framework for understanding the psychological effects of working with victims. *Journal of Traumatic Stress, 3* (1), 131–37.

McClain, E. (1979). Religious orientation the key to psychodynamic differences between feminists and nonfeminists. *Journal for the Scientific Study of Religion, 18*, 40–45.

McGee, R. S. (1990). *The search for significance*. Houston, TX: Rapha.

Meth, R. L., & Pasick, R. S. (1990). *Men in therapy: The challenge of change*. New York: Guilford.

Mickelson, B., & Mickelson, A. (1986). What does *kephale* mean in the New Testament? In A. Mickelson (Ed.), *Women, authority and the Bible* (pp. 97–110). Downers Grove, IL: InterVarsity Press.

Miller, J. K. (1991). *A hunger for healing: The twelve steps as a classic model for Christian spiritual growth*. New York: HarperCollins.

Mollenkott, V. R. (1989). *Godding: Human responsibility and the Bible*. New York: Crossroad.

Moltmann, J. (1975). *The Trinity and the kingdom*. San Francisco: Harper and Row.

Moltmann, J. (1985). *God in creation*. San Francisco: Harper and Row.

Morris, R. (1988). *Ending violence in families: A training program for pastoral care workers*. Toronto: Women's Inter-Church Council of Canada.

Nason-Clark, N. (1995). Conservative Protestants and violence against women: Exploring the rhetoric and the response. *Religion and Social Order, 5*, 109–30.

Nason-Clark, N. (1996). Religion and violence against women: Exploring the rhetoric and the response of evangelical churches in Canada. *Social Compass: International Review of Sociology of Religion, 43* (4), 515–36.

Nason-Clark, N. (1997). *The abused woman: How churches confront family violence*. Louisville, KY: Westminster/John Knox.

Nason-Clark, N. (1997). *The battered wife: How Christians confront family violence*. Louisville, KY: Westminster/John Knox.

Narramore, C. (1978). *The submissive wife*. Rosemead, CA: Narramore Christian Foundation.

Neville, G. (1974). Religious socialization of women within U.S. subcultures. In A. Hagerman (Ed.), *Sexist religion and women in the church: No more silence!* in collaboration with the Women's Caucus of Harvard Divinity School (pp. 77–84). New York: Associated Press.

Neuger, C. (1993). In R. Wicks, R. Parsons, & D. Capps (Eds.), *Clinical handbook of pastoral counseling* (pp. 185–207). New York: Paulist.

NiCarthy, G., Merriam, K., & Coffman, S. (1984). *Talking it out: A guide to groups for abused women.* Seattle, WA: Seal.

Noddings, N. (1989). *Women and evil.* Berkeley and Los Angeles: University of California Press.

Once gay, always gay? (1994, March). *Focus on the Family, 18* (3), 2–5.

Outka, G. (1972). *Agape: An ethical analysis.* New Haven, CT: Yale University Press.

Page, C. G. (1975). *How to failure-proof your family.* Denver, CO: Accent.

Perriman, A. C. (1993). What Eve did, what women shouldn't do: The meaning of *authentes* in 1 Timothy 2:12. *Tyndale Bulletin, 44* (1), 129–42.

Perriman, A. C. (1994). The head of a woman: The meaning of *kephale* in 1 Corinthians 11:3. *Journal of Theological Studies, 45* (2), 602–22.

Pizzey, E. (1977). *Scream quietly or the neighbors will hear.* Short Hills, NJ: Ridley Enslow.

Plantinga, C., Jr. (1988, March 4). The perfect family. *Christianity Today,* 24–27.

Rainey, D., & Rainey, B. (1986). *Building your mate's self-esteem.* San Bernardino, CA: Here's Life.

Redmond, S. (1988). Despair, hope and forgiveness. In *Family violence in a patriarchal culture: A challenge to our way of living.* The Church Council on Social Development, Health and Welfare Canada. (For assistance contact The Keith Press Ltd., Ottawa, Canada.)

Redmond, S. (1990). Christian "virtues" and recovery from child sexual abuse. In J. C. Brown & C. R. Bohn (Eds.), *Christianity, patriarchy and abuse: A feminist critique* (pp. 70–88). New York: Pilgrim.

Ridderbos, H. (1975). *Paul: An outline of his theology.* London: SPCK.

Rinck, M. J. (1990). *Christian men who hate women: Healing hurting relationships.* Grand Rapids, MI: Zondervan.

Robinson, J. A. (1904). *St. Paul's Epistle to the Ephesians.* London: James Clarke and Co.

Rosenbaum, A., & O'Leary, K. D. (1981). Marital violence: Characteristics of abusive couples. *Journal of Consulting and Clinical Psychology, 49,* 63–71.

Russell, D. (1990). *Rape in marriage.* New York: Macmillan.

Saiving, V. (1979). The human situation: A feminine view. In C. Christ & J. Plaskow (Eds.), *Womanspirit rising: A feminist reader in religion* (pp. 25–42). New York: Harper and Row.

Sanday, P. R. (1981). The socio-cultural context of rape: A cross-cultural study. *Journal of Social Issues, 37,* 5–27.

Saussy, C. (1991). *God images and self-esteem.* Louisville, KY: Westminster.

Schaeffer, F. A., & Koop, C. E. (1979). *Whatever happened to the human race?* Old Tappan, NJ: Revell.

Schechter, S. (1982). *Women and male violence.* Boston: South End.

Schwendinger, J. R., & Schwendinger, H. (1983). *Rape and inequality.* Beverly Hills, CA: Sage.

Scott, C. L. (1992). *Breaking the cycle of abuse: A biblical approach to recognizing and responding to domestic violence.* Elgin, IL: David C. Cook.

Shotland, R. L., & Goodstein, L. (1992). Sexual precedence reduces the perceived legitimacy of sexual refusal: An examination of attributions concerning date rape and consensual sex. *Personality and Social Psychology Bulletin, 18,* 756–64.

Shupe, A., Stacey, W., & Hazlewood, L. (1987). *Violent men, violent couples.* Lexington, MA: Lexington.

Stack, S., & Kanavy, M. J. (1983). The effects of religion on forcible rape: A structural analysis. *Journal for the Scientific Study of Religion, 22,* 67–74.

Stern, E. M., (Ed.). (1985). *Psychotherapy and the religiously committed patient.* New York: Haworth.

Stoudenmire, J. (1976). The role of religion in the depressed housewife. *Journal of Religion and Health, 15,* 62.

Straus, M. A. (1977–78). Wife beating: How common and why? *Victimology: An International Journal, 2,* 443.

Straus, M. A., Gelles, R. J., & Steinmetz, K. (1980). *Behind closed doors: Violence in the American family.* Garden City, NY: Anchor.

Straus, M. A., & Sweet, S. (1990). Verbal symbolic aggression in couples: Incidence rates and relationship to personal characteristics. *Journal of Marriage and the Family, 54,* 346.

Strube, M. J., & Barbour, L. S. (1984). Factors related to the decision to leave an abusive relationship. *Journal of Marriage and the Family, 46,* 837.

Swift, C. F. (1988). Surviving: Women's strength through connection. In M. B. Straus (Ed.), *Abuse and victimization across the life span* (pp. 153–69). Baltimore, MD: Johns Hopkins University Press.

Thorman, G. (1980). *Family violence.* Springfield, IL: Charles C. Thomas.

Tomczak, L. (1982). *God, the rod, and your child's bod: The art of loving correction for Christian parents.* Old Tappan, NJ: Revell.

Tower, C. C. (1988). S*ecret scars: A guide for survivors of child sexual abuse.* New York: Penguin.

Van Leeuwen, M. S. (1990). *Gender and grace.* Downers Grove, IL: InterVarsity.

Van Leeuwen, M. S. (1990). Life after Eden. *Christianity Today, 34* (10), 19–21.

Van Leeuwen, M. S. (1987, July). Identifying the wife at risk of battering. *Medical Aspects of Human Sexuality*, 31.

Walker, L. E. (1979). *The battered woman.* New York: Harper and Row.

Wardell, L., Gillespie, D. L., & Leffler, A. (1982). Science and violence against wives. In D. Finkelhor, R. J. Gelles, G. Hotaling, & M. A. Straus (Eds.), *The dark side of families: Current family violence research* (pp. 69–81). Beverly Hills, CA: Sage.

Warner, T. (1991). *Spiritual warfare.* Wheaton, IL: Crossway.

Webber, R. E. (1979). *The secular saint.* Grand Rapids, MI: Zondervan.

Westerlund, E. (1992). *Women's sexuality after childhood incest.* New York: Norton.

Whipple, V. (1987). Counseling battered women from fundamentalist churches. *Journal of Marital and Family Therapy, 13* (3), 251–58.

White, E. (1965). *Marriage and the Bible.* Nashville, TN: Broadman.

Wicks, R., Parsons, R., & Capps, D. (Eds.). (1985). *Clinical handbook of pastoral counseling.* New York: Paulist.

Williams-White, D. (1989). Self-help and advocacy: An alternative approach to helping battered women. In L. J. Dickstein & C. C. Nadelson (Eds.), *Family violence: Emerging issues of a national crisis* (pp. 47–59). Washington, DC: American Psychiatric Press.

Witherington, B. (1988). *Women in the earliest churches.* Cambridge, MA: Cambridge University Press.

Yates, W. (1990). The Protestant view of marriage. In A. Swidler (Ed.), *Marriage among the religions of the world* (Vol. 2), 59–78. Lewiston, NY: Edwin Mellen.

Contributors

James R. Beck is professor of counseling at Denver Conservative Baptist Seminary. He is a clinical psychologist, an ordained minister, and the author of *Dorothy Carey*. He also is a founding board member of Christians for Biblical Equality.

Anne Findlay Chamberlain is a clinical mental health counselor who deals largely with issues of abuse. A survivor herself, she is an experienced speaker and writer on mental health and Christian issues. She has served as the Brethren in Christ representative to the Mennonite Central Committee's Committee on Women's Concerns.

Pamela C. Court ministers in Australia with her husband, John. She received her Ph.D. in marriage and family therapy from Fuller Theological Seminary.

Marge Cox served as a volunteer community advocate for law enforcement agencies in Colorado before moving to Topeka, Kansas, where she is a volunteer working with victims of domestic violence and rape.

Cynthia Ezell, a licensed marriage and family therapist at the Center for the Family, is currently serving as chair of the Nashville Psychotherapy Institute. A certified Imago Relationship Therapist, she authors a monthly column on parenting in *Nashville Parenting* magazine. Her specialities include treatment of depression and eating disorders and marital therapy.

Catherine Clark Kroeger is an adjunct professor at Gordon-Conwell Theological Seminary. She earned her Ph.D. in classics at the University of Minnesota. She is president emerita of Christians for Biblical Equality. She and her husband authored *I Suffer Not a Woman.*

Melissa Kubitschek Luzzi works with high risk and abused children as a teacher and educator in Colorado. She is director of victims' services for P.A.V.E. (Promoting Alternatives to Violence through Education).

Lydia is a survivor of extensive childhood abuse. Her recovery is ongoing.

Nancy Nason-Clark is a professor of sociology at the University of New Brunswick, Canada. She is coordinator of the Religion and Violence Research Team at the Muriel McQueen Fergusson Center for Family Violence Research at the University of New Brunswick. Her book, *The Battered Wife: How Christians Cope with Family Violence,* was published in 1997.

For ten years, **Diane Strong Nesheim** has been a therapist whose work emphasizes considerations of spirituality, with specialties in abused women, childhood trauma, and clergy counseling. She is coordinator/facilitator for the Interval House Sexual Assault Program for Lennox and Addington Counties in Ontario.

Elizabeth Pearson is a doctoral candidate in social work at Columbia University. Despite the arrival of twins, she continues to research issues related to domestic violence and child abuse.

Andrew C. Perriman is assistant pastor of the Protestant Church of Oman and a teacher of theological education through extension programs. He holds an M.A. Oxon, English language and literature, from Lincoln College and an M.Phil. in theology from London Bible College.

Margaret Josephson Rinck is a licensed clinical psychologist in private practice at the New Life Clinic in Cincinnati. Her specialities include abuse and violence toward women, and she has taught many seminars and lectured widely. She was ordained by the Evangelical Church Alliance and is best known in Christian circles for her books *Christian Men Who Hate Women* and *Can Christians Love Too Much? Breaking the Cycle of Co-Dependency.*

Joan Tyvoll is an ordained minister with the Conservative Congregation Christian Conference. A graduate of Bethel Seminary,
she currently pastors a congregational church in Spring Valley,
Wisconsin. She recently founded a retreat ministry named Rest
and Be Thankful.

Amy Wildman White is a nationally certified counselor in private
practice in individual, family, and marital counseling. She
teaches at Robert Morris College in the department of psychology and sociology.

Mary Williams is the pen name of a missionary with twenty-two
years of foreign service. A graduate of Moody Bible Institute,
she holds an MSW with a speciality in domestic violence and
engages in a counseling ministry.